INSTITUT FÜR AFRIKASTUDIEN

The peer-reviewed series "Bayreuth Studies in Politics and Society in Africa" publishes research about socio-political processes and structures in African societies. The editors welcome innovative monographs and guest edited volumes in either English or German which discuss historical and current transformations in African countries with an empirical or theoretical focus. The series is open to case studies and comparative research from the social sciences and related academic disciplines.

Bayreuther Studien zu Politik und Gesellschaft in Afrika
Bayreuth Studies in Politics and Society in Africa

is edited by

Institut für Afrikastudien (IAS) der Universität Bayreuth
Dr. Antje Daniel
Prof. Dr. Alexander Stroh

Volume 12

Alžběta Šváblová

The Peacebuilding Process in Postwar Liberia

A Tortuous Way Forward

Diese Arbeit entstand im Rahmen des Exzellenzclusters Africa Multiple, an der Universität Bayreuth, gefördert durch die Deutsche Forschungsgemeinschaft (DFG) im Rahmen der Exzellenzstrategie des Bundes und der Länder – EXC 2052/1 – 390713894.

The Deutsche Nationalbibliothek lists this publication in the Deutsche Nationalbibliografie; detailed bibliographic data are available on the Internet at http://dnb.d-nb.de

a.t.: Bayreuth, Univ., BIGSAS, Diss., 2020

Original title: A tortuous way forward: Peacebuilding process and actor interaction in postwar Liberia

ISBN   978-3-8487-8603-9 (Print)
          978-3-7489-1114-2 (ePDF)

British Library Cataloguing-in-Publication Data
A catalogue record for this book is available from the British Library.

ISBN   978-3-8487-8603-9 (Print)
          978-3-7489-1114-2 (ePDF)

Library of Congress Cataloging-in-Publication Data
Šváblová, Alžběta
The Peacebuilding Process in Postwar Liberia
A Tortuous Way Forward
Alžběta Šváblová
288 pp.
Includes bibliographic references.

ISBN   978-3-8487-8603-9 (Print)
          978-3-7489-1114-2 (ePDF)

Onlineversion
Nomos eLibrary

1st Edition 2021
© Nomos Verlagsgesellschaft, Baden-Baden, Germany 2021. Overall responsibility for manufacturing (printing and production) lies with Nomos Verlagsgesellschaft mbH & Co. KG.

To Marie,
who uplifts my heart and constantly reminds me
what really counts in life.

Acknowledgments

In the first place, I would like to express my gratitude to my supervisor, Prof. Dieter Neubert. He has always been constructive in his feedback, showing me directions and different ways, but leaving the decisions, if I want to follow them, up to me. The completion of this dissertation owes a great deal to his kindness, understanding, and explicit as well as tacit encouragement. A heartfelt thank you belongs to my mentors, Prof. Alexander Stroh, especially for his input to the theoretical and methodological parts, and Prof. Andreas Mehler for his country-specific remarks and advice related to the post-conflict peacebuilding debate. The project could not have been accomplished without the support of my research partners in Liberia. Among the many, I am especially grateful to Silke Pietsch and Debey Sayndee.

My sincere appreciation goes to German Academic Exchange Service (DAAD) and the State of Bavaria, who supported my research financially. BIGSAS, apart from the generous funding for field research and conference travels, also provided a lot of administrative backing and an outstanding working environment. The support from the side of the BIGSAS Junior Fellows was an integral part of it. Matthew Sabbi helped me to shape the theoretical position of the thesis. Stefanie Alisch and Rose Kimani provided inspiration and a great deal of motivation to stay on track with the project. A special thanks belongs to Blaise Muhire, who helped me navigate through the writing phase and reminded me of things I forgot about. Sincere thanks go to Seth Styers, who copyedited the thesis, having included a fair deal of his fine sense of humour in the process.

Needless to say, the dissertation would not come into being without the support of my family. Without my mom, who was always ready to help and never asked the forbidden question about when I am supposed to finish. Without all the grandmas and aunts, who provided hours of selfless baby-sitting. And without Miroslav and Marie. Thank you for being there in good and bad times, and for making me remember, each in your own way, the life beyond a PhD.

To include the names of all friends and colleagues, whose advice, feedback, and good company I appreciated throughout the years is impossible; the list would be too long. This, however, does not mean that I took this support for granted. Thank you all for your cheerleading along the way, your friendship, and your love.

Table of Contents

List of Figures

List of Tables

Acronyms and Abbreviations

ABA	American Bar Association
ACI	Actor-centered institutionalism
ACS	American Colonization Society
ADR	Alternative Dispute Resolution
AfT	Agenda for Transformation
ASI	African Solidarity Initiative
AU	African Union
BCR	Bureau for Corrections and Rehabilitation
BIN	Bureau of Immigration and Naturalization
CAR	Central African Republic
CPA	Comprehensive Peace Agreement
CRC	Constitutional Review Committee
CSC	Country-Specific Configuration
DaO	Delivering as One
DDRR	Disarmament, demobilisation, rehabilitation, and reintegration
DRSRSG	Deputy Representative of the Special Representative of the Secretary General
ECOMOG	ECOWAS Monitoring Group
ECOWAS	Economic Community of West African States
EU	European Union
EWER	Early Warning/Early Response Working Group
EWWG	Early Warning Working Group
FIND	Foundation for International Dignity
GBV	Gender-based violence
GC	Governance Commission
GEMAP	Governance and Economic Management Assistance Program
GIZ	Deutsche Gesellschaft für Internationale Zusammenarbeit
GoL	Government of Liberia
HU	Humanity United
ICTJ	International Center for Transitional Justice
IDPs	Internally displaced persons

IFIs	International financial institutions
IMF	International Monetary Fund
INCHR	Independent National Commission on Human Rights
INPFL	Independent National Patriotic Front of Liberia
JPC	Justice and Peace Commission
JSC	Joint Steering Committee
KAICT	Kofi Annan Institute for Conflict Transformation
LC	Land Commission
LCCs	Land Coordination Centers
LDA	Liberia Development Alliance
LDRT	Land Dispute Resolution Taskforce
LEITI	Liberia Extractive Industries Transparency Initiative
LERN	Liberia's Early Warning and Response Network
LNP	Liberia National Police
LPP	Liberia Peacebuilding Program
LRDC	Liberia Reconstruction and Development Committee
LURD	Liberians United for Reconciliation and Development
MDGs	Millenium Development Goals
MIA	Ministry of Internal Affairs
MLG	Multi-level governance
MLME	Ministry of Lands, Mines, and Energy
MODEL	Movement for Democracy in Liberia
MoF	Ministry of Finance
MoGD	Ministry of Gender and Development
MoJ	Ministry of Justice
MPEA	Ministry of Planning and Economic Affairs
MSME	Micro, small, & medium enterprises
NCDR/NA	National Center for Documents and Records/National Archives
NGP	National Gender Policy
NPFL	National Patriotic Front of Liberia
NRC	Norwegian Refugee Council
NTGL	National Transitional Government of Liberia
NTLA	National Transitional Legislative Assembly
OHCHR	United Nations Office of the High Commissioner for Human Rights
PBA	Peacebuilding Architecture

PBC	Peacebuilding Commission
PBF	Peacebuilding Fund
PBO	Peacebuilding Office
PBSO	Peacebuilding Support Office
PCRD	Post-Conflict Reconstruction and Development
PPP	Peacebuilding Priority Plan
PRPs	Poverty Reduction Papers
PRS	Poverty Reduction Strategy
PUPs	Private Use Permits
R2P	Responsibility to Protect
SC	United Nations Security Council
SIDA	Swedish International Development Cooperation Agency
SRSG	Special Representative of the Secretary General
SSR	Security system reform
TAG	Technical Advisory Group
TRC	Truth and Reconciliation Commission
UN	United Nations
UNDAF	United Nations Development Assistance Framework
UNDP	United Nations Development Fund
UNDG	United Nations Director General
UN-HABITAT	United Nations Human Settlements Programme
UNHCR	United Nations High Commissioner for Refugees
UNICEF	United Nations Children's Fund
UNMIL	United Nations Mission in Liberia
UNPOL	United Nations Police
USAID	United States Agency for International Development
WB	World Bank
WIPNET	Women in Peacebuilding Network

Abstract

The study examines the postwar reconstruction process in Liberia. It analyses the interaction of the government of Liberia, Liberian civil society, and international actors against the backdrop of four institutions, where these actors meet: the Governance Commission, the Land Commission, Gender-Based Violence Taskforce, and Early Warning Working Group. The book studies the roles of the respective actors in the four fields and attempts to identify factors behind the relatively slow pace of the post-conflict reform process. Designed as a qualitative case study with a strong descriptive component, the study used interviews and observation as the main data collection techniques.

Findings indicate that international actors sketched the broad framework of the reform process, provided financial aid, as well as human resources and know-how. The government chose more specific priorities and disposed of a substantial blocking potential with regard to the passing and implementation of the reforms. Civil society played mainly the role of a service- and information-provider. The progress of the reforms was influenced by a number of factors—the most decisive ones being the standard domestic political processes and the nature of the issue at stake. The Liberian case shows that despite a rich, critical academic debate, the current practice of peacebuilding remains shaped by the neo-liberal paradigm, focuses mainly on institution-building, and stays rather disconnected from the post-conflict realities and individuals on the ground. The blinkered perspective of external actors, largely ignoring the domestic political processes, renders the ultimate fate of the reforms uncertain.

Summary

The study focuses on the process of postwar reconstruction in Liberia, more specifically on the involvement of three groups of actors—the government of Liberia, Liberian civil society, and international actors. Against the backdrop of four selected institutions, the dissertation analyses the interaction of the respective actors, their roles in peacebuilding, and attempts to find out the factors explaining the relatively low level of progress in the reform process.

The broader debate on post-conflict peacebuilding has covered a number of topics, but recently, it seemed to become somehow self-referential. Several authors have pointed to the need to overcome this tendency and to revive the debate by including more empirical studies. This dissertation attempts to fill part of the "empirical gap".

Apart from the broader debate on post-conflict peacebuilding, the study was shaped by actor-centered institutionalism, useful for the research design, and multi-level governance, which provided a convenient analytical lens. The multi-level governance approach helps to overcome common analytical boundaries by arguing that decision-making processes transpire on a number of levels and transgress the boundaries of nation-states. They also include various actors. The same applies to peacebuilding. The second theoretical approach used in the study, the actor-centered institutionalism, developed by Renate Mayntz and Fritz Scharpf, points to the fact that when studying social phenomena, both institutions and actors should be taken into account, otherwise their analysis would be incomplete. Mayntz and Scharpf suggest to depart from a specific set of interaction in order to identify relevant actors, which was an approach used during the data collection phase.

The dissertation is designed as a qualitative case study, with Liberia as a general case. There are four embedded units of analysis, defined by selected institutions, representing the "places of encounter" for the actors in focus: the Governance Commission, the Land Commission, Gender-Based Violence Taskforce, and Early Warning Working Group. The sub-cases were chosen according to a number of criteria. All four institutions have been set up in order to deal with an issue important for building stable peace. They are different with regard to their size, degree of financial and political support, level of international presence, and political relevance.

However, they share a common feature, showing little progress in terms of results of their work in the respective fields of reform.

Expert interviews and observation were used as the main techniques for the collection of primary data. After the within-case analysis, the findings from the sub-cases were compared and examined across cases. The four empirical chapters, covering the sub-cases, are complemented by an evaluation of the documents framing the Liberian postwar reconstruction process, and by a detailed analysis of the three groups of actors in focus of the study.

Governance reform, presented in the first empirical chapter, has been a problematic issue since the establishment of Liberia as an independent state. Poor governance and over-centralisation of the state have been at the origins of the growing tensions that contributed to the outbreak of the conflict. The importance of governance reform has been repeatedly emphasised in documents framing the reconstruction, as well as by international and domestic political actors. However, the declared importance of the issue does not match the real support the Governance Commission receives. The GC is in a precarious situation. By the virtue of being an institution that attempts to change established practices, it is quite unpopular with governmental actors. With regard to civil society, they offer each other mutual support. International actors are to a large extent absent in the institution itself; however, they have determined the general direction of the whole reform process towards good governance, with transparency, accountability, decentralisation, etc. The outcomes of the Commission's work are entirely dependent on the legislature, and as such, the institution's political weight is rather low. On the other hand, it has a strong, respected leader, able to leverage support and skillfully manoeuvre the political waters.

A lot of what has been said here applies to the Land Commission as well. Apart from a capable leader, however, land reform also enjoys a fair deal of financial support in addition to the rhetorical one. As an issue with a high conflict potential, it draws the attention of international actors, whose presence at the LC is most significant from all the four selected institutions. However, similar to the GC, the policies the LC proposes have to be approved by the legislature. The experience with passing the Land Rights Act, a major project being blocked by the legislature for several years, shows that the results of the Commission's work can be easily jeopardised, especially by powerful profit-seeking actors behind the scenes.

Gender-based violence has been widespread in postwar Liberia and despite the emphasis on the issue from the side of international actors, the phenomenon is very much rooted in socio-cultural values and norms, which makes it difficult to deal with. The efforts of the GBV Taskforce, the main body in charge of the problem, are focused mainly on service provision for survivors. However, even this task is complicated by inadequate support from the domestic political actors and by the generally poor level of law enforcement. International actors provide more material backing and other forms of assistance, although they also shift the agenda by offering funding opportunities mainly for action focused on the fight against rape. On the other hand, the very presence of a UN mission and a number of international personnel is problematic, being linked to a frequent occurrence of sexual exploitation and abuse. Civil society acts mainly as an implementing partner and information provider from the grassroots level. This is especially visible in the GBV Taskforce.

Early Warning Working Group, representing the last sub-case, is an example of a Liberian-led, bottom-up initiative, based on the engagement of civil society, with international actors providing financial and technical support. The system works quite well, but its main ambition, to offer relevant information for policy-makers, remains unfulfilled. The decision-makers are not interested, and most of the other potential beneficiaries of the project are also excluded, out of different reasons. The impact of the whole initiative is therefore limited. The system is influenced by a number of features that are typical for the political realities of postwar Liberia, and for the current practice of peacebuilding, such as high fluctuation of personnel, importance of "rank", or lack of coordination among a great number of actors involved in different initiatives.

In general, despite the variation across cases, it can be said that international actors mainly provide general direction of the reforms and bring material and human resources to support the reforms. The UN is the most prominent actor on the ground and serves as a "manager" of the reconstruction process, breaking the general objectives included in the framework plans into smaller tasks and programs for a subsequent implementation. Bilateral partners are present through their diplomatic representations on the ground, and in the institutions at the supra-national and highest decision-making level. The regional dimension of the reconstruction process and the presence of regional organisations on the ground was marginal. The Liberian government decides over more specific priorities, and most importantly, disposes of a substantial "allowing" and blocking potential. Civil society, despite its higher ambitions, works mainly as an information- and service-provider, implementing the projects of bigger players. Due to the dependency on external funding and a general low level of development, its agenda is often donor-driven.

The interaction among the three groups of actors in the four sub-cases was determined by the specific nature and political character of the particular issue at stake. It is facilitated by the relatively small size of the country, and also by the very existence of the institutions and where they can meet. There seems to be a tacit understanding on this division of labour, and despite some underlying tensions, there were no signs of open conflict or rivalry among the different actors. Generally, governmental actors showed a lower level of participation than the other two categories. This might be explained as a result of a meeting fatigue, lack of "buy-in" for the reforms, or a strategy of extraversion.

The explanatory factors behind the lack of progress also varied across the four sub-cases. In the case of land and governance reforms, it was the dependency on other actors in the political process, especially on the legislature, which, out of different reasons, was not favourable. With regard to GBV, the nature of the issue, combined with a low level of priority and financial support, seem to be the problem. Concerning the early warning, the main challenge is its irrelevance for the decision-makers.

More generally, categories of "support" (both formal and financial), which seem to co-relate with the level of international presence, have been decisive for the question of progress. Another one was the nature of the issue at stake—some, such as governance or GBV, are more resistant to change, as they are closely connected to the mindset of people, or socio-cultural values and political culture. Some issues, such as land, have higher conflict potential. However, domestic political actors and processes are the crucial factor, determining the ultimate fate of the reform efforts. Surprisingly, it seems not to be considered by the architects of postwar reforms.

Contextual variables were also essential, starting from the international context, with rules shaped by the neo-liberal paradigm, global commodity prices, and stability in the region, to the domestic level, with a high fluctuation of personnel, low institutional stability, and lack of material and human resources. Additional factors with impact on the reforms were leadership and individual engagement. Many of these factors are not sufficiently reflected in the theoretical literature on peacebuilding.

The Liberian example shows how current peacebuilding practice puts a great deal of emphasis on formal coherence. However, this coherence results in the creation of a self-referential, hegemonic discourse, which does not grant space for alternatives and leads to a blinkered perspective, to a large extent disconnected from the postwar reality. There is also a clear detachment from the post-conflict individuals. The ultimate beneficiaries of the reforms are not in the centre of attention. Instead, institutional reforms are in focus, with the underlying assumption that well-functioning states are the best guarantee for stable peace.

In the academic debate, especially in the critical stream of thought, these problematic issues have been pointed to. However, due to a relatively closed nature of both the academic and practitioners' worlds, the insights and recommendations do not translate into changes of peacebuilding policies and strategies. This dissertation, by focusing on peacebuilding practice on the ground, attempts to bridge part of this gap, and provide empirical contribution for the theoretical debate, as well as useful input for the peacebuilding practitioners.

Chapter 1 Introduction

The civil war in Liberia lasted, with a short break in the 1990s, over 20 years. It led to a human tragedy of a scale hard to imagine, with massive displacement, hundreds of thousands deaths, complete destruction of the country, and destabilisation of the whole region. It is estimated that over half of the Liberian population was displaced during the conflict. The peak year was 1994, with an estimated 1.1 million IDPs and 780,000 refugees (Sawyer 2005: 209). About 250,000 people, representing over 10 percent of the pre-war population of the country had been killed (TRC 2009).[1]

After the end of the war in 2003, one of the largest and most expensive UN missions ever was deployed in the country with the ambitious goals to avoid the mistakes of previous peace operations and to prove that the UN is capable of "doing peacebuilding". Soon, the country was flooded by foreign experts, military and civilian UN personnel, as well as dozens of NGOs. Some years later, after the security situation had improved, they were joined by researchers, eager to watch this laboratory of transformation in real time.

The initial, intensive phase of international engagement has come to an end. After 15 years, the UN mission closed in March 2018. Shortly before that, in a democratic transition, the first postwar president, Ellen Johnson Sirleaf, handed the presidential seat over to George Weah. The country has certainly developed since the end of the war; however, much remains to be done. At this kind of a cross-roads, my thesis offers an opportunity to look back at some aspects of the peacebuilding and postwar reconstruction exercise.

Since the 1990s, peacebuilding, defined as "building confidence among previously warring parties, developing the social, political, and economic infrastructure to prevent future violence, and laying the foundation for a durable peace" (Doyle and Sambanis 2006: 11), has attracted considerable interest of both scholars and practitioners. Starting as an analysis of a new style of peacekeeping operations of the UN and international organisations, the scope of the debate soon broadened. Apart from the relatively uncontroversial discussions about effectivity, sequencing of the reforms, and other "technical" issues, a more critical stream of thought emerged,

---

1 The estimates vary depending on the methodology of the sources.

questioning the legitimacy and the very rationale of the interventions and their underlying values. The "local turn" in the debate has shifted the attention to the side of the actors in the countries of deployment; local voices, preferences, and solutions; and the issue of ownership in the peacebuilding process. The role of the civil society in the latter became more prominent as well.

However, in reality, peacebuilding in countries emerging from a violent conflict has so far followed the mainstream, neo-liberal, top-down approach, promoted by the UN and international agencies, with a clear set of reforms to be accomplished within the framework of a post-conflict reconstruction process. The latter is to some extent shaped by the conditions and context of a particular case, but remains very schematic in its basic setting and with a strong emphasis on institution-building.

The postwar reconstruction exercise is a complex endeavour, with a plethora of actors taking part. Three main groups are always involved in the process: the government of the state "under reconstruction", international or external actors (e.g., international organisations, usually with the UN taking the lead, foreign governments, or donors), and local non-state actors, often put together under the label of civil society.[2] Throughout the exercise, these three broad categories interact and play different parts. There are general assumptions and tacit understanding about what their cooperation should look like and what their roles should be; the international side should provide financial (and other) resources for reforms, designed according to the needs and in an active participation of the partners on the "recipient side". The latter should ensure legitimacy and sustainability of the reforms. Post-conflict peacebuilding has been acknowledged as a complex process, but has rarely been studied empirically in its multi-actor and multi-level complexities (with some notable exceptions, such as Nagelhus Schia 2015 for Liberia).

There have been a number of studies focusing on the roles of a single group of actors in postwar context, for example, on the role of the international ones (de Carvalho et al. 2018, Röhner 2012, Zürcher 2006), or on the role of civil society in the peacebuilding process (Neubert 2004, Paffenholz 2010 and 2015, van Tongeren 2005, Zanker 2017); however, the nature of interaction of all three groups has hardly been a focus of

---

2 Economic actors, such as international and transnational corporations, or local businessmen, are also an integral part of it. However, this study is first and foremost a political analysis. As such, it leaves the analysis of economic actors aside, except for the cases where they are directly linked to the issues in focus.

attention, and even more rarely formed the main focus of research.[3] This is a gap this book aims to fill, at least partly, by analysing the case of Liberia.

Liberia represents a typical post-conflict country in many respects. After a protracted civil war with no clear winner a negotiated peace agreement was signed, and subsequently, a transitional government based on a power-sharing agreement was formed. There were a number of other factors that seemed to work in favour of the reconstruction and reforms—the relatively small size of the country, a robust UN presence in the form of a peacekeeping mission with a broad mandate and good financial support, and, last but not least, a reform-oriented political leadership that emerged from the elections in 2005.

The presented study analyses the interaction of three groups of actors—Liberian government, international actors, and civil society—in the peacebuilding process in Liberia, in four selected institutions: the Governance Commission, the Land Commission, the Gender-Based Violence Taskforce, and the Early Warning Working Group. On the backdrop of the four "places of encounter", I analyse the roles of the particular actors in the four specific micro-contexts, as well as at a broader, cross-case level. The four institutions are all closely related to peacebuilding reforms but vary in a number of other aspects, such as the level of international presence, material support, or the conflict potential of the issue they try to address. As such, they offer diverse yet complementary perspectives on the practice of peacebuilding.

Apart from the interaction and roles of particular actors, the study seeks to examine the relatively slow pace of peacebuilding reforms. Despite the favourable factors mentioned, the considerable efforts, elaborate planning, and substantial financial resources invested in the peacebuilding process, until nowadays, 15 years after the end of the war, there has been little advancement. The thesis tries to identify the factors that impact the pace of reforms and that can explain the reasons behind the lack of progress in the four presented sub-fields of reconstruction.

Usually, the kind of questions this study asks are approached from an abstract, general perspective, often taking a normative stance of how things should be and pointing to the fact that the reality is different from this ideal state of affairs. This book approaches the topic in a different

---

3 With a few exceptions, such as Autesserre (2017) looking at the everyday interaction of "insiders" and "outsiders" from an anthropological perspective, Heathershaw (2009), Pouligny (2006) or Sabaratnam (2017). None of those, however, explicitly used more specific categories of actors for the analysis.

way. It departs from the empirical base. Such an approach, together with the relatively long time span of seven years the study covers, represent its main strength and contribution to the existing body of research. Apart from that, the descriptive component provides a unique contribution to the body of knowledge on postwar Liberia, offering a systematic and detailed picture of the institutions in focus, and of the developments in the respective sub-fields of reconstruction.

The thesis is a qualitative case study, with Liberia as the general "case", with four sub-cases defined by the four institutions in focus. The latter serve as a base for the final analysis at the level of the primary case (i.e., the country). The primary data were collected using interviews, observation, and informal conversations, and complemented by secondary sources (i.e., official documents and plans framing the reconstruction process, grey literature, and academic literature).

As is often pointed out with regard to case study research, the tempta-tion of making broad generalisations is quite high (George and Bennett 2005: 23ff., Jahn 2006: 320ff.). While this book focuses on one country, it is obvious that the Liberian experience shares a number of characteris-tics prominent in other countries emerging from violent conflicts. The postwar political and social "landscapes" share a number of common features (e.g., fragile or non-functional state institutions, destroyed infras-tructure, political and social polarisation) or factors shaping the postwar international intervention—the "tyranny of the urgent"; fast-changing, dy-namic context; number of actors involved; coordination challenges; etc. The "peacebuilding cookbooks" are also to a large extent similar, being shaped by the ruling neo-liberal discourse (Newman et al. 2009, Debiel et al. 2016). Following the similarities of the issues to be solved and processes used for this purpose, it is clear that some findings from the Liberian case can be generalisable, and might be compared and tested in other postwar contexts.

This study, by looking at specific institutional contexts, provides insights into the limitations of the current approach to international postwar peacebuilding. By examining the policy-making processes and functioning of some of the formal institutions, it argues that issues, which are mostly not taken into consideration in the design and implementation of the postwar peacebuilding programmes, are actually crucial for the outcomes of the work of the institutions, and, consequently, for the outcomes of the peacebuilding interventions in general. The nature of a particular issue at stake, the position of the institution *vis-à-vis* the broader political context, or individual engagement and leadership are some of them. The evidence

from Liberia seems to relativise the conviction that peacebuilding as institution-building is the right and effective approach for countries emerging
from a violent conflict. In other words, the thesis suggests that putting
some institutional structures into place, to ensure creation and later implementation of a policy or reform, is often not enough and does not yield
the expected results. The blinkered perspective of the external actors, limited to the view of peacebuilding as institution-building and policy-making,
and to a large extent ignoring the domestic political processes and power
players (cf. Sabaratnam 2017), leaves the fate of the peacebuilding reforms
up in the air. The neo-liberal approach to peacebuilding has a clear set of
goals and a portfolio of strategies on how to achieve them. However, they
often have little in common with the reality into which they are planted.
Often, they are suited for rational bureaucracies of the "Western" cut and
do not take into consideration the specificities and hurdles of particular
postwar contexts, where institutional fragility meets scarcity of qualified
staff, basic equipment, high turnout of personnel, and interests of various
political (but also other) actors.

From the theoretical perspective, the research design was shaped by
actor-centered institutionalism and multi-level governance (MLG). The actor-centered institutionalism promotes the approach that takes interaction
in a specific field, representing a unit of analysis, as a point of departure
which allows us to identify relevant actors in the context (Mayntz and
Scharpf 1995). Institutions create arenas for interaction among the actors,
and hence a setting, where the rules and principles of interaction can be
observed (Scharpf 1997). The MLG approach reminds us that actors can
transgress common analytical boundaries and move among them (Marks
1991, Piattoni 2010). Peacebuilding works in a similar manner; there is a
range of actors, operating at different levels (i.e., international, national, or
sub-national) that affect their presence, engagement, and ways of decision-
making.

After the initial overview of theoretical debates about peacebuilding and
introduction of multi-level governance and actor-centered institutionalism,
the outline of the methodology follows. Chapter four presents the historical background of the case by briefly summarising basic information about
the conflict and its background, about the peace process, and the postwar
situation in Liberia. The particular focus of the chapter are the factors
and events leading to the civil war, and those pertaining to some of the
issues treated in the case studies. Chapter five examines the three groups
of actors in our focus (i.e., the government of Liberia, international actors,
and civil society) and outlines their roles in the postwar period. After that,

it introduces various "places of encounter", where the actors meet and interact. At the same time, it offers insights on the political realities of the postwar context and some of its characteristics, that substantially shape the conditions of the whole reconstruction exercise. Chapter six analyses the documents, framing the Liberian reconstruction process, starting with the Comprehensive Peace Agreement from Accra, through the Poverty Reduction Strategy, UNDAFs, and Peacebuilding Priority Plans. Apart from the analysis of the content, it points to their coherence and to the fact that the latter does not represent a strength only.

Chapters seven to 10 cover the case studies, forming the core of the book. They follow a similar structure: after the introduction of the topic, its relevance to Liberian conflict and post-conflict[4], and current debates in the field, the institution in focus, its projects, and position in the broader political landscape are presented. In the analytical part of the chapters, the interaction and roles of the groups of actors in focus are outlined. The final sections draw partial conclusions and relate the findings to the initial research questions. The first two case study chapters (on governance and land reform) examine the policy-making aspects of the respective commissions, whereas the chapters on gender issues and early warning analyse the activities and working processes of the institutions in focus. This difference is not deliberate; it is a result of different ways of functioning of the respective bodies. Both perspectives, however, complement each other in showing different facets of peacebuilding practice on the ground.

Chapter 11 represents a cross-case analysis, juxtaposing and comparing the four cases, presenting topics and factors that crystallised as important in the particular cases, and discusses the implications of the findings.

---

4 Similar to some authors, I use "post-conflict" as a noun here.

Chapter 2 Theories and concepts

"There is nothing more practical than a good theory."
Kurt Lewin: Field theory in social science (1952: 169)

2.1 Peacebuilding: Origins of the term

The term peacebuilding was coined in the 1970s by Johan Galtung, a "founding father" of the discipline of peace studies in his essay "Three approaches to peace: Peacekeeping, Peacemaking, and Peacebuilding" (Galtung 1976). Since then, the concept has become accepted and widely used in academia and among practitioners. However, its general acceptance and notoriety came first with the end of the bipolar world.

The first generation of peace operations led by the UN dates back to the early years of the Cold War and fall in the category of peacekeeping missions. The missions were deployed in inter-state conflicts to monitor ceasefires or to guard demilitarised areas and buffer zones, and had no ambition to resolve the sources of conflict or instability which, at that time, were considered to belong to the *domaine reservée* of the state. This early stage is sometimes referred to as the "Westphalian" era, pointing to the fact that states represented the main points of reference, as well as the main sources of security threats in the international system.

The major shift in the system of international relations following the end of the Cold War also created a fundamental change in the patterns of violent conflicts (Kaldor 2012, Lederach 1997: 1-18). The end of bipolarity brought an increased number of minor conflicts, with the majority of them being intra-state. The "old" peacekeeping proved to be insufficient for the different context, and a new type of peace operations emerged. Their objectives became more complex, with a broader range of activities and the involvement of more actors, including the non-governmental, humanitarian, or commercial ones. The number of operations also grew bigger, with almost 60 in years 1991–2015, compared to 13 from 1945–1991. These multifaceted missions are often called the "second generation" of peace operations and mark the transition from the classical peacekeeping to the post-Westphalian *peacebuilding*.

Since the new missions were usually deployed amidst intra-state violence, they needed a solid justification. The rationale for this kind of external involvement had two sources. Firstly, the humanitarian one. The situations of widespread violence, with refugees, diseases, famine, environmental deterioration, etc., have no longer been perceived as a concern that can be overlooked or left to be resolved by the respective states. This principle is embodied in the "Responsibility to Protect" doctrine (R2P), endorsed at the 2005 World Summit, and claims that states have to protect their populations from mass atrocities. In situations where states fail to grant such a protection, the international community has the responsibility to intervene.[5] Secondly, the principal change in the security paradigm after the end of the Cold War, but more importantly after 9/11, brought a fundamental shift in the conception of a threat. It was no longer strong states who constituted a security threat for the others, but the weak ones. Internal instability and conditions of state failure, or lack of control over their territories, made states sources of regional instability and potential sanctuaries for terrorist organisations. The new peacebuilding was one of the strategies to address this threat.

Peacebuilding in the post-bipolar world

One of the first attempts to define peacebuilding in the "new era" of the post-bipolar world dates back to the 1992 "Agenda for Peace" by the UN Secretary General Boutros-Ghali. The document that summarises the tasks of the UN in the new context of world politics conceives peacebuilding as a counterpart to preventive diplomacy, where the latter seeks to help avoid a crisis by preventing the escalation of a problem, whereas the objective of the former is to prevent the recurrence of a conflict. More specifically, peacebuilding refers to any "action to identify and support structures which will tend to strengthen and solidify peace in order to avoid a relapse into conflict" (UN 1992).

From a temporal perspective, preventive diplomacy should be the first attempt to "resolve disputes before violence breaks out" (UN 1992). In a situation of open conflict, the concept of peacemaking comes to the fore, trying to bring parties of conflict to an agreement. Once attained, peacekeeping seeks to protect the agreement, usually in a form of a de-

---

5 For more details see the Global Centre for the Responsibility to Protect website (http://www.globalr2p.org/about_r2p, accessed 23. 11. 2015).

ployment of a UN mission that prepares the ground for the post-conflict peacebuilding process.

Following the Agenda for Peace, peacebuilding has become a buzzword and was further discussed in a number of UN documents. One of those that brought a significant contribution to the evolution of the term was the Brahimi report (UN 2000) that defined the aim of peacebuilding as achieving "something that is more than just the absence of war" (UN 2000: 3), coming close to the meaning of positive peace in Galtung's sense.[6] Five years later, the Secretary General's Report "In Larger Freedom" called for the creation of the Peacebuilding Architecture to facilitate the implementation and coordination of relevant activities within the UN (UN 2005).

2.2 UN Peacebuilding Architecture

The concept of Peacebuilding Architecture (PBA), which should support "coherence and effectiveness" in post-conflict peacebuilding (UN Peacebuilding Support Office 2010), was presented at the World Summit in 2005. It consists of the intergovernmental PB Commission, PB Support Office, and a multi-donor trust fund (Peacebuilding Fund). Represented in the Commission are national governments, as well as international donors and financing institutions. The PB Support Office provides administrative support to the Commission. The Fund, established in 2006, serves as a flexible source of financing for countries emerging from a violent conflict, especially in situations where no other financial mechanisms are available. It combines the advantages of a global fund with a country-specific focus.

The original purpose and mandate of the PBA was to coordinate peacebuilding efforts, to facilitate cooperation and synergies among the relevant stakeholders, and to serve as a resource center of knowledge and expertise (Hearn, Kubitschek Bujones, and Kugel 2014). However, the combination of a broad mandate with a lack of tools and institutional weight to assert that mandate led to inactivity at the beginning of PBA's existence. The new bodies were regarded as unwelcome intruders by the established UN

---

6 Galtung makes a distinction between a "negative" peace, which means a mere absence of open violence, and a "positive" peace or, as he put it in an editorial to the first issue of the Journal of Peace Research, "the integration of human society" (1964: 2)—a situation without structural violence, where relationships among the parties are supportive and collaborative, and conflicts are being resolved constructively (Galtung 1969).

agencies and became a proxy-platform for pursuing various agendas from other venues.[7] They lacked legitimacy in the eyes of other actors engaged in peacebuilding, even within the UN system, and were therefore unable to even coordinate activities in the field, let alone to fulfill the originally envisaged leading role. The PBA spent the first years of its existence trying to find its place in the institutional landscape of the UN and developing the basic working mechanisms. From mid-2008 on, after the initial stage of "survival", it has started to pursue its mandate more vigorously, but is still far from living up to the original expectations (Jenkins 2013).[8]

2.3 AU Framework

A similar structure to the PBA can be found at the level of the African Union (AU). In July 2006, the AU adopted the Post-conflict Reconstruction and Development (PCRD) Policy[9]—intended to serve as a framework for planning and designing specific policies that "seek to consolidate peace, promote sustainable development and pave the way for growth and regeneration in countries and regions emerging from conflict" (African Union 2006). In contrast to the UN framework documents, it is far more detailed and specific.

The policy is designed as a tool for peace consolidation and prevention of relapse into violence. It should help "address the root causes of conflict, encourage and fast-track planning and implementation of reconstruction activities; and enhance complementarities and coordination between and among diverse actors engaged in PCRD processes" (Africa Governance Institute 2014). There have been some steps towards its implementation, such as the creation of operational guidelines for the implementation at

---

7 The PBA was created in the context of broader reform of the UN system, and arguments from negotiations about other reform issues (e.g., the UNHCR) often spilled over to PBA. This was used as an alternative, proxy battlefield, where losses from other venues could be counterbalanced.

8 Apart from the factors already mentioned here, there is also a weak working relationship with the Security Council and perceived lack of a strategic vision that contribute to this situation. In 2011, there was contention between the PBC and the OECD-led International Dialogue on Peacebuilding and Statebuilding, where the G7+ countries are represented, which led to further lowering of the impact of the Commission at the international level (Hearn, Kubitschek Bujones, and Kugel 2014).

9 Decision of the Executive Council EX.CL/Dec.302 (IX).

the regional and national level, the creation of a Committee within the AU, efforts to build a database of peacebuilding experts across Africa, and several "quick impact" projects and multi-disciplinary missions to assess the needs of the post-conflict countries across the African continent.[10] The African Solidarity Initiative (ASI), as a means to mobilise resources comparable to the UN Peacebuilding Fund, was established in 2012 (ISS Africa 2014). However, the overall impact of the framework is very limited. Most of the listed activities are related to the institutional or policy-development aspects. As such, there remains a lack of adequate resources and capacities, as well as a general lack of experience and engagement at the highest political level.[11]

2.4 Peacebuilding as a concept

Based on the examples mentioned here, it is clear that although peace-building generally refers to a variety of activities that contribute to building peaceful societies and addressing issues with a conflict potential, in practice the term is used predominantly for the measures following a violent conflict, that is for *post-conflict* peacebuilding.

In the discourse of the UN and other international agencies, the concept is usually employed interchangeably with the term post-conflict reconstruction, in both cases referring to "building confidence among previously warring parties, developing the social, political, and economic infrastructure to prevent future violence, and laying the foundation for a durable peace" (Doyle and Sambanis 2006: 11). As Jeong argues, the process of post-conflict reconstruction should "enhance public security, generate economic recovery, facilitate social healing, and promote democratic institutions" (Jeong 2005: 12-13).

Although it has become a common parlance, this interchangeability is, in fact, problematic, for it narrows the term to the post-conflict reconstruction projects, usually implemented in a form of a UN mission, or another externally led intervention. However, as we will see, there is an

---

10 There have been six missions of this kind: CAR (2006), Liberia and Sierra Leone (2009), DRC and Burundi (2010), and Sudan (2011). See ISS Africa (2014).

11 The PCRD Ministerial Commission, established in 2003, has been inactive. The PCRD Unit has only one employee and the outbreaks of violence in Mali (2012), CAR (2013), or Sudan (2013) proved that the PCRD is very much insufficient in its impact (ISS Africa 2014).

alternative perspective, promoted by the conflict-resolution school, critical or feminist approaches (e.g., Monk and Mundy 2014, Porter 2007), where peacebuilding can be conceived much more extensively.

A broad definition, provided by Newman, Paris, and Richmond in their edited volume (2009) summarising the recent debate about the concept, presents peacebuilding as a cluster of activities, aiming to prevent the escalation or resumption of violent conflict and to establish a durable and self-sustaining peace by addressing the underlying sources of conflict. The goal is building and rebuilding peaceful social institutions, as well as values, institutions of governance, and the rule of law (Newman, Paris, and Richmond 2009: 8). In a similar vein, though from a slightly more holistic and people-centered perspective, Schneckener (2016) understands peacebuilding as "a holistic approach to building peaceful relations among people, covering political, economic, social, cultural, symbolic, educational, and psychological aspects" (Schneckener 2016: 2).

The packages commonly implemented in postwar contexts include activities in four broad areas: the first one contains measures related to the provision of basic stabilisation and security, followed by the process of disarmament, demobilisation, rehabilitation, and reintegration of former fighters (DDRR) and a security system reform (SSR). The second field of reform focuses on politics and governance, and includes the organisation of elections, re-/building of institutions of governance, and establishing the rule of law. Justice and reconciliation is the third pillar. And last but not least, there are activities related to the economic revitalisation and development (Jeong 2005, Paris 2004).

In peacebuilding literature, one often comes across the term *state-building* (in the US context, this is also called "nation-building"[12]). Although often discussed together with peacebuilding, state-building is narrower in the scope of included activities. The main focus is the reconstruction of the institutions of governance, service delivery, and effective control of the state's territory and borders, as well as rebuilding the capacity of states in their external relations. As Dobbins puts it in the RAND "Beginner's

---

12 This terminological incoherence might stem from the use of the concept of "nation-state" in the US debate. The term has been used since the 1960s in the context of political science modernisation theories. However, using the term "nation-building" as a synonym for state-building suggests that, contrary to empirical and theoretical understanding of a nation and its emergence, external actors are commonly involved in the process of creating a nation. In addition, historically, nation-building has occurred most often through wars, which makes the affinity of the concept with peacebuilding even more problematic (Newman 2009: 30).

Guide to Nation-Building", state-building refers to the efforts to "promote political and economic reforms with the objective of transforming a society emerging from conflict into one at peace with itself and its neighbors" (Dobbins et al. 2007, xvii). The problematic point in this respect is the question, whose vision of state is being promoted. It is usually the Western secular state, based on liberal values, which is far from being universally accepted and appropriate.

2.5 Peacebuilding discourse: Scholarly perspectives

In the course of time, several schools of thought about peacebuilding have developed. The oldest, neo-liberal, or "mainstream", approach, describes peacebuilding as a mainly top-down process, with governmental and international actors calling the tune. The latter are also referred to as "track one" actors, based on Montville's (1982) distinction between the official (track one) diplomacy and the "track two", non-governmental approach to conflict. The analytical lens was further elaborated and applied to peacebuilding by Lederach (1997: 37ff.). The first track involves international actors (mainly international governmental organisations), high-level politicians, and diplomats. The second, middle track includes civil society activists, scholars, religious leaders, or opinion leaders from other fields. In the third one, actors and leaders at the grassroots level are represented.[13]

The neo-liberal approach usually accepts the principal "rules of the game" of the current peacebuilding practice as legitimate and taken for granted, and when taking a critical stance, it adopts a "problem-solving" perspective, focusing mainly on the methods or effectiveness of peacebuilding projects and the ways they could be improved in the context of the ruling neo-liberal paradigm. It deals with issues such as parameters of the missions, sequencing, or pace of the reforms. Advantages of light- vs. heavy-footprint missions are discussed, for example, by Zürcher (2006) or Röhner (2012). Paris (2004) argues for institutionalisation before liberalisation; others advocate for establishing power-sharing agreements (see Mehler 2016), emphasis on the DDR ("security first", e.g., Marten 2004,

---

13 The classification was further developed by Louise Diamond and John W. Mc-Donald into nine tracks, which include also business, education, activism, and other categories (for details see http://imtd.org/about/what-is-multi-track-diplomacy).

Etzioni 2007), or support of civil society (Pouligny 2016, Van Tongeren et al. 2005, Verkoren and Van Leeuwen 2013).

The primary actor engaged in mainstream, top-down peacebuilding is the UN, with the international financial institutions in the background, supporting the programs and reforms financially. They tend to present peacebuilding as a task of a purely technical nature, therefore value- and interest-free. However, in reality, peacebuilding is *essentially* political. Despite the "universal blueprint approach", it is certainly relevant to ask how the peacebuilding activities are designed and whose interests are being served (Newman 2009).

An alternative school, derived from conflict resolution and coming mainly from the middle-level practitioners' perspective, sees peacebuilding in a much broader light. It usually puts emphasis on the context of each case—historical, cultural, and other specificities of the societies where peacebuilding takes place (Lederach 1997, Darby and Mac Ginty 2003). It focuses more on the second- and third-track actors and includes activities taking place not only *after* the official end of hostilities, but also during and even before the outbreak of violence. The building of peace emphasises the bottom-up, rather than the top-down, approach and brings the role of local actors to the fore. The impact of the conflict resolution school, or the transformative approach to peacebuilding, as Edward Newman (2009) calls it, has permeated the neo-liberal discourse over time. Transformative peacebuilding tries to address the underlying sources of violence, to engage local institutions and communities, and to build on local customs and norms (Newman 2009: 47). In this vein, local actors, context, and local solutions should have provided a cure for some of the ailments the mainstream approach suffered from, mainly for the lack of social and political legitimacy of the institutions being created, resulting in a questionable sustainability of the latter (e.g., Chandler 2006, Donais 2009). Richmond compares the current practice of peacebuilding to building "virtual peace resting on cold institutions" (2009b: 58), where peace is designed primarily for the "benefit of the international community, in the hope that locals will benefit later when it becomes internalised and the local is 'converted'" (Richmond 2009b: 62).

To be sure, the "local turn" with the strategy of engaging local actors makes sense, especially with regard to the criticism pointed to neo-liberal peacebuilding with its "tendency to be formulaic, top-down and ethnocentric" (Newman 2009: 42, cf. Schneckener 2016) and its lack of attention to traditional institutions and local forms of authority (Newman 2009). "The locals" can provide legitimacy, and their potential to block reforms is an aspect to be taken into consideration (Donais 2009, Hughes et al. 2015). However, there are some problematic points.

Firstly, the lack of proper definition or content of the "local". Usually, local is defined in opposition to the external or international. Each one takes its counterpart as a point of reference, so the categories are mutually constitutive (Mac Ginty 2016). Schneckener (2016) reminds us that both concepts "remain overdetermined and undertheorized at the same time (Schneckener 2016: 12).

"The local" can have different meanings, depending on the characteristics or normative expectations ascribed to it, either as something that has to be reformed, or to the contrary, a resource to be built upon (MacGinty 2015, Donais 2009, Richmond 2009a). It is often pictured as being rather passive, resisting or ignoring the initiatives of the former, whereas the external peacebuilders are portrayed as acting rationally and being goal-oriented (cf. Mehler 2016). Sometimes there is a tendency to romanticise the local (Newman 2009), as of being inherently propitious to peace. However, local actors often have their own interests and agendas, and some of the latter are far from having sustainable peace as their ultimate goal. Certain "local values" can be also significantly different from the generally accepted human rights standards or practices of good governance (Hughes et al. 2015). "The locals" have often been portrayed as passive recipients, displaying little agency besides simple resistance or disinterest. However, it has been observed that the globally produced agendas and messages in peacebuilding (and in a number of other fields) are subject to substantial modification in the course of the implementation process. The process has been theorised under the "travelling models" label (Behrends et al. 2014) and analyzed by a number of authors, describing the same dynamics without using the concept.[14]

At the analytical level, it is more useful to distinguish specific actors—national elites, regional or grassroots-level actors, civil society, international NGOs, governments, armed groups, etc. (cf. Schneckener 2016: 12). Still, despite using more specific categories, sometimes it is difficult to distinguish between the local and the international at the empirical level. External actors by the virtue of their operation on the ground become a part of the "local" political landscape. There are people from the diaspora coming back to their home country for short- or longer-term contracts. There are positions at the local ministries, manned by foreign experts employed as local staff (such as the Scott Fellows, graduates from prestigious

---

14 E.g., Sharon Abramowitz (2014) for Liberia.

US universities, see de Carvalho et al. 2018, or chapter five for details). In such cases, the vague border between external and local becomes even harder to trace, as it can go "through" an individual.

In addition, peacebuilding is by nature a complex endeavour, where interactions take place on multiple levels—more than just these two. Peacebuilders on the ground have to deal not only with their counterparts in the country, but also with their headquarters (or capitals, at the level above), or, in case of "local" peacebuilders, with their constituencies (a level below). Each of the levels is driven by a slightly different logic, and the perspectives might be conflicting. Schneckener (2011, 2016) distinguishes several levels of interaction: among locals, among internationals, between local elites and international peacebuilders, among internationals "working in the same post-conflict theatre" (Schneckener 2016: 13), among actors in the capitals and headquarters (ibid.). This distinction is analytically useful and could be further refined. Going in this direction, this thesis focuses on the arena where the internationals meet locals at the working, middle level, not the "elite" one. At the same time, it pays attention to the loop of command between the headquarters and actors on the ground, as an important, yet often implicit, factor shaping the interaction.

2.6 Critical approaches

The point of departure of the critical school of thought about peace operations was the observation that the existing scholarship dealing with the topic has been undertheorised, and when tackling theoretical questions, it has overly focused on the problem-solving aspects (Bellamy 2004; Chandler 2006; Newman and Richmond 2001; Paris 2001; Pugh 2004). Generally, the critical approaches challenge the normative and ethical foundations of peacebuilding, questioning the legitimacy of the project and its underlying values, such as the ideas of liberal democracy, market economy, and state-building. It sees the current peacebuilding as a project of rich countries of the global North, reflecting and reproducing power inequalities in the world. There are several streams of the critical thinking, based, for example, on neo-Marxism, neo-colonialism, or feminist approaches.

There is a line of scholarship that completely denies the usefulness of external intervention in a conflict and suggests that it is better to "let the states fail", parties fight, and conflict burn out (Herbst 2004; Weinstein 2005). The argument follows a realist reasoning, stating that peace agreements following a military victory are more likely to last than after a negotiated agreement and states are better off when left to recover without an external intervention. This strategy, however appealing, is problematic in the post-Cold War context of protracted intra-state conflicts, which do not tend to end with a clear military victory of one of the parties and, if left to burn out, can last decades, leaving the countries and their populations completely devastated. Secondly, the argument that conflict has been historically the most efficient way to define boundaries (e.g., in medieval Europe), whereas borders in other parts of the world (e.g., in Africa) are artificial, loses a large part of its appeal in the post-bipolar world, where most of the conflicts are intra-state. Last but not least, the "hands-off" approach is highly problematic because of the concern made explicit in the R2P doctrine, which refuses to leave human suffering in an exclusive sphere of action of individual states.

The most common argument of the critical school focuses on the intrusiveness of peacebuilding missions, stating that they are overly invasive (Chandler 2000; Chopra 2000; Chopra 2002). Surely, the external engagement is substantial and in a postwar context, with lack of human resources and capacities on the domestic side, the influence of external peacebuilders on the agenda is bigger than domestic parties might like. On the other hand, the invasiveness of the missions is often exaggerated, with regard to the extent to which the intervention is able and willing to transform the states and societies of deployment. In addition, there are some authors (e.g., Oliver Richmond 2009b) who criticise the exact opposite, that the reforms are superficial and cannot bring the needed transformation in all (read: social) segments.

Interestingly, contrary to most of the critics pointing out the excessive intrusiveness, Richmond argues that the current practice of reforms is not thorough enough to achieve the desired result. He is also one of the authors pointing to the problem of over-focus on the *rights* of the post-conflict individuals and not enough on their *needs* (2009b). Welfare is relegated on the periphery of attention (2009b, cf. Pugh 2009). Charbonneau et al. (2012) point to the neglect of a post-conflict individual as well, seeing the well-being of these actors as a possible point of intersection between the top-down and bottom-up approaches. Taking into consideration the "individual turn" in security studies and some other areas, it is actually surprising that the approach has not penetrated the mainstream peacebuilding discourse, and the individuals who should be the final beneficiaries of the reforms are still relegated to the margins.

Feminist authors, such as Porter (2007), criticise the prevailing approach to peacebuilding as too narrow, not only leaving out women's perspectives and experiences, but also, similarly to the transformatory school, as conceiving peacebuilding as *post*-conflict and focusing predominantly on formal processes. Porter argues that peacebuilding has to be understood more broadly as a "process that encompasses pre-conflict, conflict and post-accord transformation in formal and informal settings" (Porter 2007: 26ff.). Only in this case does informal, grassroots-level work that is crucial for building stable peace not fall out of scope. Porter further problematises the "post-conflict" adjective, arguing that it refers to the time when the fighters cease to engage in the "official" warfare. However, this is often a case of a "negative peace", where the general feeling of insecurity still prevails and conflicts are present. Similar to some authors from the critical stream of thought (Monk and Mundy 2014, Williams 2010), she suggests "postwar" as a more apt and realistic adjective for the activities in focus (Porter 2007: 29). Secondly, the "reconstruction" part of the term implies that the goal of the whole process is to reconstruct the situation *before* the conflict, which is not only impossible, but in many cases also not desirable.

Feminist approach differs significantly from other critical approaches presented here by drawing its criticality out of the peacebuilding *practice*. The others, on the contrary, often tend to theorise "from the desk", and although their questioning of the generally "taken-for-granted" rules of the peacebuilding game is valuable, the lack of grounding of their arguments in real situations supported by fieldwork represents a serious weakness.[15] Another problematic point is the lack of constructive alternatives and solutions these approaches offer (cf. Paris 2010). This is, however, generally symptomatic for critical scholarship, whose objective is to raise issues and to pose questions, rather than to find answers. On the other hand, by transcending simple facts about peacebuilding and questioning the generally accepted rules and structures, they offer us a mirror that tells us about the nature of the whole international politics (Newman 2009).

Meera Sabaratnam (2017) stresses the need to acknowledge and dismantle the Eurocentric foundation of the current approaches to interventions and to decolonise peacebuilding. The current approaches are ineffective and methodologically weak because of their limited gaze, leaving important parts of the studied reality unnoticed due to their underlying ontology, which perceives the "non-Western" as marginal and irrelevant. This

---

15 Séverine Autesserre (2017) again represents an exception in both respects, taking practice to the center of attention and supporting her arguments by a thorough ethnographic evidence.

results, e.g., in an "absence and depoliticisation of the targets of intervention as political subjects" (Sabaratnam 2017: 23)—an aspect that proved to be present in this study as well.

All of these streams of thought are unanimous in the conviction that the hitherto model of peacebuilding has to be reformed. The desired new contract should be based not only on an international consensus, but also on communication with recipients, who could then negotiate and co-determine the nature of the peace that is being created (Richmond 2009b: 73, Sabaratnam 2017). Some authors speak about hybridisation of the whole process, or its particular parts, stressing the competition and overlaps of different notions of peace and the orders and institutions that underpin it (Schneckener 2012: 15, cf. Richmond 2009b: 55, Mac Ginty 2010, Belloni 2012, or Boege et al. 2009)

In the current practice, the legitimacy of the intervention comes from the consensus between international elites or local power holders, or from the universal claim of bringing sustainable peace for all (Richmond 2009a). However, the questions of legitimacy and the related concept of accountability have not received adequate scholarly attention rooted in empirical studies.

The same holds for the question of sovereignty. Although clearly crucial (after all, most peacebuilding interventions include a temporary suspension of sovereignty to some extent), it has been rarely examined beyond the indirect analysis in the framework of the local ownership debate.[16] The sovereignty discourse has been rooted in the international law, linked to the instances of international humanitarian interventions (Bahcheli 2004, Grant 2015, Ronen 2015), or to the exogenous nature of sovereignty, for example, in the case of African states (Englebert 2009, Jackson and Rosberg 1982). It has been acknowledged that the term in its classical meaning as a basic attribute of statehood is no longer adequate in the current international context (Keohane 2003, Krasner 2004). Sovereignty has been governmentalised (Andersen and Sending 2010, Bartelson 2014), linked to responsibility (in the context around the Responsibility to Protect doctrine, Deng et al. 1996, or see Glanville 2014, de Carvalho and Paras 2015 for a summary of earlier debates) or taken as a discursive practice, with variations across time and space (Malmvig 2006). De Carvalho et al. (2018) analyse sovereignty as an everyday practice, being constructed, re-constructed, and performed on a daily basis—an approach, in my

---

16 With a few notable exceptions to the rule, such as Andersen and Sending (2010), Heathershaw (2009), Helle Malmvig (2006), or de Carvalho et al. 2018.

opinion, particularly suited for the post-conflict settings, that often defies existing classification and the hitherto used concepts.

2.7 *Theoretical position of the study*

All the aforementioned streams of thought about peacebuilding have influenced the focus and the approach of this study, though some of them more directly. Broadly speaking, the book fits in the conceptual-analytical stream of peacebuilding, studying peacebuilding as a set of social practices, looking at the actors and their interaction, and taking into consideration multiple levels at which the former operate (cf. Schneckener 2016).

By looking at the interaction and roles of different actors engaged in peacebuilding, this study strives to offer an empirical basis for the theoretical debate to further build upon. Schneckener (2016) reminds of the need for empirical studies about peacebuilding, so that the debate does not become self-referential and detached from the reality it studies. My book follows this trajectory. It does not make a direct contribution to the theory, it rather offers explanations and empirical observations that can be further used to refine theoretical arguments (e.g., in the debate on local ownership, the binary lenses of local and international, or the process of implementation of peacebuilding reforms).

This study regards peacebuilding as a set of policies and institutional reforms that are results of joint efforts of different actors. It offers insights on the reasons behind the lack of progress in the reform process.

It acknowledges some of the arguments of the critical streams of thought, but rather than engaging in a mental gymnastics of power inequalities and normative ambitions, it adopts a pragmatic standpoint, taking the reality of neo-liberal peacebuilding practice as a matter of fact, and tries to understand its principles and rules of the game. It takes inspiration from the feminist thinking in taking the *practice* in the centre of attention.

In terms of terminology, I prefer to use the adjective "postwar" rather than "post-conflict", bearing in mind that the official end of hostilities does not mean that violent conflicts, nor political conflicts with the potential for fuelling future violence, are gone. Throughout the study, "peacebuilding" and "postwar (or post-conflict) reconstruction" and reform are used as synonyms, in line with the mainstream discourse. The focus of the study lies in peacebuilding activities *within* the framework of postwar reconstruction in Liberia. As such, despite the validity of different arguments seeing peacebuilding as a broader concept, encompassing a wider range of activities on different levels, distinguishing the two would bring no added value to the analysis.

The focus on three groups of actors builds on the binary lenses of local vs. international, but takes it further. It acknowledges Schneckener's argument that it is better to analyse single, particular actors, rather than general, poorly defined categories. Based on the empirical data and emic discourse, this study concentrates on three categories of actors:

- International ones (e.g., the UN, international and regional organisations, donors, international NGOs, foreign governments);
- Government of Liberia, including its ministries, agencies, and the executive and legislative branches;
- Non-state Liberian actors, representing and being labelled "civil society", comprising mainly Liberian NGOs.

The framing of the study, with its focus on formal institutions based in the capital, effectively means that the grassroots-level actors, including the neo-traditional authorities, are not included in the analysis. This is an effect of the research design and of their absence in the contexts I reviewed, not a judgement of their importance for the peacebuilding process.[17]

Apart from that, the study would like to draw attention to the multi-level character of peacebuilding, which is not prominent in the literature[18], yet decisive in practice, mainly when it comes to the importance of the supra-national and individual level. The supra-national level is crucial for setting a broad framework and direction of the reforms, as well as for the procurement of financial resources. The individual one, with particular personalities, their motivations, skills, and abilities, is decisive for "getting things done", that is, the progress and implementation of reforms. Last but not least, similar to Sabaratnam (2017), the study argues that political landscape and regular political processes in the countries of intervention are an extremely important, but rarely mentioned, factor impacting the outcomes of peacebuilding efforts.[19]

---

17 I conducted interviews with representatives of the National Traditional Council of Liberia, and they confirmed that the (neo-)traditional authorities have been included in the peacebuilding process at the national level. However, they were not present in the institutions in focus of this study.

18 With Autesserre (2017), again, representing an important exception.

19 For a more detailed discussion on this issue, see chapters 11 and 12.

2.8 Multi-level governance

Apart from the general debate on peacebuilding, an approach that has crystallised as useful for the study, especially after the field work, was a concept of multi-level governance (MLG). Originally formulated for the analysis of the European Union's policies by Gary Marks (1991), it is also convenient for examination of other processes and phenomena, where a wide range of actors from different levels are present.[20] In the case of peacebuilding and our focus on selected institutions in Liberia, not only are there various actors represented (e.g., the UN, international agencies, international and local NGOs, Liberian political elites, civil society actors), but as already mentioned above, for most of them, the decision-making processes and engagement on the ground is to a large extent bound by the mandates and guidelines from their headquarters.

Multi-level governance approach acknowledges that decision-making processes transgress the borders of particular nation-states. It is also actor-centered. Different levels (understood primarily as territorial, i.e., supranational, national, or subnational) are linked by actors who move among them, so the processes are not just multi-level, but also multi-actor (Piattoni 2010: 20). Simona Piattoni (2010) defines multi-level governance as "a diverse set of arrangements, a panoply of systems of coordination and negotiation among formally independent but functionally interdependent entities that stand in complex relations to one another and that, through coordination and negotiation, keep redefining these relations" (Piattoni 2010: 26).

As a concept, MLG crosses three significant analytical boundaries: the difference between center and periphery, between the domestic and the international, and between state and society. Peacebuilding policies, in their implementation on the ground, generally do the same thing. They do not fit the usual analytical categories, for they stretch beyond them. In practice, some of the cleavages listed also overlap, for example, the divide between center and periphery that goes along the same axis as the one between domestic and international level.

In the context of peacebuilding operations, there is a specific kind of governance institutions being created. Liesbet Hooghe and Gary Marks (2003) describe it as "Type II" governance structures. In contrast to conventional, established structures in nation-states (Type I), Type II represents

---

20 For application in a non-EU context see e.g., Rosenau and Czempiel (eds.): Governance without government. Rosenau and Czempiel (1992).

an emerging category of governance, occurring especially in situations of institutional vacuum, in an absence of generally accepted rules and norms. These structures are typically task-specific, flexible, and have intersecting memberships (Hooghe and Marks 2003: 9ff.).

Skelcher (2005) distinguishes three categories of Type II entities: a club, an agency, and a polity-forming entity. From these three, agency[21] is the category particularly applicable to the context of postwar Liberia; agencies are bodies created in a top-down process, usually by the government, in order to come up with specific policies or solutions to problems. They are accountable upwards, to the authority that created them. In the context of a low level of institutionalisation, their legitimacy and overall performance depends to a large extent on interpersonal relations, navigational skills, and qualities of their management (Skelcher 2005).

2.9 Actor-centered institutionalism

Apart from the multi-level governance, the second approach that proved to be useful for the design of the research and the analysis is the actor-centered institutionalism, developed by Renate Mayntz and Fritz Scharpf. One of the streams in the new-institutionalist paradigm, it assumes that social phenomena are results of interaction of intentional actors. Both interactions and actors are influenced by the settings in which they occur. Therefore, in an analysis, both actors and institutions have to be taken into account, otherwise the picture would be incomplete (Mayntz and Scharpf 1995: 46).

In practice, actors are usually not individuals, but organisations (or composite actors), defined as "social entities that are capable of purposive action" beyond the individual level (Scharpf 1997: 38). They are further characterised by specific capabilities, perceptions, and preferences.

In actor-centered institutionalism, institutions stand for the principal rules of the game, that "structure the courses of action that a set of actors may choose" (Scharpf 1997: 38). They might be clearly defined, such as legal norms, or more tacit, such as social norms. They facilitate or restrict a certain kind of behaviour, but do not determine actors' behaviour completely.

---

21 In contrast to sociology, regarding agency as an ability to act and make choices, in Skelcher's terminology the concept denotes a specific kind of organisation, a formal institution, which is a part of a particular polity.

Institutions create arenas, where actors meet and interact. They are hence of crucial importance for the formation of composite actors, because the latter are created according to pre-existing rules, in a particular institutional setting. As such, they are the best sources of information on actors and their interaction. The rules are common knowledge among the actors, which means that they are also relatively accessible to a researcher (Scharpf 1997).

There are different types of settings, depending on the level of institutionalisation, ranging from anarchic fields and networks, to hierarchical organisations and the state. The institutional setting is further decisive for the modes of interaction available to the actors.[22]

Mayntz and Scharpf consider their approach a useful tool for empirical studies: "...a tailor-made approach for research on the problem of governance and self-organisation on the level of entire social fields" (Mayntz and Scharpf 1995: 39). The point of departure for a research design is then the focus on specific set of interaction (i.e., the unit of analysis) that helps to identify relevant actors. This approach was indeed helpful for the research design of this study, especially for the empirical chapters (Chapters 7 through 10). Here, the set of interaction in a particular "place of encounter"[23] was the point of departure for identification of relevant actors and the analysis of their interaction. The research design and overall methodology of data collection and analysis will be the focus of the following chapter.

---

22 Scharpf (1997) distinguishes four basic modes of interaction: unilateral action, negotiated agreement, majority vote, and hierarchical direction.

23 In one of the institutions in focus of the study—the Governance Commission, the Land Commission, the GBV Taskforce, and the Early Warning Working Group.

Chapter 3 Methodology

> "It has always been my habit to hide none of my methods, either from my friend Watson or from anyone who might take an intelligent interest in them."
> Sherlock Holmes: The Adventure of the Reigate Squires

3.1 Case study design and its use

Case studies represent a format useful for in-depth description of complex social phenomena in their real-world context. As such, they are particularly suited for analysis of current, contemporary issues, where the researcher has little influence over the phenomena in focus (Yin 2014). John Gerring (2004) defines a case study as *"an intensive study of a single unit for the purpose of understanding a larger class of (similar) units"* (Gerring 2004: 342, emphasis in original). The unit represents a "spatially bounded phenomenon—e.g., a nation-state, revolution, political party, election, or person—observed at a single point in time or over some delimited period of time" (ibid.).

The format offers the possibility to study phenomena in detail, in order to build explanations, test theories, and explore complex causal relations. George and Bennett (2005: 19ff.) consider case studies especially suited for theory development. They can also achieve high conceptual validity by assessing concepts in their particular context (George and Bennett 2005: 10ff.).

Despite being a common, established format of research in a number of disciplines, case studies have often been criticised as well, for not being representative enough, prone to biases related to purposive case selection, or for having issues with validity (Jahn 2006: 320-336, George and Bennett 2005: 23ff.). These critiques partly reflect the different perspectives of qualitative and quantitative approach to social sciences. There are good arguments, showing that case study is indeed a sound method, with specific advantages, well suited for certain research objectives (see e.g., Yin 2014, George and Bennet 2005, Gerring 2004). There is a justified criticism pointing to the fact that this format of inquiry is very much dependent on the researcher, which increases the danger of biases and potentially wrong inferences (Jahn 2006). These issues are partly inherent to every qualitative inquiry, and they can be mitigated by a conscious, careful research design, and techniques of analysis (George and Bennett 2005). Probably the most common objection is directed to single-case studies, as being little predicative and prone to a number of biases.[24]

3.2 Case selection: postwar Liberia

This book is a qualitative case study, with postwar Liberia representing the case, and containing four embedded units of analysis, or sub-cases, defined by four specific institutions: the Governance Commission, the Land Commission, Gender-based Violence (GBV) Taskforce, and the Early Warning Working Group. Liberia has been selected as a typical case (according to Gerring 2004), representing a post-conflict country with a number of features to be found in other similar contexts: there was a protracted civil war with no clear winner, followed by a negotiated agreement as a base of the peace negotiations. Subsequently, a large UN peacekeeping mission was deployed and a comprehensive package of reforms, based on the "institutions first" approach, has been implemented. The UN involvement was subject to high expectations from the side of the international community—the UN was under pressure to prove its capability in the field of post-conflict peacebuilding, after several failures in the past decade. The conditions seemed to be very favourable for such an exercise—there were no spoilers seriously threatening the peace in the country, the Liberian political leadership was willing to accept the reforms, and there was enough financial and political support for a long-term UN engagement. A relatively small size of Liberia was also considered an asset (Abramowitz 2014: 19ff.).

Seawright and Gerring (2008) note that case selection always departs from a reference to a broader population and an implicit cross-case analysis of cases that are usually not included in the study itself. Therefore, the clas-

---

24 To be sure, research design with multiple cases offers interesting avenues for comparison. On the other hand, a number of influential studies, for example in political science, were single-case studies; Graham Allison's analysis of the Cuban missile crisis or Arendt Lijphart's study of Dutch democracy come to mind as first-hand examples.

sification of a certain case depends to a large extent to the characteristics of the "population" of cases and our assessment of the latter. Depending on the criteria and reference cases, a particular case can be classified in different categories. With regard to Liberia, if approached from a different perspective, the country can also be seen as an example of a deviant case (Gerring 2010). Deviant cases demonstrate a "surprising value" (Gerring 2010: 655), an anomaly assessed against a general model (ibid.). An important aspect of deviant cases is their relativism; they are always measured against a general model or a theory. If the theory changes, such as in our case, if we cease to anticipate that the logical way to expect in post-conflict countries is the progress of peacebuilding reforms, then the case becomes a typical one (Gerring 2010).

Applied to Liberia, taking into consideration all the favourable conditions, the expectations based on common sense would be that the country will follow a trajectory of recovery and more or less swift implementation of the reforms. However, there is very little progress in this regard. If we accept the change and implementation of reforms as our reference, then Liberia falls into the category of a deviant case. If, on the contrary, we subscribe to a more pessimistic opinion that does not expect much change in post-conflict context, then, just by virtue of changing the model of reference, Liberia becomes a typical case again. Taking both the perspectives outlined above, I still see Liberia as a representative (or typical) case of a post-conflict country, with all related challenges to be found in similar contexts. In terms of its performance in post-conflict reconstruction, however, it does show the "surprising value" of no progress and therefore clearly fits the deviant category.

Among various types of case studies as presented by George and Bennett (2005: 74ff.), defined by their research objectives and ambitions in the field of theory-building, this study fits in the category of configurative-idiographic design, with a strong descriptive component that can be used for theory building, but not contributing to the theory-building directly (George and Bennett 2005: 75). There is a heuristic component to it as well, identifying "inductively [...] new variables, hypotheses, causal mechanisms, and causal paths" (George and Bennett 2005: 75), in our case factors behind the lack of expected progress of the reforms.[25]

---

25 The authors consider heuristic approach especially useful for deviant cases (George and Bennett 2005: 75).

3.3 Selection of the sub-cases

The four particular institutions forming the sub-case units of analysis were selected according to a number of criteria.[26] Most importantly, they represent arenas, where all the three groups of actors in focus of the study meet and interact. All four institutions were set up to deal with a particular issue (or set of issues) directly related to peacebuilding. Poor governance, with the concentration of political power in the capital and in the hands of the Americo-Liberians has been widely accepted as a long-term problem at the roots of growing tension in the country. Land issues fall partly into the broader field of governance, but their conflict potential stayed high in the postwar phase as well, mainly as a consequence of the return of refugees and IDPs. Gender-based violence tackles a phenomenon that was present in Liberia before the war already, but went out of scale and was used as a tactic of warfare during the conflict. After the war, GBV has still been widespread, not only menacing women's wellbeing and security, but having impact on the level of families and whole communities as well. Early warning is rather a mechanism of conflict monitoring, but illustrates very well the practices and ruling mechanisms of the peacebuilding reform in general. However, the "matter", around which the selected institutions meet, is not of primary importance. The crucial aspect is the interaction as such, as it shows different roles and capacities of the actors in focus.

The four fora differ with regard to the level of financial and political support, the level of international presence, and a number of other aspects. However, they have a common outcome—there is very little progress in their respective "fields" of reform. In other words, they represent examples of equifinality, the plurality of causes, where "the *same* type of outcome can emerge in different cases via a *different* set of independent variables" (George and Bennett 2005: 157, emphasis in original). Particularly in such cases, the case study format offers an advantage of a detailed analysis, which helps to explore and identify possible explanations, causal relationships, or variables in play (George and Bennett 2005: 205ff.).

---

26 Apart from the methodological criteria, the selection of cases was determined by pragmatic issues as well, the main one being access for me as a researcher.

3.4 Data collection

The research is based on primary data, collected during six months of fieldwork in Liberia, complemented by secondary data, coming mainly from official documents, reports, academic publications, and "grey literature".[27] The field research was divided into three parts: a pilot study in June 2011, the main phase from April to June 2012, and a follow-up visit in November 2012. The first visit was used for networking and making contacts, the second one for the main data collection work, and the last one offered opportunities for follow-up interviews and catching up on recent development. With regard to methods of data collection, I used expert interviews, informal conversations, and observation. Geographically, the main site of the fieldwork was Monrovia, the capital of Liberia, where the institutions in focus of the study are located. The study has, therefore, a clear urban focus.[28]

Understanding processes and institutions in focus in this study requires a specific knowledge that only certain people possess; that is why expert interviews were used as the main technique of data collection. Expert interviews represent a type of a qualitative interview, distinct by the selection of interviewees. In Bogner and Menz's words, *"in terms of method, it cannot be treated as nothing more than a qualitative interview with a particular social group"* (Bogner, Littig, and Menz 2014: 55, emphasis in original). The status of an "expert" is ascribed by the researcher (Meuser and Nagel 2014: 18) to "someone with a specific kind of specialized knowledge that is not available to the researcher" (Bogner and Menz 2014: 47), who has the "capacity to provide researchers with facts concerning the question they are investigating. Experts are sources of information with regard to the reconstruction of sequences of events and social situations" (Bogner and Menz 2014: 10). They do not necessarily belong to the highest positions in

---

27 Grey literature is defined as resources "produced on all levels of government, academics, business and industry in print and electronic formats, but which is not controlled by commercial publishers." (The Fourth Conference on Grey Literature in Washington, DC, October 1999, cited at Greylit.org - http://www.gr eylit.org/about)

28 This is a logical consequence of the research design, focusing on the institutions located in the capital. Despite the urban focus, I was keeping in mind that "Monrovia is not Liberia", a mantra of many Liberians who talked to me, pointing to the gap between the capital and the rest of the country in terms of development, principles of everyday functioning, and general importance for decision-making processes.

their organisations, on the contrary, most often they occupy middle- and lower-level ranks (Bogner and Menz 2014).

As a tool for data collection, expert interview is useful in the initial phase of the research to get the basic orientation in the field quickly. Later, it provides access to systematic information about the phenomena in focus. The most appropriate form is an open structure interview, since it respects the individual specificities and differences of each situation and interviewee, and gives space to the interviewee to reveal his opinions and reflections (Bogner and Menz 2014: 31). I used semi-structured interviews, with a set of guiding questions related to the particular institutions in focus, as well as to the cooperation and interaction of different actors both within the institution and in the broader field of the particular sub-case.[29]

The interviewees were employees of governmental agencies and ministries, staff of international governmental and non-governmental organisations operating in Liberia, diplomats, international consultants, and representatives of Liberian civil society. Usually, the institutions in focus served as an entry point to their particular member organisations. In some cases, a contact to the institution was facilitated by a specific member organisation or an individual, who acted as a broker or provided "credentials" for me to get access. This informal way, based on personal recommendations, proved to be generally more efficient than negotiating access through formal, "official" channels (e.g., contacting the organisation via official email address), although there were exceptions to the rule as well.

Before embarking on the field research, I made a list of institutions I wanted to contact for data collection, based on the secondary sources of information about the peacebuilding process. This initial list was modified, taking into consideration the information acquired in the field. Some of the organisations I originally targeted were non-functioning, others were not accessible, or met only very infrequently and exclusively at a high level. Apart from having an impact on the final selection of the cases, this fact also represented an additional factor for the analysis, showing the discrepancy between formal plans and their implementation on the ground, as well as practical challenges the latter have been facing.

Apart from this, snowball sampling was used as a complementary strategy. Often, the research partners themselves mentioned other people, who could provide useful information for the research. In other cases, I got suggestions upon asking.

---

29 For details with regard to guiding questions, see Annex 1.

Observation of the meetings was the second main method of data collection. It complemented the data from the interviews and provided an additional source of information for triangulation. Apart from the content of the meetings, I focused on a number of contextual and procedural aspects, such as the venue (location, state of the facility, equipment, spatial setting of the room,...), composition of participants (number of participants, their gender, age, institutional affiliation), or procedural issues (who was chairing the meeting and how, what were the decision-making procedures, overall atmosphere, nature of interaction,...). The observations provided invaluable insights into the matter. The problematic aspect was the irregularity of the meetings, which were often re-scheduled or cancelled last minute.

I collected over 60 interviews: 16 with government officials; 22 with representatives of international organisations (both governmental and non-governmental ones), diplomats, and other external actors; and 15 with civil society representatives.[30] The list of interviews is attached in Annex 2. The names of the respondents are not disclosed, their institutional affiliation for most of the cases is, unless we agreed otherwise during the interview. Some of the interviews were recorded; however, most often I only took notes, either upon request of the interviewee, or for the sake of a more open atmosphere. With regard to the records, I chose not to transcribe them verbatim, since the exact wording was not crucial for the purposes of research. I made summaries and excerpts with the most relevant information instead. I also made a short "memo" after each interview, putting down the details about the interview, such as location, atmosphere, overall impression from the meeting and other relevant points that later helped me to remember the situation in detail and put it in context for the purposes of analysis. During observation of the meetings, I restricted myself to taking brief notes and wrote down a comprehensive record after the meeting. This approach helped to keep my presence low-profile and least disturbing possible. I observed 12 meetings of different taskforces, where all the three groups of actors met.

The primary data were complemented by the secondary sources of information, mainly from academic literature, official documents, and grey literature, produced by local NGOs, civil society organisations, and international consultants. Official documents were easily accessible online,

---

30 There were also 12 interviews that did not fit any of the categories. They are grouped under the label "others" in the annex. The respondents were mainly ordinary citizens.

or upon request, from Liberian authorities. Where possible, I stayed in touch with the interviewees after completion of my field research, usually via email. This allowed me to remain updated about the development in the respective fields of inquiry and offered an avenue for an ongoing, longer-term analysis.

3.5 Data analysis

Admittedly, the analysis is "one of the least developed aspects of doing case studies." (Yin 2014: 133). Some of the guidelines in the literature are general, describing analysis in rather vague terms as a "a reflexive process in which the researcher visits and revisits the data, connects them to emerging insights, and progressively refines his/her focus and understandings" (Tracy 2013: 184, cf. Srivastava and Hopwood 2009: 77). General strategies on how to approach data in case studies as listed (e.g., Yin 2014)[31] and recommended techniques of coding, constant comparison, and iterative reference to research questions (e.g., Tracy 2013) provided general guidance to the within-case analysis, but were little useful for the cross-case level.

I followed a bottom-up approach, taking the collected data as a starting point. I followed the way suggested by Meuser and Nagel (2014: 35), ordering the transcribed interviews (or notes) according to the thematic units that appeared in them. In case of expert interviews, the sequence of the topics within a single interview is not of primary interest. The emphasis is put on the position of the expert and his statements in the institutional-organisational context. Coded topics are subsequently compared across different interviews and interpreted within the particular theoretical context (Meuser and Nagel 2014).

At the first level, the codes and themes were analysed within each of the four sub-cases.[32] There is an analytical part at the end of each empirical chapter (Chapters 7-10), summarising the main findings and relating them to the research questions. Chapter 11 focuses on the level above, and compares the findings *across* the four cases. The lines of analysis are the independent variables from the sub-cases.

---

31 Yin (2014) distinguishes among bottom-up, theory-led, descriptive approaches, or analysis based on exploring rival explanations.
32 No data analysis software was used.

Apart from the descriptive component, linked to the first two research questions (i.e., interaction and roles of particular actors, and the structure and functioning of the institutions in focus), the thesis uses an analytical perspective inspired by explanation building (Yin 2014) and process-tracing to answer the third research question of lack of progress. Process tracing, according to George and Bennet, "attempts to identify the intervening causal process – the causal chain and causal mechanism – between an independent variable (or variables) and the outcome of the dependent variable" (2005: 206). They see it as a useful method for cases with more independent variables in play and can help explain equifinality, offering "the possibility of identifying different causal paths that lead to a similar outcome in different cases" (George and Bennett 2005: 215). It is considered especially suited for deviant causes (ibid.). In this study, the need for explanation became evident over time, based on the results of the descriptive part of the thesis. The analysis does not attempt for a full-scale reconstruction of a causal chain and tracing of steps in particular cases. After all, the sequence of the steps was not crucial for the result. The intervening factors have simply been present and needed a contextual explanation. As such, the approach can be seen as a variation of a process tracing, in a form of a detailed narrative, with some parts accompanied by causal hypotheses and explanations (cf. George and Bennett 2004: 206ff.).

In addition, a comparative approach has been used at the cross-case level.[33] Since all four cases had a similar outcome, displaying no or very little progress in the implementation, the focus of analysis were the independent variables, particularly their variation (differences and similarities) across cases.

3.6 Challenges and biases

At the level of research design, there has been a fair amount of criticism pointing to the weaknesses of single-case studies (see section 3.1). Apart from taking into consideration the general arguments and mitigation strategies mentioned in the first section of this chapter, this study tried to minimise "the danger of wrong inferences" by including four sub-cases, selected consciously in order to provide both representativity and variation in the areas of analytical interest (Gerring 2010). They are, in the first step,

---

33 The method of controlled comparison, see George and Bennett 2005 (especially chapter 8).

subjected to a within-case analysis, before embarking on the cross-case level.

For the collection of the data, the primary challenge was to actually be able to collect them, to get access to the relevant people and institutions. By the nature of their positions, the interviewees often had busy schedules and were difficult to reach. One strategy to overcome this condition was to approach them in an informal setting first. Another one was the use of snowball sampling mentioned previously, which provided me with a reference that often offered an entry point to other interviewees. Generally, most people were willing to schedule an appointment. However, the tight schedules and frequent travelling of many of them made the planning difficult. In this respect, the division of the field research into three phases proved to be useful. Another challenge was caused by the high level of personnel's fluctuation, especially in the case of international expatriate workers. Often, it took them considerable time to find their bearings in the plethora of institutions at the local scene, which impacted the scope of knowledge and information they were able to provide. This aspect, apart from a problematic issue for data collection, turned out to be an important factor shaping the interaction among the actors in focus.

A second set of challenges was linked to my position as a foreign, white, young, female researcher coming from the global North. The role of age, gender, and racial bias, and positionality in conducting research, has been well addressed in the literature (e.g., Abels and Behrens 2014, Belur 2013, Berger 2014, Eagleton-Pierce 2011, Noh 2017, Pezalla et al. 2012, Stanley and Slattery 2003, Hawkins 2010, Underwood, Satterthwait and Bartlett 2010). Abels and Behrens argue that female researchers get better feedback because they are perceived as "less threatening" (Abels and Behrens 2014: 142ff.). Certainly, it had an impact on the kind and scope of information I was given. As Abels and Behrens (2014) note, women, especially in male-dominated fields, are often treated as "acceptably incompetent" (Abels and Behrens 2014: 142-145). My position of a foreigner sometimes incited answers the interviewees anticipated I wanted to hear. Some of the factors mentioned here have been mitigated by a thoughtful selection of questions and by building a base of trust with research partners. On a positive side, my status also facilitated the access to the research partners at times, especially in the case of actors dealing with gender-related issues, or generally, in terms of networking along the "women's lines".

These factors also played a role in the subsequent analysis of the data. Here, I simply attempted to keep my biases in mind and, where possible, used data triangulation or requested feedback on my findings from the research partners.

Chapter 4 Historical background

"The past is the key to the present."

Many times during my interviews, before actually embarking on the questions I asked, my informants started their answers by a shorter or longer excursion to Liberian history, pointing out that the civil war and the post-conflict arrangements that followed were rooted in the trends and events that accompanied the evolution of Liberian statehood from its very beginning. This "popular" emphasis on the *longue durée* has been mirrored also in the scholarly literature on Liberia, particularly in works trying to explain the causes of the civil war. The different explanations of the reasons behind the war will be briefly presented after the first part of the historical overview, covering the period from the 19th century to 2003, when the civil war officially ended. The second part of the chapter focuses on the postwar political development in the country.

4.1 Birth of the republic

The origins of the first independent African republic, as Liberia is often referred to in scientific and popular writing, date back to the beginning of the 19th century[34], when the American Colonization Society (ACS), sponsored by the US government started to look for a place, where a colony for freed slaves[35] from the American South could be established. After several unsuccessful attempts along the Gulf of Guinea, the ACS

---

34 For an earlier history of the area before the arrival of the American settlers see e.g., Yoder 2003, Moran 2006, or Sawyer 1992.
35 Resettlement in Africa should have provided a solution for the growing numbers of freed slaves in the American South, regarded as problematic by some of the plantation owners (Moran 2006). Between 1822 and 1867, 12,000–13,000 settlers came to Liberia from the United States. From them, some 4,500 were born free, the others were freed on the condition that they immigrate to Africa (Liebenow 1987: 19). They were joined by about 6,000 so-called "Congos"—recaptives saved from the slave ships crossing the Atlantic Ocean. The term "Congo" later started to be used for the whole settler elite, as opposed to the indigenous population.

made a deal with one of the indigenous rulers[36], and purchased a piece of land, where in 1822 they established the first settlement of the colony that later became Liberia. From the beginning of its existence, the colony had to face attacks of the indigenous polities around. In spite of that, the settlements of ACS had gradually expanded and a number of its colonies grew up along the coast in the next two decades.

In the context of constant conflict over land with indigenous polities but also with France and Great Britain, who continued their colonial expansion in the region, Liberian colonies needed a guarantee of their territorial borders and security for trade.[37] Independence, with the protection of the territory of a sovereign state coming from the international law, was finally opted for and in 1847, Liberia became an independent republic, the first one on the African continent.[38] The country was, however, far from an embodiment of liberal democracy as we know it today, despite its republican label. In the early years of the colony, the power was firmly in the hands of the "white men", the representatives of the ACS, who drafted its constitution and were also the sources of legislative, executive, and judicial power (Sawyer 2005). Despite a gradual transfer of governance to the hands of the Americo-Liberians, the majority of the republic's inhabitants were excluded from the political participation, based on the fact that citizenship was granted only to Americo-Liberians and Congo settlers (Kieh 2008).

Following its independence, Liberia expanded geographically further along the coast and also to the hinterland.[39] As an armed tool for the expansion, the Liberia Frontier Force (LFF), an ancestor of the Armed Forces of Liberia (AFL), was established in 1907. The force soon gained a reputation for its ruthlessness and violence *vis-à-vis* the indigenous popula-

---

36 As an infamous historical anecdote goes, Robert Stockton, the Navy officer in charge, made the ruler, King Peter, sign the deal at gunpoint.

37 Since 1838, a "Commonwealth", a form of federal agreement among the colonies was in place; however, it was not regarded as a sovereign state.

38 France, Great Britain, and the German Hanseatic Federation were the first countries to recognize Liberia. Amusingly, the US recognition only came 15 years later, with the presidency of Abraham Lincoln and the abolition of slavery.

39 Strategies of expansion varied from land purchases through founding alliances with indigenous polities, to incorporation of the latter through a system of patron-client relations (Sawyer 2005).

tion (Akpan 1973, Liebenow 1969). These traits and the general *esprit de corps* were later passed on to its successor, the AFL (Berkeley 2001).[40]

In the first decades of the 20th century, Liberia effectively underwent the process of internal colonisation of its hinterland counties and applied the system of indirect rule to govern them (Mamdani 1996, Clapham 1978, Abasiattai 1988, d'Azevedo 1989). The ACS had gradually withdrawn and handed the power over to the settler elite. With regard to political rights, the population of the country became divided into two groups, for whom different political and legal structures applied—the "civilised" ones, descendants of the original settler elite, with citizen rights granted by the constitution and statutory legal system, and the indigenous population, relegated to the subjects and governed by a distinct set of rules.[41] The latter group, the original inhabitants of the country, constitute over 95% of its population. Among them, 17 different ethnic groups can be distinguished (LISGIS 2009).[42]

Liberia has developed into a unitary, centralised state, governed by the settler elite and dominated by a single political party, the True Whig Party founded in 1869. The Liberian political system has been modelled after the one of the United States, with a concentration of power in the executive branch, represented by the president. The country was characterised by political stability, peaceful transitions of power, and relative prosperity throughout the 20th century. It was incorporated into the world economy as one of the leading producers of rubber but also of other natural resources, such as iron ore, timber, and agricultural products. However, the facade of stability and prosperity, maintained at the expense of domination and political, economic, and social marginalisation of the majority of the population, began to crumble in the 1970s, in the context of the international economic recession and domestic voices demanding reforms of the political system. Popular movements calling for democratic reforms were

---

40 Apart from the pacification of the interior, LFF also extorted taxes, where it used violence against the civilian population as well (see e.g., Berkeley 2001, Utas 2003, or Liebenow 1969).

41 In 1949, they were enacted as the "Rules and Regulations Governing the Hinterland of Liberia".

42 The largest ethnic group is Kpelle with 20,3%, followed by Bassa (13,4%), Grebo (10%), Gio (8%), and Mano with 7,9% (LISGIS 2009: 84-87). Apart from these, there is also a relatively small, yet economically significant, community of Lebanese, who due to their non-African origin, are not Liberian citizens.

founded in 1970s and assertively demanded change (Moran 2006, Sawyer 2005).[43]

Despite the gradual opening of the political system, the dominance of the settler elite was omnipresent and popular discontent grew. In this context, a group of non-commissioned officers from the AFL, led by Sergeant Samuel Doe, overthrew President Tolbert in a military coup in April 1980. This event marked a rupture of the existing political order in several ways. Firstly, the military was introduced as a political actor, a trend that was going to continue in the decades to come, seeing gangsterism as an efficient tool for acquiring power (Sawyer 2005: 18). Secondly, the coup brought the domination of the Americo-Liberian elite to an end. Doe, of Krahn origin[44], promoted himself as the representative of the "ordinary people". However, his rule soon turned out to be based on brutal repression and offered no constructive alternative to the criticised patrimonial practices of Tolbert administration.

The democratisation tendencies of the 1970s were crushed. A new constitution, chopping off political rights was drafted and subjected to referendum. Doe was getting rid of all potential enemies and put together an administration largely composed of people of his own ethnic group, the Krahn. The military became gradually Krahn-dominated as well. In 1985, an election was organised to provide the military regime with legitimacy. Although obviously rigged, the election was claimed free and fair by international observers. The regime was also backed by robust financial support from the United States.[45] Shortly after the election, Thomas Quiwonkpa, one of the members of Doe's putschist group, also recognised as the mastermind behind the coup, attempted to overthrow Doe. But his plot was discovered, Quiwonkpa executed, and a mass campaign of retaliation launched. For the first time, the revenge also targeted the home area of the "perpetrator"—Nimba county and ethnic Gio and Mano. This

---

43 MOJA (Movement for Justice in Africa) in 1973, PAL (Progressive Alliance of Liberia) two years later.

44 The Krahn ethnic group constitutes about 4% of the Liberian population and is also found in the neighbouring Côte d'Ivoire. Although there are Krahn people dispersed all over the country, most of them live in Nimba and Grand Gedeh counties.

45 Doe's regime, perceived as a crucial ally of the US on the African continent in the Cold War context, received an unprecedented amount of military assistance from the Reagan administration. From 1980–84, the US military assistance to Liberia amounted to more than 400 million USD and became the second, after Israel, on the list of aid-receiving countries. See Moran 2006 and Sawyer 2005.

is the first instance of a trend, where ethnic divisions were tapped upon and instrumentalised in the struggle for power.

In the second half of the decade, the regime loses most of the external support from the US, as well as the rests of the popular support. In this context, Charles Taylor with a small group of armed men trained in Libya crosses the border from Côte d'Ivoire on the Christmas Eve 1989 and starts a successful military campaign. Taylor's National Patriotic Front of Liberia (NPFL) grows quickly, with mostly Gio and Mano people, holding deep resentments *vis-à-vis* Doe's regime, joining his forces. Taylor also capitalised on his image of the "heir of Quiwonkpa" in gaining popular support against Doe's military dictatorship. In July 1990, a faction led by Prince Johnson splits from NPFL and the Independent National Patriotic Front of Liberia (INPFL) is created. Soon after that, other armed factions mushroom.[46] By June 1990, NPFL controlled most of Liberia's territory and arrived at the outskirts of Monrovia. An intervention force under the auspices of ECOWAS was authorised and deployed in August 1990. The primary objective of ECOMOG (ECOWAS Cease-Fire Monitoring Group) was to stop Taylor from taking over the country. However, the poorly equipped mission with a lack of intelligence and no ceasefire to keep was soon drawn into the conflict as one of the parties and adopted the strategy of fighting NPFL by proxy, founding alliances with various armed factions (Gerdes 2013).

Throughout the 1990s, there were efforts to end the violence[47], several peace agreements were signed, and two transitional governments installed, but the deals never lasted long. The last, 13th peace agreement signed in August 1995 in Abuja paved the way for the third transitional government, chaired by a civilian[48], but manned with the heads of the warring factions. The demobilisation and disarmament process began in November 1996 and armed factions were partly transformed into political parties. In the election that followed, Charles Taylor, the leader of the strongest armed faction, was elected president of the country in a landslide.[49]

---

46 For a good analysis of all the relevant factions and the military aspects of the conflict, see e.g., Gerdes 2013 or Adebayo 2002.

47 For a detailed overview of the war in terms of moving fronts, influential battles, etc., see e.g. Utas 2003 or Adebayo 2002.

48 Former Senator Ruth Perry.

49 Taylor received 75,3% (Gerdes 2013: 59). Despite his reputation and warlord past (or rather *because* of them), the majority of Liberians were convinced that he is the person, who can keep the country at peace and his exclusion from political power would lead to further unrest and violence.

Between 1997 and 1999, there were occasional skirmishes in some parts of the country, but generally, war was regarded as being over. However, the fragile peace did not last long. Taylor's brutal campaign against his opponents soon produced armed opposition by LURD (Liberians United for Reconciliation and Democracy) and MODEL (Movement for Democracy in Liberia). The conflict began to spill over to the neighbouring countries and the whole Mano River Basin was caught up in a conflict complex, of which Liberia was the core. Despite embargoes imposed by the UN, international trade with Liberia in its natural resources (especially timber, iron ore and diamonds) flourished and the revenues from the trade were used (in addition to President Taylor's personal enrichment) to foment the regional instability.[50]

2003 turned out to be the year of change. In the situation, where both rebel groups (LURD, supported by Guinea; and MODEL, backed by the Côte d'Ivoire) were approaching Monrovia, a negotiated agreement was actually the most convenient option for the warring parties. Further fighting would be risky not only because the results were hard to predict, but also because the international community had signalled that they would not support a government that seized power by force. On 18 August 2003, the final comprehensive peace agreement (CPA) was signed in Accra. Compared to the peace agreement from Abuja, the CPA from Accra offered more prospects for a sustainable peace. Firstly, Taylor, as the main potential spoiler, was indicted by the Special Court for Sierra Leone and forced into exile, thus effectively removed out of the game. Secondly, the power ambitions of the warring parties were fulfilled by the positions in the transitional government. Civilians also played a more important role in contrast to the 1995 Abuja peace agreement, chairing the National Transitional Government (NTGL), holding a majority in the National Transitional Legislative Assembly (NTLA), as well as some important positions at different ministries and governmental agencies. In September 2003, the United Nations Mission in Liberia (UNMIL) was established by the SC Resolution no. 1509 and deployed in the country to assist with the implementation of the peace agreement and the whole process of postwar reconstruction.

---

50 Gerdes (2013) provides a thorough analysis of the economic dimension of the conflict, as well as of the political economy of Taylor's rule.

4.2 Explanations of the war

As already briefly mentioned in the beginning of the chapter, the works dealing with the origins and causes of the Liberian civil war[51] emphasise the importance of the factors and trends with the roots in the early years of the formation of Liberian statehood. There is a broad consensus that the initial division between the settler elite and the majority population, the concentration of power in the hands of the former and marginalisation of the latter, together with non-functioning political and other institutions were the major causes of popular resentments that led to the violent conflict. However, some authors recognise specific additional factors as the decisive "ingredients". Amos Sawyer (1992, 2005) points to the institutional choices and overly centralised governance arrangements. Kieh (2008) follows a similar trajectory, seeing the first Liberian civil war as a result of "multifaceted crises of underdevelopment – political, economic, social, and cultural – engendered by the failure of the country's neocolonial state" (2008: 13). His analysis from the perspective of Marxist tradition, however, omits other important factors and his application of the concept of class to Liberian society is also questionable.

Yoder (2003) blames Liberian political culture and its underlying values, such as overemphasis on authority, order, and hierarchy, that are inherently undemocratic and illiberal, for they do not provide space for a critical discussion, which is at the core of functioning democracies. Utas (2003) reminds that a thorough militarisation of Liberian society was an important factor, shaping the way to the war, as well as the patterns of the conflict itself. Ellis (2007) follows a tradition of emphasis on the cosmological and religious factors in Liberian politics, arguing that the war mirrored the anarchy in the spiritual world. Richards (2005) stresses the agrarian dimension of the conflict and of land as a conflict factor.

Although all of these opinions have a point, the Liberian civil war was too complex a phenomenon to be explained by a single factor. The war grew from a spawn, where long-term tendencies and suppressed tensions stemming from a large-scale marginalisation and exclusion were nurtured and catalysed by proximate factors, such as personal motives, economic opportunities and tactical decisions. An additional factor, often omitted in

---

51 Although the 14 years of the conflict are often divided into the "first" and the "second" war, the conflict will be referred to in a singular form throughout the text, as the two-year intermezzo between 1997 and 1999 was rather a nominal form of peace.

the literature on the origins of the war, is the impact of external actors, most importantly the more or less overt forms of American support to different "camps" in the course of the time.[52]

The war itself then turned out to be "an elite struggle for political-military power and associated opportunities for personal enrichment" (Gerdes 2013: 32), rather than a fight for a "just cause" or more or less noble principles. Once rolling, the war machinery, fuelled by opportunities for economic gains, was difficult to stop. The peace negotiation that produced a lasting agreement came only after 14 years of pillage and carnage. The war took its toll mainly on civilians. Extreme brutality, mass atrocities, sexual violence, and exploitation led to thousands of deaths, trauma, and large-scale displacement. Up to 15,000 child soldiers (United Nations 2003) are estimated to have taken part in the conflict.[53] The absence of basic health services and sanitary provisions only added to the appalling effects on the population. The widespread looting stripped the country of everything that could have been sold.[54]

4.3 Postwar phase

It is worth reminding that the official end of the war did not mean an instant improvement of the security situation on the ground—quite the contrary. The first three years after the CPA (2004–2006) are remembered as particularly dangerous and terrifying by Liberians, with violence and insecurity levels comparable, if not worse, than during the "official" time of conflict (Abramowitz 2014). Violence penetrated all spheres of everyday life, armed robbery and banditry were widespread and the absence of functioning systems of order and judiciary only made the situation worse.

---

52 The role of the US stands out in particular in this respect. The US supported the Doe regime in the 1980s but soon switched sides and backed Charles Taylor, facilitating his prison break and subsequent military training in Libya. It is, however, fair to note that these kinds of *realpolitik* strategies were not limited to the US-Liberian relations, but were commonplace in the context of the Cold War and are, even today, far from lying idle on the shelf of obsolete tools of international politics.

53 The number of combatants is estimated to exceed 100,000, representing about 3% of Liberian population (http://www.peacebuildingdata.org/research/liberia/result s/civil-war/ex-combatants).

54 E.g., the country's landline telephone network has been completely destroyed; the copper wires were sold as scrap metal.

After the years of violence, the country was completely destroyed. Basic infrastructure and services were missing. The population was uprooted, traumatised, and in a bad health condition. The sovereignty of the Liberian state was effectively abrogated, due to the total destruction in political, economic, social, and administrative fields. The UNHCR coordinated a massive repatriation exercise, facilitating the return of more than one-third of the country's population, living in the neighbouring countries or being displaced internally.[55] International humanitarian NGOs stepped in as providers of basic services (from education and food distribution to reconstruction of road networks), effectively acted instead of the state, which had no capacities for coordinated action.

At the international level, UNMIL was perceived as a practical test of the Responsibility to Protect doctrine, where the international community is responsible for protection of civilians against war crimes and other atrocities, with the success of the mission being an imperative, proving the UN's capabilities in the context of its recent failures in other post-conflict settings (e.g., Bosnia, DR Congo, Haiti, or Somalia). The mission was a flagship of the "new style" of UN peace operations, with a strong civilian component and an integrated leadership.[56]

The time of change had begun. The early post-conflict period was effectively cut out as a specific period, "a time of exception (....) a time out of time, a time-bounded zone of social, political, and legal experimentation" (Abramowitz 2014: 30), and Liberians were "transformed into beneficiaries of a massive, uncoordinated, and decentralized project of humanitarian social engineering" (Abramowitz 2014: 25). In line with Collier's and others' recommendations, the first (respectively the second) five years after the end of war were regarded as decisive for the country's future and as such adopted as benchmarks for the projects of humanitarian actors on the ground.[57] In December 2003, the process of demobilisation, disarmament, rehabilitation, and reintegration (DDRR) began as the first one

---

55 According to the estimates, the displacement in 1994 (the "peak year"), reached more than one million IDPs and 780,000 refugees (World Refugee Survey, cited in Sawyer 2005, cf. Abramowitz 2014 and Ellis 2007).

56 The initial strength of UNMIL was 15,000 military personnel and 1,115 civilian police (http://www.un.org/en/peacekeeping/missions/unmil/background.shtml). The mission began to downsize gradually in 2007. The deployment came to an end on 30 March 2018, after the inauguration of George Weah to the presidential office.

57 Another, although vaguer, benchmarking often used in the literature on postwar reconstruction is the change from the "humanitarian" to "development" phase.

from a series of programs and reforms from the "peacebuilding package".
Approximately 120,000 former fighters were demobilised and disarmed
(Abramowitz 2014: 60). Originally, a comprehensive approach including
components of psychosocial counselling was envisaged; however, due to
various reasons (mainly financial and administrative ones), it was never
implemented and the process was more or less reduced to the exchange of
arms and ammunition for money (Abramowitz 2014: 161ff.).

In September 2005, the Governance and Economic Management Assistance Program (GEMAP) was imposed on Liberia. It was a form of international supervision and assistance in financial administration of the country, launched as a reaction to a large-scale misappropriation of public funds
and massive corruption. Although officially presented as a "partnership
between the Government of Liberia and the international community"
(GEMAP Website), the mission of the project—"to promote accountability
and transparency in fiscal and financial management to enable Liberia to
use its resources in the interests of its citizens"—clearly shows the reason
behind its creation. International staff were tasked to improve financial
management of the country, and as such placed in financially strategic government positions, where their co-signature was required for all important
decisions.[58]

Elections were held in October 2005, and Ellen Johnson Sirleaf, an
internationally well-connected economist with extensive experience with
the UN and the World Bank, was elected president. In the Parliament, 21
out of 94 seats[59] were won by the personalities linked to the parties of
conflict.[60] Although her international reputation worked as a kind of guarantee, attracting donors' support and investment to the country, it did not
spare Ellen Johnson Sirleaf from criticism for corruption and nepotism.

---

58 Unsurprisingly, the program quickly generated considerable resistance from the
   local side (for more details, see Gerdes 2013). Although originally planned for
   three years, the program was maintained until mid-2010.
59 The seats in the lower house of the Parliament are distributed among the 15
   Liberian counties according to the size of their population. In the Senate, each
   of the counties is represented by two Senators. The MPs are usually elected based
   on their ties to their respective constituency, which is evaluated by their willingness to provide material support or other kinds of benefits to the communities
   (Gerdes 2013: 209).
60 Although representing more than 20%, this share does not stand out in comparison with legislative assemblies in other post-conflict countries. In the next
   legislature, the number dropped 16, a decrease that illustrate that success at war
   did not necessarily translate into a successful long-term ticket to a political career
   (Gerdes 2013: 2014ff.).

Gerdes (2013), however, notes that firstly, her appointments were mainly qualified professionals, and secondly, the fact that she established a personal network of power is easy to understand – networks are built faster than institutions, and in the post-conflict settings it is the most efficient way to promptly put governance structures in place. The building of institutions requires time, whereas informal networks work instantly.

In line with the mainstream approach of post-conflict peacebuilding, a cascade of further reforms and projects was launched. DDRR was followed by the security sector reform, reconciliation exercise, massive capacity-building across sectors, programs promoting the rule of law, and reconstruction of road networks, infrastructure, and services. Although conceived and presented as a purely "technical" assistance, the underlying message of this large-scale exercise was with no doubt highly political and 100% normative: a profound change in people's attitudes was necessary as a precondition for peace to last (Abramowitz 2014).

The trajectory and slow-but-steady pace of reforms was disrupted by the outbreak of Ebola in the spring 2014. The epidemics lasted over a year[61] and swallowed a great deal of financial resources intended for other projects. Although more than 10 years after the war, it still showed the weaknesses of the state institutions, and the inadequacy of the health care system (Tokpa et al. 2015). Another turning point was the presidential election and transfer of presidential office from Ellen Johnson Sirleaf to George Weah, who came to the Executive Mansion in January 2018. April 2018 also marked the departure of UNMIL—a milestone that was carefully planned for, but still brings consequences in terms of security provision and availability of stable funding.[62]

---

61 The epidemic started in March 2014, gaining strength in the second half of the year. The number of cases dropped significantly in early 2015. There were, however, occasional flare-ups with limited cases throughout 2015. The WHO declared Liberia Ebola-free only in January 2016. (WHO, http://www.bbc.com/ne ws/world-africa-28755033)

62 For more details about the different funding schemes, see the section 5.2.1.

Chapter 5 Actors in focus: An analysis

> "After eight months in the country, I still feel like I do not know what is going on."
> (Interview ABA, 29 May 2012, Monrovia)

This chapter gives a detailed overview of the three groups of actors in our focus. First, it examines the government of Liberia in the early postwar period and offers some background information about the specificities of the Liberian political system. Second, it focuses on the international actors, with the UN as the most prominent one, followed by others (bilateral partners, supranational actors, regional organisations, and international NGOs). Next, it analyses the Liberian civil society and its functions, both on a general and a case-specific level. It concludes by introducing "places of encounter" of the actors in focus: the Joint Steering Committee, the Liberia Reconstruction and Development Committee, and the Peacebuilding Office, as a unique structure straddled between the governmental and international sides.

5.1 Government of Liberia

During the conflict, the government (GoL) was practically non-functioning. It was nominally in place, but did not fulfil its core functions. After the end of the first civil war and the election of Charles Taylor for president in 1997, the regime turned into a highly personalised autocracy, focused mainly on the president's personal profit. After the signing of the CPA and Taylor's exile to Nigeria, an interim government was put into place. The National Transitional Government (NTGL), as a body that should have led the country until the democratic elections in 2005, was appointed in October 2003, with its members supposed to reflect "national and gender balance in all elective and non-elective appointments" (CPA 2003, Article XXVIII).[63]

---

63 It was not possible to find information about the gender ratio. What is certain, however, is the fact that the composition of the NTGL reflected mainly the

The CPA included no restrictions for political participation of the members of LURD and MODEL in the postwar phase. The only limitation was put upon people appointed to high positions within the NTGL—the Chairman and the Vice-chairman, principal cabinet ministers, as well as Chief Justice and Associate Justices (CPA 2003, Article XXV, XXVII), who were not allowed to contest for any elective office in the 2005 elections. Gyude Bryant, a business man with a neutral political record and therefore a figure acceptable for all parties involved, became the chairman of the NTGL. The Transitional Government, however, soon gained a reputation for large scale mismanagement, corruption, and misappropriation of public funds.[64] As a consequence, the original "technical support and assistance" by the international experts, foreseen in the CPA, was soon replaced by GEMAP (Governance and Economic Management Assistance Program), a programme designed as a form of assistance with the everyday administrative and financial management. However, the assistance was rather a form of international trusteeship with the main task of assuring transparency and proper management of financial affairs. Opinions vary about the impact of the program with regard to corruption, but there is a consensus about the added value in terms of increased transparency of financial flows and improved governance, as well as training and development of professional skills of the governmental employees (USAID 2010).[65]

After the inauguration of Ellen Johnson Sirleaf to the presidential office in January 2006, the regular administration started to operate, although in extremely modest conditions and still under GEMAP.[66] Ministries and governmental agencies were dilapidated and lacked basic equipment. It was difficult to staff all the institutions due to the scarcity of competent professionals available for the jobs. Decades of violent conflict meant not only interruption of education for a whole generation, but also led to a brain-drain of qualified individuals. Programs were established to attract Liberians in diaspora to come "back home" and help to rebuild Liberia

---

power balance between the three main armed factions: LURD, MODEL, and GoL (see e.g., Bøås and Dunn 2013, or Bøås 2015).

64 In 2007, Bryant himself was tried for large-scale embezzlement of funds.

65 The international staff worked closely with the Liberian counterparts and besides the "official" training, the latter group received a fair deal of training "on-the-job", in everyday interaction (USAID 2010). For more details on GEMAP, see chapter four or Gerdes (2013).

66 It was lifted only in 2010.

in a form of short- to middle-term contracts.[67] Seconded experts from international organisations and development partners flowed in the country to assist with capacity building.[68] Such measures provided the much needed human resources in the short term, but did not offer a sustainable solution:

> "They [the experts coming to the country] all have their lives back in the US. In a few years, they are coming back and let's see who comes to replace them." (Interview #54, Director of LEITI, 22 November 2012, Monrovia)

In other instances, the transfer of knowledge between the "outsiders" and locals did not really take place:

> "There was little contact between Mr. Pink [a Scott Fellow, an international expert] and national staff, and they [the latter] did not seem very eager about learning." (de Carvalho and Nagelhus Schia 2011:22)

Lack of interest on the Liberian side has not been the only challenge to capacity-building:

> "Mr. Blue went on to stress the 'huge disconnect between national and expat staff.' The few locals working for the UN, he said, are largely left to their own devices and not mentored by anyone. The lack of transfer of knowledge was once again brought up. The same applied for NGOs, who leave nothing behind once their programmes are over: 'After the UN and NGOs leave, whose capacity have they built?' " (de Carvalho and Nagelhus Schia 2011: 13)

The situation during the time of my fieldwork in 2012 was certainly better than at the beginning of Sirleaf's mandate; however, the gap in human resources was still a serious problem in the bureaucracy. The top positions in the ministries and governmental agencies were staffed, but the mid-level bureaucrats were missing:

---

67 TOKTEN (Transfer of Knowledge through Expatriate Nationals) or SES (Senior Executive Service) were two such programs.

68 Despite the undisputed added value of these efforts and involvement of many qualified professionals with knowledge and skills to share (e.g., the Scott Fellows, graduates of top American universities, placed in a number of Liberian ministries), there were also instances of capacity-building by relatively inexperienced young international staff, who resembled enthusiastic gap-year volunteers rather than expert professionals (personal observations and informal conversations #23, #24, #41, #53, April–June 2012, Monrovia).

> "We would be interested in the direct, government-to-government cooperation, but the capacities are simply not there yet. It would be much cheaper, but we are not there yet. There is a thin layer on the top, where the capacities are there, but it is as thin as paper; you pierce it and there is nothing underneath. You can see a minister making photocopies, because there is no one else who can do it. There needs to be a cadre of new professionals built." (Interview #61, USAID employee, 30 November 2012, Monrovia)

There was a general decrease of international presence in political institutions after the lifting of GEMAP. The presence and level of support in terms of personnel and training has further varied across the ministries and governmental agencies, where in some of them, the presence of international experts and consultants has been relatively high (e.g., in the Land Commission, with the Land and Policy Institutional Support Project described in more detail in chapter eight, or in the Ministry of Finance, Ministry of Justice or Foreign Affairs), whilst others, such as the Ministry of Youth or Gender, remained out of the spotlights.

A general challenge, related to the missing human capacities, has been the issue of performance and productivity. Very often, a position at a ministry is regarded as a status symbol rather than a post that requires "getting things done":

> "The working ethics of some of my colleagues at the Ministry is to appear around 10 o'clock, to check emails, news, Facebook, have a coffee...then, around 1 or 2 pm they work a bit, and then they go home." (Interview #32, ABA, 29 May 2012, informal conversation #58, #65, Monrovia)

Despite the weak record in terms of human capacity, there is a perception of the top-level Liberian leadership as "outspoken and very assertive in defining what they want. The government is very much in charge." (Interview #38, foreign embassy, 7 June 2012, Monrovia)

Another aspect worth mentioning with regard to political institutions is their strong centralisation. There is little presence of the state institutions beyond the capital. Some ministries and governmental agencies have decentralised to some extent and established offices in the counties, but the bulk part is still concentrated in Monrovia. A related issue is a poor distribution of information from the centre to the counties.[69] Documents and policy decisions are not routinely translated to local languages, nor simplified, which makes the implementation, not to mention the general level of civic awareness, problematic.[70] The over-centralisation has been one of the factors behind the conflict and although there is a decentralisation policy (for details, see chapter seven), the supremacy of the centre is still an issue generating resentment among the citizens. This is reflected in the saying "Monrovia is not Liberia", frequently used especially in conversations with foreigners. There is also a general feeling of a "deep mistrust to everything that comes from Monrovia, based on the historical experience" (Interview #61, USAID employee, 30 November 2012, Monrovia, cf. #27, civil society representative, 18 May 2012, Monrovia), an attitude that manifested clearly during the Ebola pandemics, when measures to halt the virus coming from the capital were met with resistance at the local level (The Nordic Africa Institute 2014, Reuters 2014).

The government, and practically, the functioning of the whole country, is to a large extent dependent on external financial resources. In fiscal year 2015/16, the grants and loans from the development partners represented over 90% of the total domestic revenues. In 2016/17, the ratio of in-budget support decreased to 65% and for the 2017/18, it is foreseen to drop to 2,25% only, coming entirely from USAID (Budget Framework Paper 2017).[71] Equally, the off-budget support tends to decrease. This is partly due to the Ebola epidemics (when the donor assistance was frontloaded), but also due to the uncertainty surrounding the political transition and departure of UNMIL, resulting in donors' reserved stance to spending on the country. This uncertainty will, of course, have a major impact on the whole postwar reform process and its pace.

The Liberian political system is a presidential democracy, similar to (and openly referring to) the US model, with the directly elected president and the executive branch as the strongest component. The legislature consists

---

69 Radio represents the main source of information for the majority of the population. Printed newspapers are hard to access outside the capital. Although internet access has been increasing steadily (between 2012 and 2016, the population with internet access more than tripled from an estimated 2,6% in 2012 to 8,6% in 2016; http://www.internetlivestats.com/internet-users/liberia/), it is still far from being the mainstream way of acquiring information, especially in the rural areas, where the connection is slow.

70 The level of illiteracy further adds to the problem. In 2015, an estimated 47,6% of the population (15 years and older) could read and write (CIA World Factbook).

71 For more details on budget, see Annex 3.

of a bi-cameral parliament. There are several political parties; however, they are not crucial for the everyday political life. They are activated mainly around the election time, and the party affiliation of the politicians does not represent the primary variable during elections, nor does it determine the voting of the MPs.[72] The president and the cabinet are supported by the ministries and specialised government agencies. For the majority of them, the president appoints and calls off the leadership.

Concerning the four bodies in focus of this study and their place in the formal political structures, the Ministry of Gender is a common ministry. The Governance Commission and the Land Commission fall in the category of specialised governmental agencies, they also fit Skelcher's (2005) definition of agencies.[73] The former is a stable structure with an unlimited mandate, whereas the latter's life span was originally determined to five years. After a year-long prolongation it was replaced by a permanent successor institution. Both commissions are advisory, policy-making bodies with no implementation power. The Early Warning Working Group is not a part of the political system. It has grown as a bottom-up, informal initiative and is connected to the politics only indirectly, through some of its members (e.g., Liberia National Police or Bureau of Immigration and Naturalization).

5.2 International actors

International actors were, right after the end of the war, in charge of almost everything, starting with security, provided by the UN peacekeepers, to the basic services and humanitarian relief, with the international NGOs in charge. They were organised in clusters, with each cluster bringing together various actors focused on a particular issue —shelter, health, nutrition, telecommunications, etc. (Abramowitz 2014: 20). The cluster structure facilitated coordination and "policy discussions" (Abramowitz 2014: 46) among the different actors, and shaped to a large extent the sub-

---

72 For the voters, personalities matter more than parties, especially the link of a candidate to a particular locality, and the benefits related to this relationship play a role. In the parliament, the issue in question is the main variable that determines the vote.

73 Bodies created by the government to come up with solutions or policies addressing particular issues. For more details, see section 2.8.

sequent organisation of NGOs around particular ministries (Abramowitz 2014: 45ff.; interview #36, US researcher, 5 June 2012, Monrovia).

5.2.1 The United Nations

The engagement of the United Nations in Liberia started long before the signature of the peace agreement in 2003. The UN participated in the settlement of the first war and in the peace negotiations in the 1990s. During the second war, the UN was involved in the peace process and shortly after the peace agreement was signed, the UN Security Council approved the mandate of UNMIL, the United Nations Mission in Liberia.[74] The mission was deployed in the context of a series of recent non-achievements of the UN in other post-conflict contexts (e.g., Bosnia, Somalia, DR Congo, or Haiti) that shattered the confidence and trust in the peacekeeping capacities of the UN. There was an "imperative of success" (Abramowitz 2014: 19) for the UN engagement in Liberia: "if we can't prove that we can rebuild Liberia, then maybe we can't do this anywhere" (interview with an UNMIL official, cited in Abramowitz 2014: 19). With its initial strength of over 15,000 personnel and a budget of over 550,000,000 USD for the first year of its operation (UN GA Report 2003), UNMIL has been the largest and most expensive UN peacekeeping mission of its time.[75] Apart from the military component, the mission included up to 250 military observers, 1,115 police officers, and over 1,500 civilian staff.[76]

As Abramowitz notes: "the UN was motivated to restore the legitimacy of humanitarian peacekeeping operations in Liberia. Mindful of the criticism that UN peacekeeping interventions had focused too much on elections as a benchmark of peacekeeping success, and had left too early, the UN regarded the success of the Liberian reconstruction as a critical test of the Right to Protect doctrine and as a moral test of the international community." (2014: 22)

---

74 In a SC resolution 1509 from 19 September 2003.

75 The budget for the final year of operation (July 2017–June 2018) amounted to 110,000,000 USD (https://peacekeeping.un.org/en/mission/unmil).

76 In July 2016, there were 1,240 military personnel and 606 police (UNMIL Factsheet, https://unmil.unmissions.org/sites/default/files/unmil_factsheet_may_2017 _1.pdf). The strength of the mission in October 2017 was 1,580 in total, with 707 civilians, 306 police, and 404 contingent troops (https://peacekeeping.un.org/en/ mission/unmil).

The "drawdown phase"[77] of the mission began therefore after nine years of UNMIL deployment, in 2012—a year after the second postwar elections. There has been a lot of emphasis on the responsible departure, to avoid potential problems caused by a too fast, poorly planned withdrawal of the missions elsewhere, as well as a certain nervousness on the Liberian side, related to the fact that the mission has been functioning as the principal security provider in the country.[78] The mission also communicated and explained extensively how the system is going to work in the future, once UNMIL is gone. The UN would be represented by the agencies (UNDP, UNICEF, UN-HABITAT, etc.) in charge of the ongoing and new programs. In spite of careful planning, it has been clear that some challenges in the post-UNMIL era would be hard to avoid. A major one is a gap and a general decline in external funding, due to the fact that UNMIL has disposed of a stable budget, whereas the UN agencies have to operate in a different budgetary scheme, based on program-related funding (Peacebuilding Priority Plan 2017).

The whole UN system in Liberia is presided by the Special Representative of the Secretary General (SRSG), with two Deputy SRSGs supporting him, one in the Rule of Law, and a second one in the field of Recovery and Governance, who is at the same time overseeing the work of the UN Country Team as a Resident Coordinator. UNMIL also subscribed to the UN initiative "Delivering as One" (DaO), launched by the UN Secretary General as a response to the Paris declaration on Aid Effectiveness in 2005. The objective of DaO is to avoid duplication of work and to facilitate coordination of activities of different UN entities on the ground.[79] Liberia wanted to join the initiative as a "self-starter country"; the government decided to take part. But in reality, the UN was already working together before the official launch of the approach:

---

77 The UN prefers the terms "reconfiguration", "adjustment", or "restructuring", referring to the decrease of the military component, since "people tend to associate the words 'drawdown' and 'withdrawal' with 'premature exit' or 'departure'." (Interview #26, foreign diplomat, 16 May 2012, Monrovia, cf. UNMIL website, FAQ, https://unmil.unmissions.org/frequently-asked-questions). However, Liberians and non-UN interviewees commonly used the term drawdown.

78 Despite a relatively successful security system reform, the capacities of the Liberian National Police are rather low. Due to inadequate equipment and financial constraints, it is difficult to fulfil its functions, especially in the context of the low accessibility of remote areas in the hinterland counties.

79 DaO should have also facilitated the transition of UNMIL.

"The management wanted to work together. And the operational conditions required it—bad conditions of roads, inaccessibility of some remote areas…so we were already working together." (Interview #29, UNMIL official, 25 May 2012, Monrovia)

However, there are also challenges linked to the initiative, mainly a certain resistance from the side of the particular agencies:

"It is not always easy, although there is a lot of awareness raising. The problem is that some UN agencies would feel that their identity is being dissolved. They want to put up a flag on their thing, saying, 'we are protecting children', for example. But the goal of Delivering as One is to use the expertise of different entities. Not to unify the UN. It is not against maintaining the identity." (Interview #29, UNMIL official, 25 May 2012, Monrovia)

The role of the UN is presented in terms of support on the strategic, systemic level, especially in the activities that require extensive human and financial resources:

"We do not try to do everything. The government gives mandate, we provide support and see how the UN can contribute to government priorities. We do not want to implement all activities; some are better provided by others." (Interview #29, UNMIL official, 25 May 2012, Monrovia)

This point of view is widely shared across the spectrum of different actors, as well as by the government and civil society organisations (Interviews #20, #22, #27, #33, #56, Monrovia). The UN fills the gap in "managerial" skills and capacities:

"There are some really good people in the government. They only sort of struggle with funding and capacities. The government is committed, but there is a gap between the broad, strategic decisions, like the PRS targets, and the actual implementation. The capacity in the middle is missing: someone who actually splits the big tasks into smaller pieces, the middle level that comes between the government and the activities on the ground. And UN and UNMIL work in this way." (Interview #31, international NGO staff, 28 May 2012, Monrovia, cf. #8, #22, #27)

On the other hand, the UN is often perceived as being very slow, bureaucratic and inflexible in terms of operational capacities:

> "You know, if they are to decide over my new laptop, my contract will be over before I get it [laughs]." (Interview #22, PBO employee, Peacebuilding Office, 1 May 2012, Monrovia)

The quote above also illustrates another general aspect of the international engagement and presence in Liberia beyond the UN—the high fluctuation of personnel, to a large extent caused by the settings in the post-conflict aid industry (cf. Autesserre 2017). Contracts are relatively short, which, together with the complexity of the fast-changing environment, leads to a sub-optimal situation, where people arrive with a relatively limited knowledge about the situation in the country and have difficulties finding orientation in a plethora of institutions, actors, action plans, and initiatives on the ground: "After eight months in the country, I still feel like I do not know what is going on." (Interview #32, ABA staff member, 29 May 2012, Monrovia) Once they find their grounding, a considerable part of their contract is already over.[80] The fluctuation impacts not only on the overall level of performance, but also on the sustainability and long-term effects of their work.

5.2.2 Bilateral partners

Bilateral partners are usually more flexible than the UN, be it in provision of financial support or equipment. They are mostly represented by national development agencies, such as USAID, SIDA, DFID, Swiss Agency for Development and Cooperation, or GIZ in Liberia. Some of the key partner countries also have their embassies on the ground; in 2012, there was an American, British, Chinese, French, German, and Swedish embassy in Monrovia, and Spain was represented by an honorary consul. The diplomatic community is relatively small. With the exception of more robust American and Chinese outposts, the diplomatic representations in Liberia are usually staffed with only one or two diplomats.

The largest diplomatic post in Monrovia is the US embassy. Due to its historical links, the US is a primary country of reference for Liberia. The political system is modelled after the American one, the biggest part of

---

80 This applies mainly to the international NGO project personnel, who are in the country for 6- to 12-month contracts (some are longer, but usually do not exceed 24–30 months). International consultants, coming for specific projects (in the early postwar period for conducting baseline studies, later for monitoring and evaluation), stay usually for a few weeks only (2–3 months maximum).

the diaspora lives there, the flag displays similar symbols, etc. There was an interesting range of metaphors my interviewees used to describe the relationship between Liberia and the US:

"The US is not like a mother country in the colonial sense, but it is a first country of reference, in terms of laws, institutions and the like. At the same time, it is like if you look at the wrong side of the telescope. They are so important for Liberians, but in the US, no one really cares about Liberia, it is just one of our ventures in the world."(Interview #38, foreign diplomat, 7 June 2012, Monrovia)

"It is like if you are in love with a girl, but the girl does not love you. You are in trouble; it is not mutual. Liberia is so proud to be similar to the US, having the flag, etc., but the US just do[es] not care. If people want to get education, they go to the US. They prefer to go to a middle, not-so-well-known college in the US, then to go to LSE [London School of Economics]. They do not want to go to Europe." (Interview #54, Director of LEITI, 22 November 2012, Monrovia)

"Liberia is like a step-child. It looks up to the US, but the US is not so much involved; it does not want to take over. There are resentments that they did not stop the war. Liberia feels that it is not treated very well." (Interview #34, GIZ employee, 1 June 2012, Monrovia)

Despite the perceived lack of adequate attention from the American side, the US is one of the biggest bilateral donors and USAID represents the largest among the national development agencies present in Liberia.

The second biggest diplomatic presence on the ground is the Chinese representation. However, unlike the American one, the Chinese embassy is located on the outskirts of Monrovia, and the cooperation is focused on infrastructure and construction projects. A common criticism often to be heard from the Liberian side revolves around the fact that there are no (or very few) employment opportunities generated by the Chinese development projects. The Chinese side brings all the experts, engineers, and personnel from its homeland (Interview #27, civil society representative, 18 May 2012, Monrovia). Sweden[81], Denmark, Germany, and Norway are other countries with a significant, long-term engagement in Liberia, largely organised through their development agencies and NGOs.

---

81 Sweden has been chairing the Liberia Country Specific Configuration of the UN Peacebuilding Commission since 2012. The former head of UNMIL, Karen Landgren, also comes from Sweden.

5.2.3 Supra-national level groups and "clubs of friends"

All the countries mentioned in the section above were involved in the International Contact Group on Liberia, an informal platform established in 2002, which was actively involved in the peace negotiations process. The list of members varies across different sources, but usually the UN, AU, EU, ECOWAS, World Bank, IMF, US, Ghana, Nigeria, UK, Germany, Spain, and Sweden are listed as member countries.[82] The Contact Group was the party that signed GEMAP with the transitional government in September 2005, and stayed involved in the postwar development, closely monitoring Liberia's progress.

After 2010, when Liberia was put on the agenda of the Peacebuilding Commission, another "coalition of friends" was formed on the supranational level: Liberia Country-Specific Configuration (CSC). Based in New York, it consists of over 50 members, some of them representing multilateral organisations, some national governments. There is a Steering Group within the CSC, with the most active members: China, Germany, Japan, Norway, Sweden, UK, and the US. The CSC was often mentioned during the interviews as a major structure that contributes to mobilisation of political and donor support for Liberia: "There is more [diplomatic] work being done in New York than in Liberia" (Interview #26, foreign diplomat, 16 May 2012, Monrovia). Prince Zeid Ra'ad Zeud al-Hussein of Jordan, the first chairman of the Configuration, was frequently mentioned in interviews as being crucial for the good performance of the group (Interview #26, foreign diplomat, #22, PBO staff, #29, UN official).[83] The group comes to Liberia for regular visits for monitoring the progress of Peacebuilding Plan implementation and meeting local stakeholders.

5.2.4 Regional organisations

The representation of regional organisations on the ground in Monrovia consists of the delegation of the African Union, ECOWAS, and the European Union. The AU and ECOWAS have small liaison offices located in

---

82 Some sources include also France and Morocco among the members (https://2001-2009.state.gov/p/af/rls/36348.htm). Some do not list Spain, France, or Morocco. Roehner (2012) includes only UN, ECOWAS, AU, EU, WB, IMF, Nigeria, Ghana, and the US (Roehner 2012: 181).

83 Prince Zeid stepped down in 2012, officially due to health reasons.

Sinkor. The EU has a more robust presence, with an office in Mamba Point in downtown Monrovia.[84]

5.2.5 International NGOs

The engagement and mandates of the international NGOs are very heterogeneous, and any meaningful analysis would have to be linked to a specific case, as the empirical chapters (seven to 10) aim to do. This is why there is no detailed analysis included in this section.

5.3 Civil society

Civil society is usually defined as an "arena of uncoerced collective action around shared interests, purposes and values" (LSE Report 2006), taking various forms with a different degree of organization. It is considered distinct from the state, family, and market, although the boundaries between them are often blurred and contested. Despite its independent nature, civil society closely interacts with the state and is oriented towards it (Spurk 2010: 6-9, Kjellman and Harpviken 2010: 29-42).

Despite the origins of the concept in the Western political philosophy and Western socio-political context in general, civil society has been used as an analytical category in various regions around the globe. There are different opinions about its applicability in non-Western contexts (for Africa, e.g., Lewis 2002 offers an overview of different arguments). One objection to the use of the concept with regard to Africa is that the definition is too narrow to capture different forms of social organisation across the continent. As many others, I subscribe to the opinion of Bayart (1986), Kasfir (1998), or Appiagyei-Atua (2002), who claim that it is possible to

---

84 The location of the institutions is also an indicator of their political importance. Mamba Point has been traditionally one of the power centers in Monrovia (together with the Capitol Hill, the seat of the president and the parliament), with a number of embassies, ministries, and UN agencies. Sinkor is a residential area, neighbouring the central part of the city, hosting a number of NGOs, but also political institutions (e.g., the Governance Commission, the Land Commission, or the National Traditional Council of Liberia) and some embassies. See the map of Monrovia in Annex 4.

use the concept, if we stick to a more encompassing perspective, including traditional, voluntary, or age-based organisations.[85]

In spite of the heterogeneity of the term, not only on the civil-uncivil (Spurk 2010) continuum, but also across different geographical and historical contexts, there is a broad consensus that civil society is a crucial actor when it comes to peacebuilding. Different streams within peacebuilding discourse focus on different aspects of its importance—the liberal mainstream acknowledges its role in building democratic states, promoting principles of good governance, respect for human rights, etc.; the conflict-transformation and critical school recognise its role of "identifying human needs and listening to the previously unheard voices of the ordinary people" (Paffenholz 2015: 349).

Paffenholz (2015) came up with a typology of functions civil society can perform in peacebuilding:
1) Protection of citizens against violence;
2) Monitoring (of peace agreement implementation, human rights violations,...);
3) Advocacy (for peace and human rights);
4) Socialisation (to values of peace and democracy, or building "peace constituencies");
5) Social cohesion (bringing together people from different groups);
6) Facilitation of dialogue among actors at various levels;
7) Service delivery.

The performance of civil society is also influenced by five types of "context factors", which are (1) the level of violence, (2) the behaviour of the state, (3) media performance, (4) composition and constellation/polarization of the civil society itself, and (5) the influence of the external actors, including donors (Paffenholz 2015: 355).

During the phase of open violence, civil society can play an important role at the Track 2 level, building confidence and contributing to bringing parties of the conflict together, but "[s]o long as fighting goes on NGOs can only play a supporting role. Aid programmes, a watchdog role and other activities cannot provide negative peace" (Neubert 2004: 65). Once the negative peace has been provided, the importance of CSOs increases. Apart from the knowledge of local context and realities, it also tends to increase the level of legitimacy and acceptance of the international

---

85 Neubert (2014: 6) points to the fact that the basis of these "traditional" forms of social organizations is not voluntarism, but rather ascribed characteristics, such as ethnic origin, geographical location, or age.

intervention, acting as an implementing partner and very often as a service provider for the population. Liberia was no exception in this respect. During the conflict, civil society, especially churches and women's groups, put pressure on warring parties to get involved in peace talks and significantly contributed to the positive outcomes of the negotiations.[86] The Inter-Religious Council of Liberia and the Mano River Women Peace Network were also included among the signatories of the Accra peace agreement as witnesses.

After the war, civil society was included in the reconstruction process mainly in the role of "implementing partners" in peacebuilding projects, and as service providers, "called upon after the decision has been made" (Interview #20, Search for Common Ground employee, 27 June 2011, Monrovia). Their involvement in the decision-making processes was rather limited (cf. Neubert 2004).[87] In the early postwar time, churches were especially active and functioned as channels for distribution of humanitarian aid and "reconstruction of social, moral, and professional networks" (Abramowitz 2014: 185).[88] Apart from the provision of services, civil society performed other functions included on Paffenholz's list. Monitoring of human rights standards and democratic values, going hand in hand with advocacy, is one of them, with Monrovia-based CSOs especially taking the lead. Socialisation and social cohesion, with a number of organisations engaged in reconciliation, peace education, etc., are also relevant fields. With regard to facilitation, civil society is definitely efficient at the local and middle level. However, at the national level, *vis-à-vis* the governmental or international actors, their impact is rather limited. They are incorporated in some of the fora, but their participation is rather tokenised; they are present and their concerns are being heard, but the real impact on the decision-making is negligible. "There is no systematic involvement of the civil society in post-conflict reconstruction. They are called upon ad hoc." (Interview #20, Search for Common Ground employee, 27 June 2011, Monrovia, cf. Neubert 2004).

---

86 They were not invited to the negotiation table; however, they were able to exercise significant pressure on the leaders of warring parties. See section 9.7 for more details on the engagement of women's groups in the peace negotiations.

87 "In a peace-building process NGOs play only a supporting role. During the establishment of negative-peace and during post-conflict stabilisation the main decisions are taken at the military and political level." (Neubert2004: 72)

88 Later, new Pentecostal churches offered chances for personal transformation and re-integration of former wrongdoers to the communities (Abramowitz 2014, The Redemption of General Butt Naked 2001).

Aside from a general tendency to be excluded from the decision-making processes, a systematic involvement in peacebuilding is complicated by the fact that the civil society base is not strongly developed in Liberia. The scene is quite fragmented, with a high number of organisations[89] involved in a broad range of activities. NGOs are the prevalent form of organisation for the civil society, mainly due to the accessibility of potential funding opportunities.[90] The overall low level of development is primarily a consequence of the country's history and the system of centralised, autocratic political governance, where there was little space for organised civic activities, apart from religious organisations. The faith-based organisations have been well established throughout Liberia, even before the war, and have been actively engaged in peacebuilding in the postwar phase, mainly through reconciliation and conflict-resolution work at the grassroots level. Women's organisations are another sub-category with a lot of activity at the community level. Media stick to the provision of information, and their involvement in peacebuilding, apart from some radio stations offering programmes with peacebuilding components, is very limited.[91] Trade unions are not strongly developed in Liberia. Although there are several professional associations, such as the AFELL (Association of Female Lawyers of Liberia) or the Motorbike Union, which brings together the motorbike drivers (most of whom are former combatants), they focus on protection of their members' interests rather than on other activities.

Many Liberian NGOs are engaged in "peacebuilding"—a simple label that provides enough flexibility for different projects and increases eligibility for donor funding. The external funding is a problematic factor in many respects. For one, it drives the agenda in the direction for which donors offer support. As a consequence, it encourages "hut-changing", in other words, shifting the agenda of NGOs depending on the availability of funds for a certain kind of projects. Besides that, the context of scarcity of such financial support incites competition and the perspective of a "zero-sum-game" (Interview #20, #27, #56). Last but not least, the way that funding opportunities are advertised (mainly in printed newspapers or on notice boards of the respective donor organisations) contributes to the

---

89 In 2005 alone, there were over 1,000 new registrations of Liberian NGOs with the UN Humanitarian Information Center (Abramowitz 2014: 21).

90 Funding opportunities offered by donors often target specifically NGOs as the implementing partners (McKeown and Mulbah 2007).

91 Analysis of such programmes may represent an interesting research field. However, this goes beyond the scope of this study.

existing imbalance between the rural and Monrovia-based NGOs, with the latter having easier access to information about the offers and open calls.

Similar to other sectors, there is a scarcity of qualified personnel, exacerbated by the need of the latter in the governmental sector, which leads to a brain-drain towards state institutions. Unlike in many other countries, the strategy of co-optation is not used to appease opposition forces, but simply to fill the gaps and provide qualified workforce. The result is, however, not different from the former situation; it leads to the weakening of the civil society as a whole.

From their own point of view, the role of the civil society is to be an alternative voice, that would raise issues responsible for the state failure, so that the mistakes of the past are not repeated at the expense of a rapid reconstruction:

> "We are reminding the government about the issues of governance, human rights, issues of pluralistic participation and democracy, reconciliation at social structural level. Reconciliation has to address the institutions that failed: court system, education, health [...] International actors and government are in a hurry for a reconstruction. We are asking the question, 'What costs the failure?' So yes for reconciliation, but not in a hurry. No hurry to build roads and schools. But ask what failed. And then decide." (Interview #27, civil society representative, 18 May 2012, Monrovia)

To facilitate this, a need for a strong, unified voice of the civil society was emphasised to "make our presence felt in the discussion with the government" (Interview #27, civil society representative, 18 May 2012, Monrovia). There have been efforts to organise the CSOs, to establish an umbrella organisation that would allow them to "speak in a unified voice" (Ibid.). The underlying competition, however, complicates the task. The Governance Commission has been involved in a similar exercise, having created a directory of civil society organisations, that could be used, for example, as a resource for the government, to provide policy advice and expert knowledge from different fields (Interview #27, civil society representative, 18 May 2012, #57, GC Commissioner, 28 November 2012, Monrovia), but the results were not accepted by the CSOs:

> "It did not go through the rank-and-file. Some vital institutions were left out and there is a need for us to own the process. So it was a triggering moment for us [to start a process of establishing an umbrella organisation]." (Interview #27, civil society representative, 18 May 2012, Monrovia)

With regard to the relationship *vis-à-vis* the government, leaders of the civil society block are said to be "generally negative and critical about the government" (Interview #56, university lecturer, 27 November 2012, Monrovia):

> "There is some personal envy. They sometimes think that Ellen [Johnson Sirleaf] is given too much glory for nothing. They have also taken part and are not given enough attention and opportunities." (Ibid.)

Relation to international actors has been succinctly summarized by a civil society representative: "We do have contacts, but in the donor-NGO atmosphere" (Interview #27, civil society representative, 18 May 2012, Monrovia). The roles of both groups are clearly demarcated. International actors are perceived mainly as donors, civil society as the "implementing partners", who are also able to provide information from the areas, where the international actors have limited presence, suchs as from the grassroots level, or from remote parts of the country.

5.4 Where do they all meet: Arenas of interaction

There are a number of fora, where people from all the three "camps" described above meet and interact. Leaving the informal and purely "social" sphere aside[92], there are essentially two other levels: one, usually referred to as "the high level", with the representatives of the cabinet and top leadership from the international side, where broad, strategic decisions are being made; and a second one, the "working level", with the focus on coordination and information-sharing. The interaction at the middle level represents the focus of the four empirical chapters that follow. This section will therefore focus on the top decision-making level.

After the inauguration of the Sirleaf government in January 2006, the locus of cooperation between the government and international actors at the high level became the National Joint Steering Committee (JSC)[93], where the highest-level representatives of both domestic and international actors have been meeting. There are representatives of six government ministries,

---

92 An ethnographic study of this kind would, however, provide very interesting information that would complement the dominant, political science-based perspective on postwar interventions.

93 Apart from this, there have also been regular, weekly meetings of the president with the SRSG (the head of UNMIL) and the US Ambassador.

with the Ministry of Planning and Internal Affairs co-chairing the group, Deputy Representative of Secretary General and UNMIL for the UN side, and key bi- und multi-lateral partners: the UK, Sweden, China, Japan, Nigeria, EU, USAID, or the American Bar Association.[94] There are also two slots reserved for civil society (one of them for women's organisations) and one slot for INGOs. Meetings of the group are generally not accessible to the public:

> "The meetings, they are public, yet a little bit restricted. The room is arranged in such a way that it does not give much more room for other people. Usually, there is one senior level representative and sometimes one more. The idea is that all projects, proposals, and reports, everything will be on the website, accessible for anybody." (Interview #22, PBO director, 1 May 2012, Monrovia) [95]

Below the JSC, there is the Justice and Security Board, with the highest leadership in the justice and security sector represented. The group is co-chaired by the Minister of Justice, the Chief Justice, and the Deputy Representative of the Special Representative of the Secretary General (DRSRSG) for the Rule of Law. Other members include the representatives of the LNP, BIN, BCR, Ministry of Planning, UNMIL (2) and UNDP (2), and donors supporting the sector. There are also two slots reserved for non-state actors, one from the Liberian side, one for an international NGO.[96] Other actors (such as NGOs or international partners) can participate as observers, but do not have decision-making power. The Justice and Security Board meets usually twice a month (UNDP 2013).

Civil society is also represented at the level of Technical Advisory Groups (TAGs) to the JSC. There are two TAGs, one for justice and security issues, and a second one for reconciliation. Their task is to provide policy advice to the JSC. TAGs meet once a month. Here as well, represen-

---

94 As a US professional association, with a core mandate of serving its members and improving the legal profession focused on the national (i.e., the US) level, ABA is not a typical entity on such a list. However, ABA is involved in projects promoting justice and the rule of law in a number of countries around the world. In Liberia, ABA is highly recognized for its projects in the fields of access to justice, alternative dispute resolution, or pre-trial detention (https://www.americanbar.org/advocacy/rule_of_law/where_we_work/africa/liberia/news.html).

95 To my knowledge, there is no functioning website of the PBO.

96 Organizations working in this field have nominated a representative from among themselves, the Foundation for International Dignity (FIND), to represent the Liberian side, and the Carter Center as the international one.

tatives of the whole spectrum are included, from the senior staff of MoJ, LNP, BIN, MIA, Ministry of Public Works, PBO, and INCHR, through GIZ, Carter Center, ABA, ICTJ, FIND, Justice and Peace Commission, to UNMIL, UNPOL, UNDP, or UNICEF (UNDP 2013). The administrative support is provided by the Liberia Peacebuilding Support Office, usually referred to as "the Peacebuilding Office" (PBO), which serves as a secretariat to all the previously mentioned bodies. There is a structure with an identical name (Peacebuilding Support Office) in New York, being a part of the UN Peacebuilding architecture (see section 2.2 for more details). Throughout the study, the Liberia-based Peacebuilding Support Office will be referred to by the emic term "Peacebuilding Office", since the former, official form has never been used by any of my interviewees on the ground.

5.5 Peacebuilding Office

The Liberia Peacebuilding Office (PBO) is a unique structure that does not easily fit the usual categorisation trichotomy between domestic, international, and civil society actors. Formally, the PBO serves as a local secretariat to the New York-based Peacebuilding Fund, overseeing the distribution of funds to the UN agencies on the ground. At the same time, the office is formally a governmental organisation, located at the premises of the Ministry of Internal Affairs, and its employees, including the leadership, are Liberians.[97] It also fits Skelcher's (2005) category of agency. According to the Chairman of the PBO, the office is a "UN project attached to the government, but the exact position of the PBO [in the domestic political landscape] has still to be defined"[98] (Interview #22, PBO director, 1 May 2012, Monrovia). It was established in 2009, around the time when Liberia

---

97 They are supported by international consultants coming for short-term assignments mainly in monitoring and evaluation. (Interview #22, PBO employee, Peacebuilding Office, 1 May 2012, Monrovia)

98 The Office suffered from the effects of political manoeuvring and changes on the Liberian political scene. Originally, it was attached to the Ministry of Planning, but the minister was appointed to the Ministry of Finance. Due to that, and to the involvement of the former minister to some projects, "most of the things you want to get done in PBO have to go through the Ministry of Finance. So the exact position of the PBO has to be still defined. I don't think that planning is the best place for the office. But the politics is also involved in it." (Interview #22, PBO employee, 1 May 2012, Monrovia)

received the first tranche of PBF funding and in 2012, there were about nine permanent employees (Interview #22, PBO employee, 1 May 2012).

The rationale behind the creation of the PBO was to overcome fragmentation of peacebuilding activities and to foster coordination and collaboration among the actors on the ground, especially between civil society and international NGOs (Interview #22, PBO director, 1 May 2012, Monrovia). Another reason was the issue of measuring the cumulative impact of peacebuilding interventions, or, "how the various interventions address the root causes of conflict. Cumulative impact is difficult to measure in a situation where everyone does their own thing." (Interview #22, PBO director, 1 May 2012, Monrovia)

The Office was the main actor behind drafting the Reconciliation Roadmap (see chapter six for more details about the document). It also aims to strengthen the local capacity for peace, mainly by ensuring the inclusion of civil society and community-based organizations in their work[99] and implementation of the Peacebuilding Priority Plan:

> "While it is true that the PBF targets the pressing Liberian conflict factors, bridging the critical peacebuilding gaps, one of the things that was also very critical for PBF, was to strengthen the national capacity for peace, or local capacity for peace. And when you think in terms of strengthening the local capacity for peace, civil society institutions and community-based institutions are the ones who reach much more to the local level, in terms of conflict management, or conflict prevention." (Interview #22, PBO director, 1 May 2012, Monrovia)

In order to reach out to the civil society, the PBO has set up regular monthly meetings:

> "[A part of our task is] to see how CSOs can participate in the implementation of the Peacebuilding Priority Plan for the country. And also through that to enhance the capacity to deliver. They share their experiences from the field, to see where we are, in the overall peacebuilding agenda of the country. The meetings were intended to give them [the CSOs] updates on what has been achieved, but also to listen to them, as they work in different parts of the country, give us updates, and the rest of the CS, to share their experience on what was

---

99 The PBO is also linked to the LERN project focused on early warning (see chapter 10 for details).

happening across the country. And to see if all of the actors speak to each other." (Interview #22, PBO director, 1 May 2012, Monrovia)

In addition to coordination, the meetings also serve to identify capacity gaps on the side of the CSOs, so that the PBO can provide training to address them.

Civil society has been recognised as a crucial stakeholder in the activities of the PBO. CSOs[100] were involved in the drafting process of the Reconciliation Roadmap; they have also been engaged in monitoring and evaluation of the Peacebuilding Plan. The employees of the Office pointed out that peacebuilding as a topic is not granted adequate attention in the post-conflict reconstruction agenda from the highest decision-making level:

> "There is no structure at the highest level [focusing] on peacebuilding and reconciliation, no advisor to the president on peacebuilding issues. [...] Generally, what I see, the Office is moving in the right direction. The whole issue of peacebuilding came to the level of full national permanence. Thanks to Wilfred [Wilfred Gray-Johnson, the director of the PBO] [101], we have that connection to the high level. Because of the UN support the PBO has, Wilfred is able to go [to] high places. But it's not high enough. Wilfred is not high enough. So in terms of real policy-making, we are just another office, another ministry." (Interview #22, Nat Walker, Peacebuilding Office, 1 May 2012, Monrovia)

Interestingly, the PBO staff conceived of peacebuilding rather in the Lederachian sense, with a focus on local level, conflict prevention, and management. Often, they used the term together with reconciliation. In this respect, the PBO's perspective represents a kind of counterweight to the prevalent top-down, mainstream approach to peacebuilding, emphasising justice and security, represented by the Joint Steering Committee.

---

100 It was not possible to get specific information about the organisations involved.
101 Mr Gray-Johnson currently serves as one of the commissioners at the Independent National Commission on Human Rights. Since May 2016, the PBO is led by Edward Mulbah, formerly employed in the PBO as a Senior Technical Advisor (Johnson 2016).

5.6 Liberia Reconstruction and Development Committee

To facilitate coordination on the donor side, the Liberia Reconstruction and Development Committee (LRDC), where donors used to meet the representatives of the GoL, was established in 2004. The Steering Committee of the LRDC was chaired by the president and included four ministers (of defence, finance, planning, and public works) and four main donors (the US, UN, World Bank, and the European Commission), together with representatives of the AU and ECOWAS. At the beginning of its operation, the Committee used to meet every other week, later it used to meet monthly to discuss broad policy decisions. The Committee included four "Pillar Groups", reflecting the pillar structure of the Poverty Reduction Strategy, chaired by the respective ministers. This structure, with the GoL chairing and a small steering group ensuring the possibility of fast decision-making, was adopted as an alternative to the models usually seen elsewhere in developing countries, with either donors meeting among themselves and coordinating with the government, or with a high-level government official (usually the Minister of Finance or Planning) chairing the meetings (Radelet 2007). The Liberian model proved to be well-functioning. After eight years, in late 2012, the LRDC underwent a major restructuration. A new entity, the Liberia Development Alliance (LDA), was established in early 2013 to bring together government representatives, donors, civil society, and the private sector, and to oversee the implementation of the Agenda for Transformation, Liberia's current framework development plan. The members of the LDA include the representatives of the United States, China, several European countries, the European Union, African Development Bank, World Bank, international NGOs, private sector institutions, and Liberia's civil society (Executive Mansion 2014).

Figure 1: Liberia Reconstruction and Development Committee

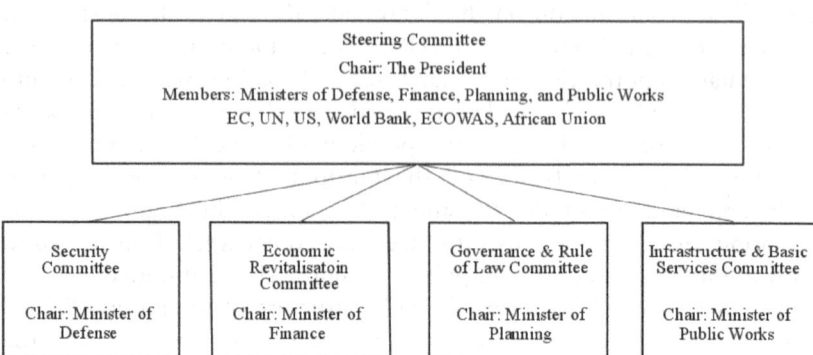

Liberia Reconstruction and Developement Committee (LRDC)

Steering Committee
Chair: The President
Members: Ministers of Defense, Finance, Planning, and Public Works
EC, UN, US, World Bank, ECOWAS, African Union

Security Committee	Economic Revitalisatoin Committee	Governance & Rule of Law Committee	Infrastructure & Basic Services Committee
Chair: Minister of Defense	Chair: Minister of Finance	Chair: Minister of Planning	Chair: Minister of Public Works

Due to the closed character of the meetings and the high-level member-ship, it was not possible to directly access information and data about the interaction in LRDC. Similar to the Joint Steering Committee, the plat-form remained a black box, with only secondary or tertiary information available. My interviewees themselves did not have access to the meetings and the only hints with regard to interaction were vague statements about the "assertivity" of Liberian leadership (Interview #37, foreign embassy, 7 June 2012, Monrovia) or a tokenized presence of civil society representa-tives (Interview #27, civil society representative, 18 May 2012, Monrovia). This might have stemmed from the lack of knowledge, as well as from the ultimately sensitive nature of the information.

At the middle, "working" level, the coordination among donors takes place in an informal way:

> "It is a small community here, so it is not that you don't know what the others are doing, there is a lot of conversation. You always have conversations." (Interview #31, employees of an international NGO, 28 May 2012, Monrovia)

5.7 Case-studies: selection criteria

The "middle level" of policy-making processes represents the main focus of the empirical chapters. The "highest level" is too exclusive and closed in terms of access for researchers. The criteria for selection of the four

empirical cases have been outlined in section 3.1, so here only a brief recapitulation is included:
- all four institutions have a direct link to peacebuilding and try to address conflict-triggering factors in Liberia;
- in all of them, a regular interaction between the actors in focus takes place;
- they were perceived as relevant by the actors on the ground;
- there was little progress in terms of specific results or impact of the institutions' work.

With regard to the last point, despite the general lack of progress, the selected sub-cases still represented institutions with a comparatively high performance, measured against the rest. It would have been methodologically interesting to include some cases with substantial progress, however, they were not there.

Apart from these common denominators, the cases are also diverse in different aspects and represent:
- a nominally important issue in the broad, neo-liberal peacebuilding discourse, prominent formally, but with little donor and international interest in practice. Still, it addresses one of the key factors related to the conflict (governance reform);
- a prominent issue, with a lot of donor funding and international interest, with a high conflict potential and crucial implications for economic development of the country (land issues);
- an issue related to social and cultural norms and values, therefore difficult to be influenced by an external intervention, with no relation to the conflict factors, but strongly linked to the consequences of the war and postwar living conditions of a large segment of Liberian population, with a relatively substantial external support, rather nominal domestic support, and results in terms of dealing with the effects rather than addressing the causes (gender and gender-based violence);
- an issue not featured on the typical post-conflict "to do" lists in the mainstream neo-liberal peacebuilding discourse, but showing a good example of peacebuilding initiative from below, with support from outside, involvement of civil society, with a focus on conflict prevention—but almost completely disconnected from its beneficiaries (early warning).

The relevance and particular relationship to the conflict and peacebuilding of each of the fields is outlined at the beginning of each empirical chapter. The interaction and roles of actors in focus are analysed against the backdrop of a particular institution within each "field"—the forum, where the actors in focus meet. Conclusions of the chapters include partial analysis and case-specific findings for each case study. Chapter 11 offers a cross-case analysis and draws conclusions at the broader level, so that we are able to see not only what roles different actors have in the process and how they "behave" *vis-à-vis* the others, but also what the latter tells about the post-conflict practice, and about the factors that can explain a lack of progress in the peacebuilding reforms.

Chapter 6 Framework documents

"Change does not come from outside, it comes
from the grassroots efforts. Any change I have
seen was self-initiated."
(Interview civil society representative, 23 June
2011, Monrovia)

The following chapter provides an overview of the key documents, framing the postwar reconstruction in Liberia. The list starts with the Comprehensive Peace Agreement (CPA) from Accra and continues with the Poverty Reduction Strategy (PRS), Agenda for Transformation (AfT), and a long-term-oriented Vision 2030. In the second part of the chapter, the UN documents linked to the reconstruction process are analysed; the UN Development Assistance Framework (UNDAF) for the years 2008–2011, and its successor, the UN One Programme, for the following period (2013–2017). The Peacebuilding Priority Plans, developed in cooperation with, and for the purposes of, the projects financed from the UN Peacebuilding Commission, together with the recent Reconciliation Roadmap, represent the last items on the list. The documents are analysed in terms of their content, their relationship to each other, and, last but not least, the temporal perspective (how the scope and priorities of the documents have changed over time) is taken into consideration.

There is a surprising lack of literature that would analyse them and to my knowledge, they have not been examined in a batch, despite the fact that the documents form a coherent framework of well-interconnected plans, which make reference to and build upon each other. Framing the whole peacebuilding process, the 10 documents in focus in this chapter still represent primary reference points for anyone trying to understand what has been done in Liberia after the war. However limited their explanatory power might be with regard to the actual progress of the reform on the ground, they do offer interesting insights to the meta-level of the peacebuilding exercise.

6.1 Comprehensive Peace Agreement

The Comprehensive Peace Agreement (CPA) signed on 18 August 2003 in Accra is a standard document of its kind, ending the Liberian civil war. It was signed between the Government of Liberia, two warring factions (LURD and MODEL) and political parties, witnessed by a number of actors, including the UN, AU, ECOWAS, or MARWOPNET (Mano River Women Peace Network), among others. Apart from its primary purpose, it outlines the key processes of the early postwar period: cantonment, demobilisation, disarmament, and reintegration of former fighters; repatriation of refugees and IDPs; humanitarian relief work; and the security system reform. It foresees several institutions, that should facilitate the reconstruction process: the Governance Reform Commission (GRC, created in 2005), Truth and Reconciliation Commission (TRC, also established in 2005), the Independent National Commission for Human Rights (INCHR, established in 2009 by an Act of Government, with the Commissioners appointed in 2010), or the implementation of a Palava Hut Program, led by the latter.[102]

CPA also lays out the political "rules of the game" for the period before the national election, planned for 2005. The document creates the National Transitional Government of Liberia (NTGL) that later gained a reputation of being corrupt beyond measure, and virtually blocking the reform efforts of the international community in the first years after the war, or the National Transitional Legislative Assembly, where the parties of the agreement, together with other interest groups (women, youth, trade unions, civil society, etc.), were to be represented.[103] With regard to

---

102 Palava hut is a traditional means of dispute resolution and seeking justice, used for dealing with minor offences in Liberia. Palava huts are round buildings, where a community gathers in order to solve a dispute. Due to its popular legitimacy, it was included as an option for transitional justice and reconciliation processes. However, the institution has not been universally accepted all over Liberia, nor is there a unified way of practicing it. There are some other problematic aspects of the scheme, such as the implicitly discriminatory principles guiding the decision-making. For more details, see e.g., Raddatz 2013, Chereji and Wratto King 2013.

103 The arrangements around the transitional executive, legislative, and judiciary bodies required a temporary suspension of particular provisions of the Liberian Constitution, as specified in Article XXXV (CPA 2003).

the future political and public engagement of the warring parties, the CPA put no restrictions in this regard.[104]

The CPA was the first document to contain a list of institutions designed to govern the country in the post-conflict phase. It includes prospects for several institutions with a peacebuilding mandate, which will be shortly introduced in the following paragraphs. Some of them were supposed to have a short lifespan and to be dissolved after fulfilling their goals (such as the National Commission for Disarmament, Demobilization, Rehabilitation and Reintegration for the DDRR process), temporal mandates of some others were not specified.

NTGL as the first institution to govern the country in the postwar phase has been introduced in more detail in section 5.1. The same is valid about the Governance Commission (chapter seven). The following paragraphs will therefore give a brief overview of two bodies with mandates directly linked to peacebuilding: the Truth and Reconciliation Commission (TRC) and the Independent National Commission on Human Rights (INCHR).

The Truth and Reconciliation Commission, foreseen by the CPA as a platform that would "address issues of impunity as well as an opportunity for both the victims and perpetrators of human rights violations to share their experiences, in order to get a clear picture of the past to facilitate genuine healing and reconciliation" (CPA 2003, article XIII), was established two years later in 2005. Despite the original intention to include people of "credibility, high integrity and honour" (TRC Act 2005), the newly established entity soon discredited itself in the eyes of the public by infighting and unethical behaviour of its members. Due to those reasons, but also to financial constraints, the body stopped working before being reactivated in 2007—this time with more adequate support from the international community. The final report of the TRC was released in June 2009 and apart from a historical record of the civil war and a list of recommendations for addressing impunity (e.g., creation of an international and domestic criminal court, using the traditional institution of "palava hut" for reconciliation at the grassroots level), it included recommendations of particular individuals for prosecution, lustration, and ban of public office, with the incumbent President Ellen Johnson Sirleaf included in the latter category. There were a number of innovative aspects in the process (such as inclusion of diaspora, taking a gender perspective into account, and containing a record of economic crimes), and the final report was praised

---

104 The only limitation was imposed on people in high positions in the transitional government. See chapter five for more details.

internationally. But there were a number of shortcomings with regard to the work of the Commission and the report itself, which seriously undermined the credibility and impact of the document.[105]

The Independent National Commission on Human Rights (INCHR) is a body that should build upon the work of the TRC and implement its recommendations. The INCHR has been tasked with the monitoring and promotion of human rights standards. The law establishing the Commission was passed in 2005, but it took another five years to really create the body and make it operational. In addition to the initial general lack of progress in its work in terms of the TRC report implementation, the Commission suffered from a controversial leadership. The first head of the INCHR was a man of dubious reputation, holding a high-level position in the Ministry of Justice in Charles Taylor's government. The composition of the Commission was, however, changed in 2015, after the mandate of the first leadership expired, and since early 2016, Rev. Colley, a respected civil society activist, took up the position of the acting Chairman.[106] The body under the new generation of appointees have become comparatively more active and visible.[107]

6.2 *Poverty Reduction Strategy*

After the election and inauguration of Ellen Johnson Sirleaf to the Executive Mansion in 2006, the preparations of another key document started—the Poverty Reduction Strategy (PRS), serving as a development roadmap for the years 2008–2011. Nominally, it is focused on poverty reduction and development, but *de facto*, the document frames the whole process of reconstruction after the war. It served as a primary reference for the organisation of donor assistance in the early postwar period.

Poverty Reduction Papers (PRPs) are a standard tool, used by the IMF and the World Bank for the countries that want to be supported by the

---

105 The methodology was criticised as non-transparent, a number of key testimonies were missing, and two of the 10 commissioners distanced themselves from the report upon its publication.

106 The "regular" chairman elected in early 2016 was retired by the government in August 2016 and a new one has not been chosen.

107 It has a functional website loaded with information, including the latest Annual Report.

international financial institutions.[108] The papers are to be prepared by the member states in an inclusive, participatory process and should outline the plans and policies to address poverty and support a broad-based macroeconomic growth. According to the World Bank, all relevant stakeholders, including the international development partners, local population, and civil society should be included in the drafting process. National ownership should be the key principle underlying the preparation of the documents (World Bank website).[109]

In Liberia, the initiative to create the PRS came from the UN—the UNDP in particular. Although the participatory consultation process is very much hailed in the document, the content was provided mainly by the Liberian political elites and other, domestic as well as international, experts (Roehner 2012, interview #8, university lecturer, 14 June 2012, Monrovia). The input from the grassroots level, which comes to mind as an attribute of any "participatory consultations", was in fact very limited. A draft version of the document was brought to the county and district level to add the input from the population and local authorities. Focused consultations with specific groups (e.g., women, youth) were also organized. The input from the county level then translated into the County Development Agendas, where the national priorities have been adapted to local context and specific needs. While it is true that the population got a chance to "have their voices heard and incorporated into the PRS" (PRS 2008: 45), the participation at the consultations was in fact limited by many factors, with logistical challenges at the first place.[110] On the other hand, it is fair to say that in the situation, where Liberia was at that

---

108 The IMF and WB introduced the PRS-approach in 1999, as a part of the Heavily Indebted Poor Countries (HIPC) initiative. It has been criticized as another tool imposing conditionality on the development funds. Currently, 68 countries are included in the scheme (IMF website).

109 Whether or not these principles are respected in practice is, however, a different thing. Some countries (e.g., Uganda or Rwanda, although in the Rwandan case the opinions are sometimes varied, cf. Renard and Molenaers 2003, Bugingo 2002) included the local level in the drafting process to address the population's needs. Others (e.g., Mozambique) just paid lip service and prepared the PRPs without any meaningful local participation (Bugingo 2002). There is also a varying degree of linking the parallel, already established strategies and development policies planned by the national government to the PRS papers (Driscoll and Evans 2005).

110 The extent and real impact of popular participation in developing poverty reduction strategies has been raised as an issue both by practitioners and academics (Green 2006, Mukendi 2010, OECD et. al 2006).

given time, it was unlikely that more extensive input from the population would identify markedly different priorities than the government and other experts brought up. There were not many alternatives to the "national consensus around the country's development strategy" (PRS 2008: 45). The country was in a state of complete disarray and everything one could think of had to be fixed. The PRS was finished in 2008 and outlined the development plan for Liberia for the next three years.[111]

After giving some background information on the civil war, including a solid analysis of the structural and other drivers behind it, and a general introduction, the document is organised into four pillars: (1) Peace and security; (2) Economic revitalisation; (3) Governance and rule of law; and (4) Infrastructure and basic services. The annexes list five additional "cross-cutting issues", featured in all the pillars: gender equity, peacebuilding, environmental issues, HIV/AIDS, and children and youth. Specific objectives for each pillar are included as well.

With regard to peacebuilding, the concept is defined neither as a specific knowledge, nor as a foreign concept imposed on Liberia from the outside. It is rather presented as a way of doing things, not defined by *what* is being done, but *how*, so that poverty reduction and development are "weighed against the peacebuilding objectives of whether such efforts aggravate conflict situations or help to strengthen the foundations for peace and a respect for human rights" (PRS 2008: 170). Even the process of creation of the PRS itself is presented as "an exercise in peacebuilding", with its inclusive consultative process, transparency, and accountability in decision-making that "inspires confidence in the government and in peaceful coexistence" (PRS 2008: 170). Peacebuilding "embodies a vision of a society that is peaceful, respects and protects the rights of citizens and ensures that disputes and tensions which are normal to any society are handled in a way that prevents their escalation into organized violence" (PRS 2008: 170). Six areas are identified as still problematic with regard to stability and maintaining peace: land conflicts, youth, political polarisation, national resources management, weak system of justice, and the relationship between the state and its citizens.

The adherence to MDGs spirit is also stated in the document, however, the PRS openly admits that reaching the Millennium Development Goals is unrealistic in the case of Liberia, due to the country's difficult starting position, with almost two-thirds of its population living under the poverty

---

111 It was preceded by an Interim PRS and a 150-days Action Plan.

line. It lists, however, several sub-targets, where it is able to reach the goals.[112]

There were periodic reviews of the document assessing the progress made by the International Monetary Fund. In 2011, the final year covered by the PRS, the progress report stated that 53% of the planned outcomes were reached. Among the areas that performed well was the economy, especially the macroeconomic stability, which was praised in the report for its balanced budgets, reduction of external debt, low inflation rate, and expansion of the financial sector. On the other hand, in the field of infrastructure and basic services there was a lot left to be done, as well as in the governance sector (with the principal issue of decentralisation) and the rule of law, with access to justice as the main concern. Among the lessons learned, a prominent place belonged to the cross-sector coordination, as challenges in one sector could influence the outcomes in the others.[113] Secondly, the evaluation reports recommend the arrangements around funding to be improved. The fact that the funding scheme was not organized in advance led to a significant delay in implementation during the first year (IMF 2012).

One of the problematic aspects with regard to PRS was that many of the objectives listed in the document were preparatory measures, such as developing plans of action, establishing procedures, passing laws, and creating policies. Or, in the language of the international donor community, there was a weak link between the "outcomes", that is the objectives given in the PRS, and "deliverables" (IMF 2012). Another pitfall was the fact that the PRS was perceived as the government's prerogative and primary responsibility. From the ministries, the tasks derived from the PRS were regarded as an additional workload, not as a genuine priority, which led to a slower implementation. Missing capacities, especially (but not solely) at the county level, posed a problem to the implementation as well (IMF 2012).

Unsurprisingly, many things were left unfinished. Liberia was so devastated, that the first development plan was simply a plan of a complete reconstruction. Despite the massive international assistance, obviously not everything could be done in only three years. The objectives that were not

---

112 They refer to hunger, access to safe drinking water, HIV/AIDS, reduction of child mortality rate under five years of age, and reduction of gender disparities in primary and secondary education (PRS 2008: 33).

113 E.g., missing or unsatisfactory roads have an impact on agriculture, economy, or education.

accomplished within the PRS time were included in the next plan, the Agenda for Transformation.

6.3 Agenda for Transformation and Vision 2030

The Agenda for Transformation (AfT) took over where the PRS had ended, covering the period from 2012–2017. Its subtitle "Steps toward Liberia Rising" hints to another document, the long-term "Vision 2030", or "Liberia Rising". Similar to other countries on the African continent and worldwide (e.g., BRICs, Singapore, Israel), Liberia launched a national visioning exercise in 2011 and 2012. Based on an analysis of the past and present, four scenarios of Liberian future offer the possible paths for Liberia, depending on how the two main variables—politics and economy—might develop.

6.3.1 Vision 2030

In the "Thank God Oh" scenario[114], some economic changes and infrastructure development transpires, but no societal transformation takes place, which leads to slow and erratic growth and development. In the second one ("Ain't that bad"), a lack of economic transformation meets opening in the political sphere, resulting from the domestic and international pressure.[115] The most pessimistic option, "Everything chakla-oh"[116], combines an authoritarian state with a resource-based economy, which results in a situation where political, economic, and social tensions are managed by force (or a threat of it), a decline of central state authority, and emergence of local strongmen, challenging it. The most optimistic scenario, and therefore obviously the preferred one, where also most of the population's aspirations are reflected, features a shift from a resource-based to a knowledge-based economy, and a developmental state—strong, capable, and open to new political elites. An improved judiciary; reforms in the

---

114 "Oh" is an expression used in colloquial Liberian English adding emphasis to a statement.
115 The political transformation as a result of either domestic or international pressure does not seem very realistic, though, especially in combination with the absence of substantial economic changes.
116 "Chakla" is a colloquial synonym for mess.

governance sector, including the constitutional one; vibrant, independent civil society; and much more are envisioned. The document admits that this particular option, labelled "It's not for fun – A tall order", is not likely to be reached even by 2030, but hopes at least for significant changes in the outlined direction. The scenario is not all about sunshine, however. Societal tensions, likely to appear, are acknowledged, and so is the initial frustration of the youth and poor (representing the majority of the population), stemming from the fact that the changes will bring little tangible benefit in the short term.

In contrast to PRS, Vision 2030 is a genuine Liberian product. The Governance Commission, together with the Ministry of Planning and Economic Affairs, were the main institutions in charge of the exercise.[117] The fact that voices of donors and international partners were not sufficiently included was acknowledged in the document as one of the limitations of the drafting process. The second drawback, less amusing, is the fact that youth had not been consulted as extensively as wished for, due to a limited time frame. Contrary to omitting the international community, which can actually be perceived as an advantage, making the document more of a "domestic product", exclusion of the youth is a major drawback of the exercise, since youth (defined culturally and socially as population between 15–35 years) represents one-third of the Liberian population (LISGIS website, data from 2012).[118] All in all, there were 18 months of consultations at the regional and district levels, complemented by focus group discussions and input from the diaspora. In the document, the drafting process is praised as participatory and facilitating dialogue.

6.3.2 Agenda for Transformation

The Agenda for Transformation, then, represents initial steps to achieve the long-term vision outlined above. Subtitled "Steps toward Liberia Rising 2030", the AfT epitomises Liberia's medium-term economic growth and development strategy. Besides the Vision 2030, the document refers also to the "New Deal for Engagement in Fragile States", a document produced by the G7+ group[119] in 2011 at the Fourth High-Level Forum

---

117 Together with the Ministry of Internal Affairs and Ministry of Finance.

118 Cf. https://populationpyramid.net/liberia/2016/.

119 The G7+ Group is a group of fragile and conflict-affected states, currently consisting of 20 countries. The group was established in 2010 as a platform for

on Aid Effectiveness in Busan.[120] The Agenda for Transformation focuses on similar issues as the PRS. The document covers five years instead of three in the case of PRS. However, and more importantly, compared to the PRS, the AfT conveys a very different message. It does not refer to the conflict, as the PRS did, nor much to the past in general. Rather, it turns to the future. Instead of poverty, it speaks about economic growth and development: the recovery and reconstruction time is over. Now it is time for inclusive, endogenous growth and wealth creation. The tone of the document is so optimistic that it almost gives an impression that all the war damages have already been repaired and the country, renewed and ready to move on, is just waiting for opportunities to come:

> "Images from the Liberia of today—crops growing in replanted fields; traders doing business in the markets of Monrovia; cars driving through clean and repaired streets; children rushing to school in their uniforms—are all clear signs that recovery has taken hold." (AfT 2012: 1)

However, this illusion does not hold up to a closer look. Even in the document itself, the *allure* of introduction stands in a strong contrast with the list of objectives that follows. The AfT gives an overview of the achievements of the PRS together with the challenges that still persists, for example, the road network (a priority area for the period under consideration), the power supply, and unclear property rights. It outlines the aspiration of Liberia to become a middle-income country by 2030 (with the GNI per capita over 1000 USD), peaceful and economically growing, with inclusive politics, a diversified economy, stable institutions, and healthy, capable people.

It refers substantially to Liberia Rising 2030 and brings up the consultative nature of the process behind both documents, which should ensure a high level of political buy-in. The AfT focuses on those outcomes of PRS that were classified as of "marginal impact" and "unsatisfactory" (IMF 2012), with an explicit task to finish what the latter had started. It acknowledges the fact that many PRS outcomes were in fact only preparatory mea-

---

sharing experience and collective advocacy. For more info, see http://www.g7pl us.org/.

120 Liberia is a pilot country for the implementation of the New Deal. The document outlines priorities in the field of peacebuilding and state-building and calls for an improvement in aid effectiveness with regard to both areas. (http://w ww.newdeal4peace.org/)

sures, and draws lessons from implementation of the former. It promises to pay more attention to results, to prioritise and achieve quick wins, to pay more attention to cross-sector coordination and capacity development.

Among the priorities, infrastructure to unblock growth, such as roads and power supply, together with human development occupy the prominent position, followed by others, such as management of natural resources or support of small to medium enterprises. The objectives are organised in five pillars:

I. Peace, Security, and Rule of Law (featuring professionalisation of security forces, strengthening reconciliation and access to justice);

II. Infrastructure and Economic Transformation (focus on energy, roads, bridges, increase of MSME, improving results of small-holder agriculture, support for export, continuation of conservative macro-economic management, mineral development and management);

III. Human Development (with a special focus on youth, improved access to basic education, healthcare, water, and sanitation);

IV. Governance and Public Institutions (with an overarching goal of greater inclusiveness, broadened and deepened provision of services, and social safety nets for people at high risk);

V. Cross-cutting Issues (to be taken into consideration in all other pillars: environment, human rights, labour and employment, HIV/AIDS, and four specific demographic groups: women and girls, children, youth, and disabled).

Although organised in a slightly different way, the issues are actually very similar to the objectives of the PRS. An extensive chapter on monitoring and evaluation is also a part of the plan, including reflections on the challenges from the PRS period.[121] A matrix listing potential risks to implementation with suitable mitigation strategies is included at the end of the document.[122]

The Ebola outbreak in 2014 and 2015, however, dealt a heavy blow to the AfT plans, especially in combination with a difficult situation on global markets, with a substantial drop in commodity prices. In April 2015, the government of Liberia introduced a Stabilization and Recovery Plan (the so-called Ebola Recovery Plan) for the fiscal years 2015/16 and

---

121 These are, for example, the absence of an integrated strategy, unclear institutional roles, lack of clear division of tasks, and of human resources (AfT 2012).

122 The PRS also entails a similar (however less comprehensive) section on risks and constraints management.

2016/17, adjusting the planning to the new situation with the aim to bring the economy back on track.[123]

6.4 United Nations Development Framework

There is a set of documents created by the UN for countries, where the organisation is involved in the field of development cooperation, called the UN Development Assistance Frameworks (UNDAFs). They are complementary to the domestic development plans and define a framework of action for the UN, based on the priorities defined by the local government.

The first UNDAF for Liberia "articulates areas of UN action in response to national priorities" for the period between 2008 and 2012 (UNDAF 2008: 3) and "sets out the coherent pragmatic response of the United Nations to Liberia's national development strategy captured in the PRS" (UNDAF 2008: iii). Guided by the international human rights standards and by a conflict- and gender-sensitive approach, the document identifies five outcomes. Four of them (Peace and security, Equitable socio-economic development, Good governance and Rule of law, Education and health—with a focus on child and maternal mortality) reflect the national priorities listed in the PRS, the fifth one (HIV/AIDS) was chosen with regard to potential consequences of an epidemic that could break out unless adequate measures are taken (UNDAF 2008).

The priorities were validated in a process of regional consultations with county and district authorities in 2007. The document stresses that the UN would engage in the areas where it has a comparative advantage, which has, in practice, meant mainly capacity building and technical support during various processes (UNDAF 2008). There are also six cross-cutting issues listed, to be taken into account in all outcome areas: youth, gender, environment, conflict-sensitivity, human rights, and capacity development. The structure of the document clearly reflects its "primary reference", the PRS. It also mentions five Joint UN-Government programs, in the fields

---

123 The Ebola crisis turned out to be a catalyst bringing the problematic issues in the country to the surface again; apart from the insufficient health care provision, there was also fundamental distrust and suspicion of citizens, especially in remote areas, *vis-à-vis* the state apparatus, which manifested itself in the reactions of the population to the emergency measures. See e.g., report of Liberia Country configuration chairman Olof Skoog (UN Peacebuilding Commission 2015), or an article by Tokpa, Kaufmann et al. (2015).

of HIV/AIDS, youth, gender and gender-based violence, food security, and nutrition.[124]

The next issue of UNDAF for the period 2013–2017 reflects the priorities of the Agenda for Transformation. This time, UNDAF is officially the first part of the "One Program" of the UN in Liberia, complemented by the Costed Action Plan as its second part.[125] The four One Program Pillars include (1) Peace, Security, and Rule of Law; (2) Sustainable Economic Transformation; (3) Human Development; and (4) Inclusive Governance and Public Institutions. The adjectives "sustainable" and "inclusive" are added, otherwise the labels are the same as in the AfT. The cross-cutting issues are not listed in a separate chapter, but mainstreamed into the pillars already. The new UNDAF claims to be more strategic[126], using the UN's comparative advantage, and based on the principles of Delivering as One.

In both UNDAFs, there are extensive references to the PRS and AfT, with government priorities listed and matched with the respective UN contributions. The latter consist mainly of capacity building and programs of raising awareness, but there are also a number of technical tasks, or tasks requiring specific skills and knowledge.

Generally, there is a lot of emphasis on coherence. It is reiterated that every document is fully in line with the others, most importantly (but not solely) the "locally produced"[127] ones. This is valid not only with regard to the PRS and AfT, as the primary references for UNDAFs, but also for a number of other documents cited—Vision 2030, MDGs, different international treaties and documents produced by the UN Peacebuilding Commission. It gives an impression that the whole reconstruction has been a well-integrated project, where the responsible people know not

---

124 The second UNDAF mentions only three joint programs, on justice and security, land, and youth (UNDAF 2013).

125 The difference is rather a formal one. The idea underpinning the "One Programme" is to streamline the interventions of various UN agencies and programs into one strategic framework. The emphasis on "oneness" reflects the momentum within the UN, putting the coordinated, coherent nature of UN's engagement to the fore. It has also been manifest in the "Delivering as One" (DaO) initiative of the UN. The initiative was launched in 2006 at the UN-level (UNDG). In 2010, the government of Liberia requested to be a DaO "self-starter country". The objective of the concept is to "deliver a more coordinated, effective and efficient assistance" (UNDAF 2013: 24).

126 It does not, however, explain in what way exactly.

127 As mentioned above, it is arguable in how far is the process of setting national priorities led by the domestic (let alone local-level) actors and how much it is influenced by the external ones.

only their respective area of expertise, but are aware of other initiatives going on in the country and beyond, on the global level.

6.5 Peacebuilding plans

The last set of documents treated in this chapter are the Peacebuilding plans, produced in cooperation with and for the purposes of the UN Peacebuilding Commission. Liberia was placed on the agenda of the PBC in September 2010 and had already received the first tranche of financial support from the PBF in 2008. Based on the visit of the PBC Country Configuration[128] in August 2010, three key priority areas (security, rule of law, and reconciliation) were identified in the field of peacebuilding. The first Peacebuilding Priority Plan (PPP) was developed in 2011.

The PPP was created with the ambition to provide a broader vision for peacebuilding that "extends beyond the support requested of the PBF and encompasses vital programmatic elements that can sustain the broader peace upon which the GoL's viability depends" (PPP: 5). Based on the latter document, the Liberia Peacebuilding Programme (LPP) was developed in the first half of 2011 under the lead of the Liberian government, as a "basis for intervention by the PBF in Liberia" (PPP 2011: 5). It includes specific, achievable objectives for the three years between 2011 and 2013. In the final draft of the LPP, the input from the government, civil society, international partners, and the PBC Liberia Country Configuration has been included. The document represents "the overall medium term peacebuilding programme of the Government of Liberia, of which support from the PBF will be an important element" (LPP 2011: 5-6).

There are two main sections in the document: the first and the key one is the Justice and Security component, embedded in the joint Justice and Security Programme of the government and the UN. The second, admittedly more modest component, focuses on national reconciliation, with the note that more emphasis on the issue is envisaged for the near future, once the results of the national visioning process are available. In the security and rule of law segment, the crucial outcome is an "enhanced access to justice and security at regional and county level in preparation for

---

128 The members of the Country Configuration are, besides the members of the Organizational Committee of PBC, also the representatives of key (sub-) regional and international organizations, as well as major finance- and troop-contributing countries (http://www.un.org/en/peacebuilding/countryconfig.shtml).

UNMIL transition" (LPP 2011: 6). This should transpire mainly through the operationalisation of the regional security hubs, a project that should improve the population's access to justice and security.[129] Reconciliation projects' ideas revolve around addressing issues of land disputes and disaffected youth mainly by the means of building platforms for dialogue and capacities for dispute resolution at the local level.

The second Peacebuilding Priority Plan for 2013–2016 (PPP II) focuses more extensively on the issue of reconciliation. There is, of course, the usual emphasis and extensive referencing to other framework documents, with which the PPP II is aligned—the AfT, Vision 2030, the National Reconciliation Roadmap, the One Programme for Liberia 2013–2017, and the New Deal for Engagement in Fragile States. A lot of emphasis is also put on synergies and building upon existing projects and work that has already been done.

The PPP II admits that reconciliation projects are difficult to be financed, since not many donors are willing to engage for "initiatives that are complex by nature and generally take more time than other programs to show clear results" (PPP 2013: 7) and proposes the establishment of a funding mechanism for reconciliation purposes, similar to the Justice and Security Trust Fund. The plan outlines a number of project ideas to foster reconciliation. For most of them, the objectives are "to resolve and transform local conflicts through mediation, early warning and response systems, as well as through community dialogue initiatives" (PPP 2013: 12). The document suggests to build on the existing system of palava huts implemented by the Independent National Human Rights Commission, peace huts[130], County Peace Committees (CPCs), and a functional system

---

129 The hubs should provide an integrated approach to security and justice and, at the same time, decentralize, or rather deconcentrate the justice and security provision in the country. They are places where Liberians will be able to access the integrated services of police and correction forces. The staff of the hubs include police officers, human rights monitors, public defenders, probation officers, and prosecutors, among others. There are plans to have five hubs in total. The first one was opened in April 2013 in Gbarnga, two more are to be opened in the remote locations of Harper and Zwedru. Initially, there was not enough awareness raising around the project, which resulted in a lack of knowledge and distrust of people. There is also the question of sustainability of the whole concept in the long-term. (Maina and Sherif 2013, PBC 2010, interview #22, informal conversation #24, civil society representatives, Monrovia 2012)

130 A concept similar to palava huts, providing an adequate space for women, which is quite limited in the former.

of early warning and early response. It is also proposed that these initiatives should be linked with the regional security hubs. Other areas of focus include the National Youth Service Programme, land issues (with a focus on urban land), or support to law reform, underlying, for example, the constitutional reform, decentralization, or many of the land disputes.

6.6 *The Reconciliation Roadmap*

The Reconciliation Roadmap, or "A Strategic Roadmap for National Healing, Peacebuilding, and Reconciliation" is the last document analysed in this chapter. Covering the period from 2012 to 2030, it aims to fill a gap in the field of peacebuilding and reconciliation, urgently felt mainly by the Liberian civil society in the context of other reforms and reconstruction efforts (Interview #24, KAICT international staff member, 14 June 2012; #56, university lecturer, 27 November 2012; #22, employees of the PBO, 1 May 2012, Monrovia). The Roadmap aims to address the lack of coordination and coherent strategy in these fields. Reconciliation is defined broadly, as "a multidimensional process of overcoming social, political, and religious cleavages and mending and transforming relationships; healing the physical and psychological wounds from the civil war, and confronting and addressing historical and structural wrongs, particularly conflict root causes including ethno-politics, religious, social, and regional exclusion, corruption and impunity as well as human rights violations." (Reconciliation Roadmap 2012: 12). Although it acknowledges the progress that has been made in the fields of security and rule of law, the Roadmap also tacitly criticises the fact that reconciliation has been so far neglected in the process of postwar reconstruction:

> "Peacebuilding and reconciliation begins with confronting and ensuring redress for wrongs and violations committed at a historical juncture of a society. Bypassing this first step in pursuit of economic growth and development (inclusive or not), urgent and important as they are, often establishes post-war societies on feeble grounds." (Reconciliation Roadmap 2012: 15)

The Roadmap is shaped more by ideas promoted by the conflict resolution school, than by the mainstream peacebuilding discourse, as a consequence of the involvement of the PBO in the drafting process (see section 5.5). As such, it can be perceived as an alternative to the neo-liberal approach, which it also criticises in the quote above. The topic of reconciliation has been largely neglected in other framework documents. The vision of peaceful, "healthy" society was mentioned many times, but all the documents before the Roadmap focused on the "mainstream" development, though implemented in a conflict-sensitive manner and with "peacebuilding in mind", as suggested by the PRS. The Roadmap reminds that "capable and resilient security and justice and rule of law sectors, social and economic infrastructures, and economic growth" are "enablers for sustainable peacebuilding and reconciliation; they are not in themselves peacebuilding and reconciliation. Peacebuilding and reconciliation begins with confronting and ensuring redress for wrongs and violations committed at a historical juncture of a society." (Reconciliation Roadmap 2012: 15)

It took considerable time to "push" the creation of the document through, and even now, the implementation is very much behind schedule, as other, more pressing issues keep emerging in the post-Ebola time —for example, the UNMIL transition, or the presidential election 2017.

The LPP has identified youth empowerment, land disputes, and social cohesion as priorities in the field of reconciliation. There was some progress with regard to the first two issues (establishment of the Youth Programme and a functioning Land Commission); however, the social cohesion component has not been emphasised. One reason behind it was "the presence of multiple actors and programmes on reconciliation across Liberia, leading to inconsistent efforts, increased duplication, waste, and unnecessary competition" (Reconciliation Roadmap 2012: 7). Therefore, the government, together with the PBC Country Specific Configuration for Liberia, decided to develop the Roadmap as a coherent strategic framework, with clearly specified roles and responsibilities.

The implementation of the Roadmap is outlined along six three-year cycles, with the first two of them (unsurprisingly) aligned with the AfT and Vision 2030. All the activities should be people-centred and bottom-up and have the objective to (1) transform individual, community, and societal mindsets; (2) rebuild and strengthen inter-group relationships; and (3) replace polarising institutions with more inclusive ones as an assurance for "never again" (Reconciliation Roadmap 2012: 16). This should be done by confronting the legacies of the past, by mitigating present tensions (especially in land and other community conflicts), and by forging a common, peaceful, reconciled future (ibid.). The specific measures envisaged in the roadmap range from truth-telling and documentation, facilitation of dialogue, community-based conflict resolution, and memorialisation, to land dispute management system and transformative education, including peace curricula.

Table 1: Overview of the framework documents

Document	Time frame covered	Specification	Content	Conveners
CPA from Accra	2003–nn (early post-war period)	Peace agreement	- processes of early post-war period: DDRR, SSR - institutions: GRC, TRC, IHCHR, NTGL, NTLA	GoL, LURD, MODEL, political parties Witnesses: UN, AU, ECOWAS, MARWOP-NET
Poverty Reduction Strategy	1. 4. 2008–30. 6. 2011	Development plan/comprehensive plan of reconstruction	Four Pillars: I. Peace and Security II. Economic Revitalization III. Governance and Rule of Law IV. Infrastructure and Basic Services Cross-cutting issues: Gender Equity, Peacebuilding, Environmental Issues, HIV/AIDS, Children and Youth	IMF/WB, GoL, UN (UNDP)
Agenda for Transformation	2012–2017	first steps to Vision 2030, continuation of PRS	Five Pillars: I. Peace, Security and Rule of Law II. Infrastructure and economic transformation III. Human Development IV. Governance and Public Institutions V. Cross-cutting issues (environment, human rights, labour and employment, HIV/AIDS, 4 demographic groups: women, children, youth, disabled)	GoL, MPEA, supported by WB

Vision 2030	2012–2030	long-term vision of development	- analysis of past and present - four scenarios of country's future: 1. Thank God-Oh 2. It's not for fun – A Tall Order 3. Ain't That Bad 4. Everything Chalk-la Oh	GC, MPEA, MoF, MIA
Peacebuilding Priority Plan	created in 2011	broadly conceived peace-building plan		
Liberia Peacebuilding Programme (LPP)	2011–2013	middle-term peacebuilding plan with specific objectives; based on PPP	1. Justice and Security (main focus) 2. National Reconciliation (briefly)	PBC, GoL
Peacebuilding Priority Plan II	2013–2016	continuation of the LPP	1. Reconciliation 2. Management of natural resources (incl. land) 3. Sustainable livelihoods 4. Constitutional and legal reform 5. Support to Liberia PBO	PBSO/PBF
Reconciliation Roadmap	2012–2030 (six three-year cycles)	plan for national reconciliation	people-centered, bottom-up activities to: 1. transform mindsets 2. rebuild relationships 3. build inclusive institutions	GoL, Liberia Country Configuration

Figure 2: Time frame covered by the documents

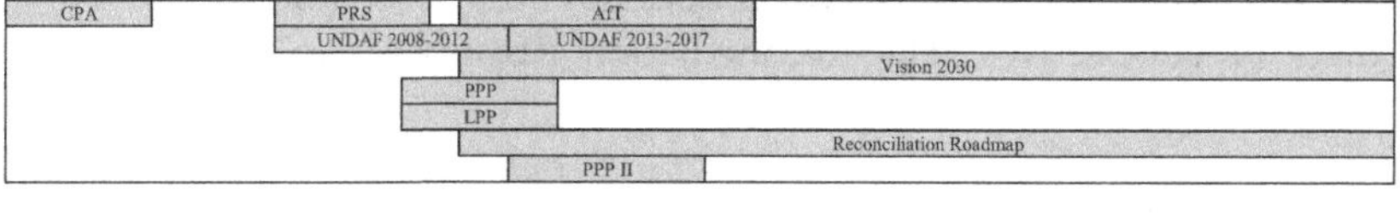

Table 2: Participation in drafting process

	Citizens	Civil Society	GoL	International Actors, Donors	Specific groups	Diaspora
CPA	-	x	x	x (witnesses)	-	-
PRS	x	x	x	x	x	-
AfT	x	x	x	x	-*	-*
Vision 2030	x	x	x	limited	youth (insufficient)	x
PPP	-	x	x	x	-	-
LPP	-	x	x	x	-	-
PPP II	-*	x*	x*	x*	-*	-*
RR	x	x	x	N/A	N/A	N/A

x active participation (defined as a direct one, i.e., in the case of CPA, citizens or women as a specific group are marked with "-", as they were not consulted directly; however, they were represented by civil society)
- no direct participation
* not specified in the document; assumption based on the background information

6.7 General analysis

All the previously presented documents share several common features. First and foremost, they extensively refer to each other, creating a bullet-proof system of aligned, coherent strategic plans, being aware of and building on each other, not only at the country level, but also beyond (with references to MDGs, New Deal, Paris declaration on aid effectivity, etc.).[131] Although it might be superfluous to say, it is worth noting that the formal coherence does not automatically reflect in the implementation process and the reality, for various reasons, can be far from the "ideal", anchored in a plan. It is unlikely that the results were better if underpinned by a chaotic system of incoherent, fragmented, and isolated framework plans. However, the result of this air-tight coherence is a kind of a "hegemonic discourse" on peacebuilding, which does not offer space for any alternative voices or perspectives. The Reconciliation Roadmap can be considered

---

131 Interestingly, there is no reference to initiatives and documents from the regional level produced, e.g., by the ECOWAS or the AU.

such an alternative, finally adopted to the mainstream discourse thanks to the support of the Peacebuilding Commission.

Secondly, the documents (the UN ones especially stand out in this regard) meticulously reiterate the emphasis on national ownership and exclusive responsibility of the Liberian government for setting the priorities and implementation oversight. Where the external partners come into play, their exclusively supportive role is emphasised and a sense of partnership as a leading principle of the mutual cooperation is brought to the fore. Unsurprisingly, the tacit but determining role of international financial institutions to the whole framework is not mentioned at all.

Besides avoiding too much initiative-taking, the UN language also stresses the "oneness" of engagement on the side of the UN family, stressing coordination and cooperation as cornerstones of UN's work. Although this is certainly true at the level of everyday interaction (e.g., in logistics or communication), my informants often admitted, that there is a slight sense of competition with regard to the results of the work of particular UN agencies. Not in a manner of open rivalry, let alone conflict. It is rather manifested in an ambition to "put up a flag" over projects and to receive adequate credit for the work done by a particular agency (informal conversation #29, UN official, 25 May 2012, Monrovia).

"Liberian" documents (i.e., those produced by the domestic institutions) always give background information on the process of their creation, emphasising its participatory nature and consultation of relevant stakeholders. Here, it is important to bear in mind that the factual "inclusiveness" may often consist merely of the opportunity to express an opinion to the presented document. How many people actually seize this opportunity is yet another issue. Moreover, the fact that people were consulted does not automatically imply that their input was taken into consideration and included in the document. Another factor worth remembering is that the influence of external actors (e.g., in terms of setting the agenda or control, even indirect or unintentional) over the drafting process is hard to assess.

Another striking aspect is the absence of human, individual perspective in the plans. The focus is on reforming institutions, developing mechanisms, and delivering services; however, the citizens, as the final beneficiaries of the reforms, are hardly mentioned. In this respect, the fact that despite all the formal progress in the implementation of the framework plans, the living conditions of Liberians, especially in rural areas, have not shown a substantial improvement, leaving the "peace dividend" card unmaterialised for the majority of the population, does not come as a major surprise.

With regard to the content, the early documents (PRS and UNDAF 2008) are very broad in scope and have no real priorities; they were simply comprehensive, all-encompassing plans of reconstruction. Not surprisingly, after the years of the war the country was destroyed in every conceivable aspect and virtually everything had to be rebuilt from scratch. In the later documents, some priorities did crystallise. Some of them were carved out by completed tasks, many others dictated by external circumstances, be it the planned UNMIL transition, or more unpredictable major forces, such as the outbreak of Ebola or regional instability.

Apart from this, logical sequencing of the peacebuilding exercise also shaped the changing areas of focus, where the attention and financial resources were being directed. The crucial processes and reforms (e.g., DDRR, security system reform, return of refugees and IDPs) from the early period, cornerstones of the following ones, have later been replaced by other, "softer" issues, such as governance and rule of law, or broadly conceived reconciliation and peacebuilding.[132] At the same time, one can trace some trends in the form, or in the general approach to planning over time, trickling down from the global level. In the Liberian case, the early "wave" of Poverty Reduction imperative, dictated by the IMF and WB, was replaced by a long-term-vision-approach, in fashion in many other countries in Africa and beyond.

The documents do not feature much of a critique, not even in the evaluation reports, and when they do critique, they do so in very diplomatic terms. Some of the challenges are, however, admitted even in these official pieces of writing. Inconsistent financial support is one especially hard obstacle to overcome. The PBC Peacebuilding Priority Plan, for example, mentions the problem of financial support, and how difficult it is to bridge the period of time between the early humanitarian phase and the later development one, or the fact that donors are not generally willing to support the initial, "hardware" phase of project creation. Instead, they prefer to join the game later and contribute with technical expertise, know-how, or personnel.[133]

---

132 Using the term "softer", however, does not imply that they are less important, it only catches the aspect of being less "exact" in definition, more difficult to grasp and operationalize. They represent context-specific topics that do not fit the mainstream, ready-made categories and approaches.

133 This was, for example, the case of setting up the first Land Coordination Center in Zorzor, where no one wanted to finance the construction of the facility. After the initial support from the PBF, however, several donor agencies expressed the willingness to provide personnel, equipment to the office, etc. (PPP 2013).

Often, the lack of clear division of tasks and inter-agency coordination is mentioned as a factor hindering progress, together with a lack of qualified human resources. These issues have been analysed in more detail in the preceding chapter, focusing on the factors characteristic to postwar Liberia, not only as attributes of a specific context, but also as powerful factors that significantly shape the general context and, consequently, the way peacebuilding is being done.

As mentioned in the beginning of the chapter, there is a lack of literature[134] assessing the framework documents of Liberian reconstruction, with the exception of CPA, which, after all, falls into a slightly different category. Likewise, there are not many papers, reports, or secondary literature assessing the PRS, in contrast to other countries on the African continent. One source of information in this respect are the IMF Annual Progress Reports. The authorship of these documents is not clear[135]; however, they provide a solid base with regard to the accomplishments and challenges of the PRS implementation. The reports are based on data collected in the four pillars of PRS and a number of field visits. They follow the structure of the PRS and include a realistic account of both progress and challenges of the implementation process. Other sources of information (e.g., various interviews) also support the accuracy of the reports, especially with regard to persisting challenges.

Mats Utas (2008) offers a valuable, highly critical analysis of the PRS. From an anthropological perspective backed by a profound knowledge of the region, he convincingly argues that documents, such as the PRS, and the official, formal political processes are only one facet in the picture of the Liberian political reality. Liberian politics are organised on the base of complex networks with "Big Men" as nodal points. Utas argues that the external actors, by not taking these structures into consideration, ignore the basic principles of functioning of the Liberian state. In such a

---

134 A notable exception in this regard is Mats Utas (2008), see below.

135 Although the LRDC and MPEA are named as actors involved in the preparation and drafting of the report, it is unlikely that the IMF would leave the evaluation process entirely in Liberian hands. The use of plural "we" in the following quote suggests that the authors are not part of the MPEA personnel: "We would like to extend additional thanks to the MPEA PRS Annual Progress Report Team" (IMF 2011: 4). On the other hand, the final sentence "We can deliver and ensure success in the third and final year of the *Lift Liberia* agenda if we remain diligent in the implementation!" (Ibid.), or "The road to development still stretches far ahead of us" (IMF 2010: 5) sounds like a statement by the Liberian side.

situation, "blueprints, such as the PRS papers, cannot become more than blueprints" (Utas 2008: 2) and "unless Western official actors seriously involved with informal Big Men (often the same as the formal actors, but with a different motive) little change will come about" (Utas 2008: 7). His analysis reminds us, that the core of the political processes and decision-making in Liberia (but also in many other countries) lays outside the polished tables and conference rooms of the ministries and governmental agencies—a fact that is only sporadically mentioned by the mainstream literature on post-conflict reconstruction. Taking into consideration the inaccessibility of this realm for outsiders, Utas's argument relegates large parts of the research of the formal political structures to the position of a superficial analysis, missing what actually transpires. To be sure, this is a valid perspective. However, in spite of that, these formal structures or, in this particular aspect, documents, create a space where the informal interaction takes place and through which the actors have to navigate. In this respect, it does shape their behaviour and matters as a topic for analysis. Utas's perspective, in addition, leads us to another set of questions: Do they know? Do all the international experts, consultants, and other peace-building folks know about the importance and weight of the informal networks? It would be surprising if they did not. For everyone who has been in the country for some time, it sooner or later becomes clear that if the country is to function, there must be something more than the often insufficient structures visible at first sight. Apart from that, the bigmanship as a major principle of social and political organisation is not reserved to Liberia, but is quite common throughout Africa and beyond.

The second question that comes to mind is then: Why do they keep ignoring it? First of all, to start a dialog with the informal networks, as Utas suggests, one has to "enter the game" and become a part of a complex web of interdependent loyalties among different big (wo)men. This is not easy in terms of getting access and might be problematic in terms of professional ethics and codes of conduct. International personnel is quite exposed and taking into consideration that the networks often have parts involved in illegal activities (cf. Utas 2008), engaging with them may well be problematic. Moreover, no matter how much the networks represent the "local context", significantly emphasised in all the programmatic documents, their mode of functioning is clearly contradictory to the principles of transparency and good governance the international agencies try to promote—they are "too local" to be incorporated. As such, it is more likely that they will stay reserved for the practitioners from the middle track, rather than for the UN personnel and international partners, as the former are less in the spotlight and hence less constrained by danger of being blamed for engaging in "dirty" practices of politics, corruption, or nepotism.

Chapter 7 Governance: a stubborn step-child

"Liberia cannot be restored; it can only be reinvented."
Stephen Ellis: The Mask of Anarchy (2007: xxvi)

This chapter presents the first of the four empirical chapters, dealing with specific institutions, where the government, international actors, and civil society meet in the Liberian post-conflict peacebuilding context. All four chapters follow the same structure, starting by introducing the main concept and its link to the broader field of peacebuilding, as well as to the particular case of Liberia. Then, the institution in focus (in this chapter, it is the Governance Commission) and its work are introduced, followed by the analysis of factors that support and hinder the progress of the reforms. The roles of the selected actors are examined and in the last section, some case-specific conclusions are drawn.

Poor governance and disrespect for the rule of law have been frequently listed on top of the issues that contributed to the outbreak of the Liberian civil war (Ellis 2007, PRS 2008, Sawyer 2005, interviews #8, #22, #27, #52, Monrovia, April–June 2012). During the conflict, political institutions and structures governing the country were completely destroyed and had to be built up from scratch afterwards. Apart from this effort, falling under the discourse label of "state-building", there are a number of other projects with a broader objective of addressing the underlying causes, which had led to the conflict and eventually to the disintegration of the state structures.

Despite the fundamental importance of governance declared in the ruling discourse on peacebuilding (Doyle and Sambanis 2006, Jeong 2005, Newman, Paris et al. 2009) and in the documents framing Liberian reconstruction (CPA 2003, PRS 2008), in practice, governance reform seems to be treated like a step-child among other areas. Despite the herculean dimension of the task, governance reform in Liberia does not receive adequate attention, nor practical support from either the national, or the international level. Compared to other case studies in this work, governance is the one most closely connected to the fundaments of the political system, one shaped by the political culture in place and therefore difficult to be subjected to a deliberate change. Although presented as a purely "technical" reform by the international agencies (cf. e.g., Abrahamsen 2001, Chandler 2006, Doornbos 2001, Hesselbein 2008, Hewit de Alcántara 1998), it is highly political in nature and touches the core of the sovereignty of the postwar Liberian state.

7.1 Governance: Evolution of the term

Governance has been a buzzword in the development industry since the beginning of 1990s, in the context of profound changes of the international system, related to the end of the Cold War, democratization processes in Central and Eastern Europe, and, in African context, the fall of apartheid in South Africa in 1994.

Good governance represented a brand new approach, a tool that made *"internally* directed political conditionalities concerned with the structuring and operation of recipient countries' institutions" the main criteria for development aid (Doornbos 2001: 97). In contrast to previous approaches in the development branch, good governance provided the necessary cover, a "fig leaf" (Grindle 2010) that enabled donors and international financing institutions (IFIs) to engage in political work and domestic affairs of states, hitherto considered a *terra prohibita* (cf. Doornbos 2001, Hewit de Alcántara 1998).

Two general lines of thought about the concept have developed: the first one, linked to academia, has been more concerned with the relations between the power and authority, whereas the policy-related line has been focused rather on state, market, management, and accountability issues (Doornbos 2001). In practitioners' circles, governance has become a panacea for the problems Africa was dealing with, especially with regard to development, or rather a lack of development of the continent (Booth and Cammack 2013, cf. World Bank 1992). However, since 1992, when the World Bank (WB) defined good governance as a necessary precondition for development, there has been an increasing consensus acknowledging that good governance is not necessarily the best path to the development of a particular country, or, in other words, that *good* governance is not the same thing as governance for *development* (Booth and Cammack 2013: 9-10, emphasis added by the author, Hesselbein 2008).

Governance is broadly defined as a "conscious management of regime structures with a view to enhancing the legitimacy of the public realm" (Hydén 1992:7) or the "manner in which power is exercised in the management of a country's economic and social resources for development" (World Bank 1992). Apart from the obvious aspect of exercise of power, it includes elements of reciprocity, authority, accountability, and trust (Hydén 1992).[136] The WB further specifies the term as including three aspects: "(1) the form of political regime; (2) the process by which authority is exercised in the management of a country's economic and social resources for development; and (3) the capacity of governments to design, formulate and implement policies and discharge functions" (World Bank 1992).

Good governance, as defined by UN ESCAP (United Nations Economic and Social Commission for Asia and the Pacific), includes the following characteristics of a political system: "participatory, consensus oriented, accountable, transparent, responsive, effective and efficient, equitable and inclusive and follows the rule of law. It assures that corruption is minimised, the views of minorities are taken into account and that the voices of the most vulnerable in society are heard in decision-making. It is also responsive to the present and future needs of society" (UN ESCAP, n.d.). At the level of actors, good governance seeks to bring civil society and the private sector into play as partners of the government (Sawyer 2005).

With all these elements, good governance has been therefore perceived as an approach that can facilitate development, or, in post-conflict contexts, to contribute to peacebuilding by overarching the gap between the state and its citizens. This conviction has, however, several weak points. One of them is the underlying neo-liberal orientation of the approach. The structural adjustment programs of the 1980s and 90s promoted by the Bretton Woods Institutions aimed for a minimalist state and market-led solutions. The experience from elsewhere (be it the "tigers" of South-East Asia, or, historically, Europe and North America), however, shows that the successful economies, who can afford a minimalist state today, started in a very different setting. Political institutions were not their point of departure; on the contrary, the latter followed the development in the economic sphere. It is the "full-blown *capitalism*" that "creates the social structures and organisational capabilities that lead to democratic governance, not the

---

136 Other definitions of governance are more or less similar, having in common the elements of control, authority, and management of common affairs. The Commission on Global Governance (1995) defined governance as "the sum of the many ways individuals and institutions, public and private, manage their common affairs". For the UNDP, governance is "the exercise of economic, political and administrative authority to manage a country's affairs at all levels" (UNDP 1997). OECD defines it as "the use of political authority and exercise of control in a society in relation to the management of its resources for social and economic development" (OECD 1995).

other way around" (Booth and Cammack 2013: 1, emphasis added by the author, cf. Hesselbein 2008, Chang 2002). Secondly, with regard to the way of managing a nation's affairs, good governance programs promote one specific form of governance, rooted in the Euro-American political tradition. Although omnipresent as a colonial import to Africa, it has not taken its roots on the continent, nor has been growing organically; it is still being perceived as a foreign concept that, in addition, has never really worked (cf. Bach and Gazibo 2012, Bayart 2009, Chabal 2009, Chabal and Daloz 1999, Mamdani 1996, Mbembe 2001, Médard 2002). To be sure, taking into consideration other forms and systems of political organisation, there is no real alternative to democracy in today's political landscape around the globe. On the other hand, the perverted universalism of the term, using criteria derived from the established democracies of the global North as a benchmark and an ultimate goal, irrespective of the cultural context or the level of development of target countries, stays problematic (cf. Doornbos 2001, Hesselbein 2008). The same applies to the implicit normative and evaluative connotation of the concept, implying judgment about how "good" the governance in a particular country actually is (Doornbos 2001).

In this regard, Grindle's contributions especially (2004, 2007, 2010) pointed to the fact that the concept is so vaguely defined and potentially all-encompassing, that it does not provide any guidance for implementation. In order to overcome the normative quest for an ideal type and to make the goals realistic, she proposes the concept of "good *enough* governance", that refers to "minimal conditions of governance necessary to allow political and economic development to occur, contrasting with the long and still growing list of normative requirements included in the traditional good governance agenda" (Grindle 2004). The "good enough" approach should take into consideration the particular context of target countries and be pragmatic with regard to the priorities and general feasibility of the reforms (Grindle 2004, 2010).

The fact that governance programs should take into account and build upon a specific context has been widely acknowledged. However, the acceptance remains largely rhetorical, as it relates in the best case to the institutional structures of a particular country. The *practices* rooted in local political realities seem to fall out of the category of an "accepted divergence", mainly because they represent exactly the elements of political systems governance reforms aim to eradicate (corruption, neo-patrimonial, or nepotist practices come to mind as first-hand examples).

Another crucial aspect is the legitimacy of the reforms. In the eyes of citizens, the legitimacy of the state is closely connected to its per-formance—provision of services and creating employment (Abrahamsen 2001, Hesselbein 2008, informal conversations #3, #5, #14, #28, June 2011, April–June 2012, Monrovia), rather than from the way offices and pos-itions are being distributed. Such a discrepancy between citizens' demand and the supply portfolio of donor programs not only undermines the sense of ownership of the reforms and sustainability of the measures (Dolzer 2007), it creates a paradoxical situation, where donors hold the states accountable and replace citizens in the position of primary constituents of the state (Abrahamsen 2001). Moreover, the reforms oriented towards rolling the state back further undermine the potential of the latter to gain legitimacy by fulfilling citizen's expectations about what a state should provide.

Despite the rhetorical emphasis on the importance of local context and political realities, good governance reforms are, in practice, often reduced to a mere "mimicking [of] the institutional patterns attained in some of the most economically advanced countries in their very recent history" (Booth and Cammack 2013: 11). Sawyer (2005) and others (Hesselbein 2008, Peterson 2010) also point to the fact that implementation of good governance programs can lead to instability, as it can exacerbate existing political struggles and tensions. Instead of achieving good governance, Sawyer calls rather for attaining *self-governance* (2005: 102, emphasis added by author) as a desirable goal.

Governance reforms and programs promoting rule of law have become a standard part of post-conflict packages (Brinkerhoff 2007, Debiel and Terlinden 2005, Doyle and Sambanis 2006, Jeong 2005, Newman, Paris et al. 2009, UN 2007), for they are supposed to contribute to creating sustain-able peace. This assumption is partly based on the premise of democratic peace, a thesis that democratic states tend to be more peaceful, as they offer ways to address tensions and grievances in a non-violent way and respond to the needs of citizens (cf. Newman, Paris and Richmond 2009). Additionally, it is also assumed that effective governance can eliminate underdevelopment and poverty as potential conflict-drivers and factors that can catalyse a relapse into conflict (e.g., Collier 2003). However, some critical voices (e.g., Kartas 2007) claim that post-conflict peacebuilding is so much caught up in the good governance discourse, that it tends to resolve conflict by promoting Western democratic institutions instead of dealing with the often complex underlying issues. Sawyer also notes that, implemented in a hasty manner in societies, whose social fabric was torn by violent conflict, such reforms can do more harm than good, restoring the state that often has been part of the problem, or "pursuing great ideals without framing them in appropriate institutional arrangements" (Sawyer 2005:139). This tendency is a consequence of an unfortunate trend to focus mainly on the top-level "track" in Lederach's (1997) sense and to implement the reforms in a top-down manner, leaving the crucial middle and grassroots level out.

The mainstream neo-liberal premise of a minimalist state has been, however, quietly challenged, for example, from the non-Bretton-Woods institutions. The African Union's Post-Conflict Reconstruction and Development (PCRD) framework, for instance, admits that "successful PCRD is dependent on good political governance", but at the same time argues that the "African" peacebuilding approach (as expressed in the documents on PCRD) emphasises the role of the state, contrary to the view prevalent in the international institutions, the WB or IMF, promoting the liberal approach and the idea of minimalist state (Landsberg: 2012).

Practically, governance reforms in post-conflict contexts, as well as beyond, include projects focused on rule of law, decentralisation, constitutional reforms, anti-corruption strategies, institutional reforms (or institution-building), programs focusing on increasing popular participation, accountability, and legitimacy of the state.

7.2 Political development and governance reform efforts in Liberia

In Liberia, as chapter four demonstrates in more detail, a long period of poor governance was at the core of the issues that eventually led to the civil war. Over 150 years of autocratic rule left the citizens and political elites with a legacy that is difficult to change. There is a tendency of a strong concentration of power in the hands of the head of state that started with President Tubman[137], who laid down the base of presidency as a personal cult, governing the country in a very classical patrimonial way. After the Second World War, there was a further increase in presidential power thanks to a direct control over financial means coming from the concessions for natural resource extraction, which reduced presidents' dependence on the taxes collected at the county level. During the Tubman administration, the centralisation of the country also rose substantially.

---

137 In office from 1944 to 1971.

William Tolbert, who replaced Tubman after 1971, continued in the way paved by his predecessor, although the political system he inherited was already shaking with instability. The marginalisation of the indigenous population and the exclusive control of power by a small, Americo-Liberian elite in a one-party system, combined with an expansion of education opportunities for the masses inevitably led to rising demands for greater political participation, articulated through the popular democratisation movements. The pace of reforms (e.g., the decentralisation policy or the "green light" for multi-party elections at the end of the 1970s) did not keep up with rising pressure from below. The April coup in 1980, however, put an end to democratisation tendencies and threw the country on a completely different path—the one of a violent dictatorship. Despite its oppressive character and open brutality, the Doe regime also engaged in governance reform work; a year after the coup, Doe appointed a 25-member body, the National Constitution Commission (commonly referred to as "Con-Com"), engaged in drafting a new constitution for Liberia.[138] In 1985, responding to the domestic and international pressure, demanding a return to the constitutional rule, Doe organized an election that confirmed him in his presidential position.[139]

In the following two decades filled with violence, governance reform was not the order of the day. A genuine program of reforms in this field started only after 2003 and was partly envisaged already in the Comprehensive Peace Agreement from Accra (CPA 2003: Article XVI). The document foresaw the creation of the Governance Reform Commission (GRC), a body tasked with promoting the principles of good governance, ensuring transparency and accountability, and designing plans for the reform of public sector management and decentralisation. The Commission started to operate in early 2005 and got a proper statutory standing in 2007, by the Act of the National Legislature. This transformed the body into

---

138 The results of the work of the Commission were, however, implemented in a very limited way. For more details, see Sawyer 2005: 102-111.

139 Despite the fact that the election was obviously rigged, international observers concluded that the result of 51% for a presidential candidate is, in comparison to other African countries, where leaders routinely claimed to receive over 90% votes, actually quite free and fair (cf. Sawyer 2005). In 1997, a similar strategy was used, and the election provided legitimacy to Charles Taylor, another strongman, who seized power by violent means.

the Governance Commission (GC), chaired by a politician, academic and seasoned civil society activist, Dr. Amos Sawyer.[140]

A broader program of governance and rule of law reform was also included in the Poverty Reduction Strategy (2008). Here, the issue of governance forms one of the four key pillars of the document and is recognised as such for its crucial importance for the future of Liberia, addressing structural conditions that hinder the potential of the country, its development and prosperity. The goals in the field of governance include enhancing participation, building effective and efficient institutions (including the legal and judicial ones), fostering transparency and accountability, and promotion and protection of human rights (PRS 2008). These rather general goals are also partly operationalised in the document, for example: enhancing participation by the means of decentralisation, fostering national integrity and confidence in government by tackling corruption, driving efficiency and effectivity in public institutions through the reform of the public sector, and privatising service delivery in combination with capacity-building programs (PRS 2008).[141] The issue features also in the Agenda for Transformation, a successor document of the PRS, and has been included in both UNDAFs[142] as well. In terms of realisation, GEMAP, imposed on Liberia in 2005 as a reaction to the mismanagement of public funds, was the first instrument implemented in the field of good governance in the postwar period.[143]

7.3 Governance Commission

The mission of the GC, as defined in the Act establishing the Commission (2007), is to work towards "a holistic system of good governance that is inclusive, participatory and just, and which promotes national oneness, sound public sector management, efficient and fair allocation and use of

---

140 Before him, Ellen Johnson Sirleaf was chairing the GRC and gave up on this position to run for the presidency.

141 There are two major programs in capacity building, Senior Executive Service (SES) and Transfer of Knowledge through Expatriate Nationals (TOKTEN). There was also a successful effort to engage the Liberian diaspora to provide the missing capacities, especially by recruiting highly qualified professionals.

142 Documents outlining the framework of action for the UN, for more details see chapter six.

143 For more details about the program, see chapter four (section 4.3) or Gerdes (2013).

resources, and a culture of honesty and integrity" (Republic of Liberia 2007).

The Commission is located in Sinkor, a residential area of Monrovia, in a renovated building close to the seashore. There are about 30 professionals working for the Commission, with four commissioners and a chairman, each coordinating her segment of the agenda. There are five mandate areas: 1) political and legal reform; 2) national integrity; 3) civic engagement, national visioning, and identity; 4) public sector reform; and 5) monitoring, evaluation, and research (Governance Commission Website). The commissioners are appointed for four years by the president, with the advice and consent of the Senate, with a possibility of one reappointment. Moral integrity and professional competence of the candidates, as well as geographic and gender representation, are the major factors to be considered in the process of their nomination (Republic of Liberia 2007). The current commissioners are all respected figures with backgrounds in civil engagement, education, civil service, and journalism, among others.[144]

The Board of Commissioners meets monthly and its sessions are led by the chairman, or by the vice-chairman in the absence of the former. There are weekly meetings within the five program areas, chaired by the respective commissioners or, in most cases, by the program manager, where the everyday issues on the agenda of the GC are discussed and the agenda for the coming week is set on the base of the completed tasks from the week before. In addition to that, there is a Project Accountability Team (PAT), a kind of internal quality control mechanism that ensures that the activities in the program areas are in line with the overall goal and mandate of the Commission. It also makes recommendations to the commissioners and seeks funds for the specific programs (Personal correspondence with a GC employee, December 2014, February 2017). With regard to the decision-making process, decisions are taken by consensus; a vote is a rare incident, since "issues are dealt with through rigorous consultations before reaching to the commissioners" (Personal correspondence with a GC employee, December 2014).

---

144 On a methodological note, the field of governance was the most challenging one in terms of gaining access as a researcher to collect primary data. The "official" way to get in did not work and even after I succeeded in getting a contact to one of the commissioners, arranging an interview was possible only after being personally introduced by a trusted "broker". With regard to the meetings of the GC, they are not public and I was not able to get access to them for the purposes of observation. The data covering this area therefore had to be obtained through interviews.

Quarterly or twice a year, general staff meetings are held, where all the "program staff" of the Commission meets (employees ranging from the support staff to the commissioners) and once a year, an annual retreat of the GC is organized. In this forum, all personnel of the Commission, "from the lowest rank janitors to commissioners" (Personal correspondence with a GC employee, February 2017) discuss the work of the GC in general, the progress, challenges, and future prospects, and set agenda for the year to come.

Chairman Amos Sawyer had been involved in the process of political reforms since the 1970s and represents a credible figure for both Liberians and international partners (Interviews and informal conversations #22, #27, #43, #44, #57, April–June 2012, Monrovia). He has a clear vision of the Commission's task, featuring inclusiveness and consultation of stakeholders as an essential aspect of the reform process. By the means of holding meetings with stakeholders, explaining and taking time to build constituencies, he succeeds in creating a fundament for a credible and legitimate reform (Interviews with civil society representatives, #27, #33, #44, #56, April–June 2012, Monrovia, cf. A. Sawyer, interview for Innovations for Successful Societies 2009).

7.4 Projects of the Governance Commission

Given this latter aspect, and also due to the fact that the agenda of the Commission comprises mainly long-term projects, it is not surprising that most of the work of the Commission is at its beginning. One of the projects that is currently most advanced is decentralisation. After an extensive, two-year consultation, the decentralisation policy was finished in 2010 and was waiting to be passed into law. In August 2013, the bill (Local Government Bill) was passed to the president, who forwarded it to the legislation for enactment in July 2016. It was stuck in the legislature for more than two years. There were a number of contentious issues that delayed the passage, with the proposition of a direct election of local officials by the citizens of their localities being the prominent one.[145] The bill finally went through the Parliament in summer 2018, and President Weah signed the act into law in September 2018 (Executive Mansion 2018).

---

145 Other issues were related to rules regulating city status or administrative division at the district level (The New Republic Liberia 2018).

Another major project related to the field of governance is constitutional reform. In 2009, the Constitutional Reform Taskforce was established to deal with the issue. However, due to poor financial support and a lack of political will from the highest level, the Taskforce could not start a proper process of constitutional review. Its work resulted in the proposal of four amendments to the constitution, subjected to referendum in 2011. The proposed changes focused mainly on minor issues related to elections and the tenure of Supreme Court judges. All of them were rejected in the poll, with the exception of one (acknowledged as valid only after an appeal to the Supreme Court), changing the election system for other than presidential elections. The whole referendum process was marked by flaws and difficulties (Nyei 2014, Zanker 2011). A year later, in August 2012, Ellen Johnson Sirleaf created the Constitutional Review Committee (CRC). After a broad consultative process around the country starting in 2013, the CRC presented 25 proposals on amendments of the current constitution at the National Constitutional Conference in the spring 2015. The results were forwarded to the president in August 2015 and were discussed in the Parliament in 2016.[146]

Among the proposals, there are some related to decentralisation and self-governance (including the election of local officials), shortening of the tenure of elected officials (the president and members of the legislature) or a contested issue of citizenship.[147] There is also a proposal to declare Liberia a "Christian state" that has sparked a heated public debate. The practical consequences of such a declaration remain unclear; however, there are justified objections, warning that such a measure could exacerbate religious tensions and undermine the unity of the nation (Nyei 2016). Due to financial and organisational constraints, it was not possible to organise a referendum on the constitution changes before the presidential elections in 2017. President Weah proclaimed his support to the reform, but there have not been any specific steps taken (Nyei 2018).

Another project touching the national identity is the national symbols review process, launched in 2014. The discussion revolves mainly around the Liberian seal, displaying settlers' ship, arriving at the Liberian coast, and the motto "The love of liberty brought us here." The motto excludes

---

146 The constitutional amendments have to be approved by a two-thirds majority in both Houses and by two-thirds of registered voters in a referendum (Constitution 1984, Article 91).

147 Issue of dual citizenship and also the "Negro-clause", granting Liberian citizenship only to people of colour.

the whole indigenous population and takes only the Americo-Liberian settler elite as a reference group. Despite its indisputable symbolic value, many Liberians criticise it as inadequate in context, where the basic needs of the population (e.g., employment, health care, basic infrastructure) are still waiting to be met (Chea-Annan 2014).

In the national integrity mandate area, which is responsible for transparency and related issues, there have been two major projects. The first is the National Code of Conduct for All Public Officials, a document setting standards of professional behaviour in public positions. After more than seven years of legislative process, the bill was finally enacted into law in May 2014. The second project is the National Integrity Barometer, a tool measuring the credibility of political institutions as perceived by Liberian nationals. The Commission was also engaged in the drafting process of the Vision 2030, a highly consultative exercise aimed at articulating a shared vision of future for Liberia.[148]

All the projects of the Governance Commission are based on consultations with relevant stakeholders. Civil society organizations are the primary reference point in the early stages of the process. However, the GC is fully in charge and leads the outreach to the local level (Personal correspondence with a GC employee, February 2017, A. Sawyer, interview for Innovations for Successful Societies 2009).

The Commission has proposed the creation of several other bodies, such as the Law Reform Commission, Constitutional Review Commission, Liberia Anti-Corruption Commission, Land Commission, or Truth and Reconciliation Commission. However, the institution itself has no executive power. It is rather an advisory body, a think-tank, whose recommendations are dependent on other institutions, legislative and executive ones, to be implemented. This ultimately undermines its position and influence in the broader political system, especially taking into consideration that the Commission's major mission is to reform the existing practices of the system it operates in.

The emphasis on the legitimacy in the process of its work, the effort to consult and include views of as many stakeholders as possible, adds an important aspect of local legitimacy and credibility of the institution:

> "In this area of decentralization for example, we start off at the district level holding meetings. We send documents out, simple information about what decentralization is about. Then we follow it and have these

---

148 The document has been introduced in more detail in the previous chapter.

discussions—have discussions with local people. Then move from the district level to the county level. Then we flesh out some issues and go back and have further discussions. Similarly, these discussions take on, we move on parallel tracks, having a discussion with the Minister of Internal Affairs also with this, sometimes jointly. So it is a consultative, a constitutive and consultative process. So it takes some time." (A. Sawyer, interview for Innovations for Successful Societies 2009).

Such an approach, indeed, requires a substantial amount of time and therefore can be problematic for external donors, who are restricted by mostly short- to middle-term frameworks and deadlines:

"[...] there is always here a kind of a tension, a tension between the time it takes and the transaction cost of building these constituencies and deepening the legitimacy of these processes among the people on the one hand and the benchmarks and deadlines of both the government and the international actors, particularly the international actors" (A. Sawyer, interview for Innovations for Successful Societies 2009).

7.5 *Actor interaction in domestic political arena*

The Governance Commission is the principal actor in the field of governance reform. As already mentioned above, its relatively weak position in the political system to a large extent shapes its actual "weight". Firstly, the GC has neither executive nor implementation power. This makes its position precarious *vis-à-vis* other institutions, ministries, and governmental bodies, where the Commission demands reforms but has no leverage for their realisation. Touching the existing practices in politics is often perceived as "stepping on people's toes" (Interview #57, GC Commissioner, 21 November 2012, Monrovia). The reform initiatives are felt as attempts to interfere in an exclusive zone of influence of the ministers and leaders of other institutions: "who are these people in the Governance Commission to come and tell me how to reform my ministry"[149] (A. Sawyer, interview for Innovations for Successful Societies 2009). The result is an unsurprising

---

149 The situation of a "turf struggle" (A. Sawyer, interview for Innovations for Successful Societies 2009) was bypassed by the creation of a reform framework, where the ministries followed an agreed-upon framework but were actually able to claim the fruits of the reforms for themselves.

unpopularity of the GC with ministries and other governmental institutions, including the legislature, which further complicates implementation of the Commission's suggestions.[150]

The Sirleaf administration has officially presented governance reform as one of the priority areas of the cabinet. From the beginning, when the president launched a program of rationalisation and right-sizing of the bureaucracy, she openly declared her adherence to the principles of good governance.[151] With regard to corruption, Sirleaf has been widely criticised for a lack of a strict stance, as well as for engaging in nepotic practices (Allison 2012, Tran 2012). Despite the fact that she did not pursue an official, exemplary punishment of the exposed cases, she did discipline the culprits in a more discreet way—a common "disciplinary measure" being a relocation to a less exposed position (Gerdes 2013). Although the critical voices certainly have a point, it is important to bear in mind that, given the overall situation of the state bureaucracy and the available pool of human resources, a more consequent approach to punishments would soon make the choice of new appointees increasingly difficult.

The overall support for the governance reform from the executive branch, however, seems to be rather rhetorical, which is reflected, among others, in the budget of the GC. To keep the record fair, it is, nevertheless, necessary to take into account that the government has many other pressing issues requiring its attention. The interaction of the GC and the legislature takes place mainly on the "proxy" field of legislative process. The long spells in the approval of the policies reflect the low level of cordiality between the two entities; the Commission is "not very popular with the legislature" (Interview #56, GC Commissioner, 28 November 2012, Monrovia).

7.5.1 Role of external actors

Apart from setting the basic framework and direction of the reform, in the sense of formulating the underlying framework, its principles, and

---

150 An illustrative example is the approval of the "Code of Conduct", a document created as an "integrity check" for civil servants in order to prevent unwarranted behaviour. It took seven years to push it through the legislative process.

151 Shortly after her inauguration, she launched a reform program of the system of bureaucracy, made a purge, scratched redundant positions, and increased the salaries of the government employees. The liberal aspect of privatisation of services (in appropriate cases) was also a part of the reform (PRS 2008).

values, the actual engagement of external actors in the field of governance at the operational level is quite limited. There are many programs and projects implemented under the umbrella of governance reform, focusing on enhancing participation, promoting human rights and the like, led by international NGOs and supported by external partners. The UN also has a whole program dedicated to governance. During the time of my fieldwork, a substantial part of the support went to the rule of law programs, with the US and Germany being the most prominent bilateral partners.

At the ministries and governmental agencies, the external presence is relatively low, especially in comparison to the early post-conflict period, with the international trusteeship in the form of GEMAP. There is a large capacity-building program (TOKTEN, see above), where seconded experts from abroad work together with local counterparts in ministries and parastatals (Informal conversations and observations April–June 2012, Monrovia). In the Governance Commission itself, the international presence is largely non-existent. Occasionally, there are international consultants from the World Bank and the UN, but otherwise, the Commission is entirely in Liberian hands, following the principles of national ownership. Or, as one of the commissioners commented, "It is a Liberian institution. A Liberian problem needs a Liberian solution" (Interview #57, GC Commissioner, 28 November 2012, Monrovia). Neither the UN, nor other foreign partners, be it governments or NGOs, are consistently involved in the implementation of the reform process, which is particularly striking in comparison to, for instance, the Land Commission, where the level of foreign presence is quite high (cf. chapter eight). The question arises, whether the reasons behind are exclusively "altruistic", following the maxims of respect for national ownership, or whether other factors come into play. Some of them could be the zero relevance of governance reform for business interests and profit-making opportunities for the donor countries, or a perception of the reforms as being of a merely formal nature, paying lip-service to the global good governance discourse.

7.5.2 Civil society

In the field of governance reform, civil society is represented by civil society organisations (CSOs), mainly by Liberian NGOs.[152] The relationship of

---

152 The GoL-CSOs Partnership Policy (2016) provides an overview and a more detailed categorization of the various types of CSOs in Liberia. There are a

the GC and CSOs is friendly and based on mutual support. Most of the Commissioners, including the Chairman, have been actively engaged, or have a background in CSOs, so the cooperation is anchored in informal, personal relationships and a solid base of trust.

The GC has been committed to strengthening the role of civil society as a partner for the government, mainly in the context of policy-making processes. To facilitate this, the Commission helped to establish a CSO Advisory Council (since 2012 an independent institution) and was also involved in a mapping exercise that resulted in a nationwide directory of civil society organizations. This is supposed to serve as a primary reference for the government to facilitate contact with partners having expert knowledge in a particular field. To a similar end, and also to make the voice of CSOs stronger, independent thematic groups around specific issues (e.g., the CSO Platform on Decentralization and Governance in the case of decentralisation) have been created (Personal correspondence with a GC employee, February 2017).

In 2016, the GC's efforts materialised in the creation of two major documents, outlining the principles and modalities of engagement between the GoL and civil society: the GOL-CSOs Partnership Policy (2016) and the Memorandum of Understanding, related to the latter document, expressing the commitment of both sides to implementation of the policy. Taking into consideration that, traditionally, the relationship between the government and civil society has been highly antagonistic and confrontational, these documents represent a significant step forward.

On the other hand, there are a number of less conducive factors, such as the general state of civil society in Liberia, which is not well developed, to a large extent dependent on external financial support, and therefore very much donor-driven in its agenda.[153]

As already briefly mentioned, civil society serves as a point of entry to specialised knowledge also for the Governance Commission itself. In the process of consultations, the Commission usually starts with relevant CSOs and then moves on to the citizenry in the counties. Unlike many international partners, hiring the CSOs as implementing agents for the outreach, the GC seeks to engage directly with the population, without

---

number of individual leaders on the civil society scene; however, all of them have been connected to an organization, usually in a leading role (McKeown and Mulbah 2007).

153 The problematic factors are listed in the GOL-CSOs Partnership Policy, together with some measures suggested to improve the situation.

any intermediaries (Personal correspondence with a GC employee, February 2017).[154] This approach further adds to the visibility and credibility of the Commission at the local level. [155]

7.5.3 Challenges

The major challenge for the Commission is a structural one—the lack of executive power and its controversial position in the political system, challenging the hitherto common practices in politics and demanding unpopular reforms. There are also other issues at the level of everyday functioning of the body. The first and the most obvious one is the task it faces. Not only its scope *per se*, but also considering the number of people working for the GC and the available budget[156], which is quite modest, compared to other institutions, (e.g., the Land Commission's budget is twice as big).[157] The estimated budget of the GC for 2013 was 1,000,000 USD provided by the government and an additional 300,000–500,000 USD by international partners (Personal correspondence with a GC employee, December 2014). The government supports the day-to-day functioning of the Commission and its basic infrastructure, whereas the project part

---

154 The CSOs are, however, major participants in the consultation processes at the local level and often develop their own initiatives and campaigns around the issue at stake (Personal correspondence with a GC employee, February 2017).

155 It is difficult to estimate how much ordinary citizens know about and how they perceive the work of the Commission, since there is no data available about the perception of public institutions in Liberia in general (the National Integrity Barometer partly covers the perception of public institutions in Liberia, but does not include the Governance Commission itself). An independent inquiry into the matter would certainly be useful; however, it was beyond the scope of this study. The overall level of civic awareness in Liberia is quite low and citizens can "feel" the impact of the Commission's work only indirectly, through the work of other civic institutions. However, civil servants, people engaged in CSOs, middle-class and other citizens, interested in public affairs are those who might know about the Commission and its work (Personal correspondence with a GC employee, February 2017).

156 No official budget or financial reports are available online. More financial resources would allow for hiring more personnel and implementing the projects faster and more "profoundly", e.g., by consulting and including more stakeholders (Informal conversation #62, employee of the GC, 30 November 2012, Monrovia).

157 The budget of the Land Commission for 2014 was 2,670,681 USD (LC Annual Report 2014).

of the budget is supplied by the international partners. At the broader structural level, the main problematic issue is the mindset of the people. Throughout its history, Liberia has never come close to embracing principles of liberal democracy in Talmon's sense (1985), being based on the rule of law and accountability to the citizens. The political culture, treating the state as an acceptable (and accepted) tool for private enrichment, provided that clients benefit, is deeply embedded in the social fabric in Liberia. Prebendalism and conception of political office as a personal patrimony and a sign of social status, rather than a service for citizens, where a certain level of performance is required, is prevalent (Interviews and informal conversations #18, #24, #33, #38, April–June 2012, Monrovia cf. Bayart 2009). This, together with the legacy of autocratic rule, certainly represents a difficult context for a reform. On the other hand, demographic realities of the country might be a factor that facilitates the change. With the median age of 18,3 years (CIA World Factbook, estimates for 2016) and over 40% of the population born after the end of the civil war, the prospects for transformation are surely higher than in other countries, such as the post-Soviet Central and Eastern Europe, where the population structure is quite different, rendering the values and political culture of the communist regimes more resistant to change (cf. Pehe 1997).

The meta-question of plausibility of such a change is by all means a relevant one. Despite the demographic argument and the factual destruction of the state institutions during the conflict, the values underlying the Liberian political culture and mindset of the citizens are very stable. They have been handed down in the process of socialisation in the families and beyond, throughout the education system and in the form of everyday practices in different spheres of social organisation. In such a context, a technocratic, top-down change is hard to imagine. The only conceivable way is to start at the grassroots level, as the GC is apparently aware. This opinion was often repeated in interviews and informal conversations with civil society representatives (Interviews and informal conversations #20, #24, #25, #56, Monrovia June 2011–November 2012) and resonates also with Lederach (1997, 2002), Porter (2007), Saunders (2000), and other peacebuilding practitioners.

The informants often stressed the fact that the work at the grassroots level has to be built on trust, and that the latter can be achieved only over time (cf. Lederach 1997):

"I've been involved in this Norwegian conflict transformation programme, where there is a group of people, peacebuilders, meeting regularly and only now, after almost two years, we can start really working. Because it took them so long to start to trust each other; they come from different communities, speak different languages, have different religions. There is a lot of ground for suspicion and distrust." (Informal conversation #24, KAICT international staff member, 14 June 2012, Monrovia)

Governance is certainly a field where the potential of middle-level leaders is being tapped. The commissioners themselves are illustrative cases of opinion leaders, cross-cutting and linking various sectors and social groups. Governance reform then represents an example of a sub-system approach (Dugan 1996 cited by Lederach 1997), where a general issue of crucial importance is being addressed through a series of sectoral reforms.

7.6 Conclusion

Governance has been one of the fundamental issues laying at the heel of the slope that led Liberia to the civil war. Very much in line with Stinchcombe's concept of imprinting (2000), where institutions and regimes are shaped by the conditions at the time of their birth, the issue of governance has been present as a problem of the Liberian state from the very beginning of its existence. As such, it is difficult to be subject to change. At the same time, exactly because of that, it is acknowledged as a crucial point to be tackled if the peace is to last in the country.

Governance is one of the fields of peacebuilding, where the emphasis in policy discourse, as expressed in various framework documents for Liberia, does not translate into support in practice. Although the crucial importance of governance reform is repeated virtually every time peacebuilding is being discussed, the real involvement on the ground lags behind. The case of the Governance Commission is a typical example of this setup; the real, material support that is an essential precondition for the work of the GC and subsequently for the reform, does not match the declared and factual importance of the issue. The support from the government for the Commission's work is rather rhetorical. Certainly, it could be caused by the fact that the government is overwhelmed by a range of issues it has to tackle. At the same time, given the implicit objective of limiting the power of the executive branch, it would be also counter-productive to support the GC. The international actors had meted out the playground by defining the general objectives of the governance reform and withdrew from the scene. So seemingly, governance reform represents an exemplary case of a national ownership approach. As already mentioned, a question comes to mind, whether it is really out of respect for the ownership principles, or out of other reasons, for example, because there is little at stake for the external actors, be it in terms of short-term gains and potential monetary profit, or because of the lip-service-like nature of the reforms. Civil society represents a platform of support and at the same time, an actor to be supported. It could (and ideally, according to all stakeholders *should*) be involved to a much greater extent, but "is simply not there yet" (Interview #38, foreign diplomat, 7 June 2012, Monrovia). It is still underdeveloped and very much donor-driven in its agenda.

The primordial challenge of a giant task, for which limited financial and human resources are available, is only exacerbated by the precarious position of the GC in Liberian political system. On the other hand, the leadership of the Commission provides an efficient counter-balance, where a clear vision meets emphasis on consultative processes, necessary for building legitimacy of the reform process. Amos Sawyer, GC Chairman, is a strong and credible figure, and despite the lack of support from "above", the institution draws legitimacy from a strong backing from "below", that is, from the civil society and community level, the two sides of a tripartite-partnership that should constitute an efficient governance framework.

The process, leading to such a level of legitimacy and ownership, requires time. This aspect is, however, underestimated in the current approach to peacebuilding in general and, more particularly, in the approach of international actors and donor agencies, whose frameworks and plans are usually based on short- to middle-term planning. Liberia proves that it is possible to have a reform tailored to the local needs and context, provided the process is backed by substantial commitment and conscious leadership. Despite all the limitations, the Governance Commission represents a solid example of tapping upon the potential of middle-range leaders, a phenomenon otherwise largely absent in the mainstream approach to peacebuilding.

Governance reform in Liberia is in need of more robust support than it actually receives right now. The question is, where from. To rely on the government in this respect is unrealistic. Firstly, the Liberian national budget is quite modest[158], and there are many pressing areas, where the resources are required. In addition, the GC represents an uncomfortable agent, challenging the status quo on the political scene. To support it

---

158 For the fiscal year 2016/17, the envisioned budget amounted to 555,993,000 USD (Ministry of Finance and Development Planning 2016). For more details, see Annex 3.

would be in fact *against* the interest of the power holders. More backing coming from outside, from the international financing institutions and donors, would certainly be desirable. However, this support should be limited to a financial scope, otherwise it could be justly perceived as an intrusion on the holy shrine of state sovereignty.

Additionally, it is worth remembering that in the Liberian case, it is not enough to restore and rebuild the institutions from the pre-war times; they were, after all, part of the problem that led to the war. The real challenge lies in the development and realisation of an *alternative vision* of how the country could be administered. Despite the fact that the civil war destroyed most of the institutions, the practices of governance developed throughout the 150 years of Liberia's independent existence persist. The basic rules and principles, underlying the functioning of the political system and shaping the way power has been exercised in Liberia are deeply embedded in the mindset of people, both the ones who govern and those who are being governed. Changing the practices of governance will not be possible without changing this mindset and the whole political culture which grows from it. There is indeed a certain tension between the approach of the Commission, that focuses on reform of the official, formal structures, and the need to change the political culture, as a necessary complement of the former. Partly, the latter "soft" component of the reform is addressed by the style of GC's work, exemplifying the good practice of a participatory, consultative process. A substantial transformation of the mindset would, however, have to be addressed at the level of civic education (i.e., from the grassroots, individual level) and, ideally, to meet and be enhanced by an adequate behaviour of the political leaders. In this respect, the question arises whether a genuine project of governance reform can be successful at all and if so, in which time frame.

Before embarking on the next case study dealing with land issues, let us conclude by a short reach-up to the "general level of analysis", summarising the main factors hindering progress of the reform. For one, it is the precarious situation of the GC in the domestic political landscape, caused by the uneasy relationships with other political actors, on whose approval the work of the GC to a large extent depends. For another, it is the nature and scope of the reform, which requires a long time to be accomplished, combined with a shortage of adequate financial support.

The case of governance also offers a number of insights about the general practice of today's post-conflict peacebuilding. Firstly, it shows that despite the prominent position of a topic in the general discourse, and even more importantly in the context of particular historical circumstances (poor governance being an issue unanimously recognised as a crucial conflict driver), the importance of an issue does not always reflect the real support on the ground. Secondly, governance shows the significance of leadership and a consultative approach for a legitimate result of the reform process. Such an approach, however, clashes with the general strategies of peacebuilding, which are focused on short- to middle-term results that can be neatly ticked off in checklists and easily reported to the headquarters level. Once the issue is long-term, with results difficult to measure, the external engagement tends to diminish. On the other hand, in the particular case of governance reform, the opposite case, with the international actors engaged too much, would be a much more controversial scenario, supporting the thesis of overly intrusive outsiders, trying to implant the institutions and principles. This might work nowadays in a country with a completely different socio-economic status, but historically, this approach has not proved to hold out in situations of crisis.[159]

---

159 Europe between the wars comes to mind as a first-hand example.

Chapter 8 Land issues in peacebuilding

> "Why do we need deeds? The land is ours."
> (Interview LC, 8 June 2012, Monrovia)

8.1 Origins of the controversy

The roots of contention around land reach to the very origin of the Liberian state and to the beginning of coast settlement by the ACS. After some initial difficulties, the colonists bought land for their first settlements from indigenous chiefs. It was a common practice at that time in political entities across the continent, to give newcomers (in this particular case, immigrants) a piece of land to use. However, the customary practice in Liberia, as well as in many countries elsewhere in Africa, did not recognize private ownership of land in the "Western" sense, where individuals could privately own and dispose of a piece of land. Land belonged to the community. In this context, individuals can access and use land, but cannot own it: "land cannot be subdivided or inherited privately (...), lineage lands belong to the dead, living, and unborn." (Unruh 2008: 7). The colonists, however, coming from a completely different tradition, regarded the land they once bought from the chief as theirs forever. The chiefs, on the other hand, conceived the land as still belonging to them. This was an original point of contention that aggravated over time, when the colonies started to expand and the newly established political entity enlarged its territory mainly by the means of conquest. Another, more decisive aspect of the problem, became the legal system governing land, which was discriminatory, unclear, and rigid.

Liberia has been governed by the system of common law, received from the US, and distinguished two legal systems – one for the "civilized" settler population, and another for the indigenous people in the Hinterlands. The land in the counties along the coast, owned as a freehold in the form of deeds in fee simple[160] by the Americo-Liberian settlers, was governed by

---

160 Freehold and ownership in fee simple are terms coming from the common law tradition, being more or less identical (in terms of rights of the owner) with today's notion of private property in continental legal systems. The owner of

the statutory law. All other land in the country was considered "public land" and fell under the category of customary law: "All other land in the interior was, and continues to be, primarily occupied by indigenous Africans under customary land tenure, but is legally considered the property of the state and therefore public land" (Unruh 2008: 12). The legal reference for land issues were the Rules and Regulations Governing the Hinterland from 1949 (revised in 2001), a law primarily created to deal with governance in general, rather than with land specifically. Hinterland counties were administered under the system of indirect rule, with chiefs acting on behalf of the state. Land was left to be managed by local chiefs, according to specific customary practices.[161]

The parallel existence of two legal systems would not be problematic *per se*; it has been a common practice in a number of African countries. The troublesome aspect in Liberia was, according to some authors, that the two systems existed in a deliberate isolation (Unruh 2008, World Bank 2008).

The inequality in land tenure reflected the generally unequal status of "civilized" and "native" Liberians:

> "The overall perspective of statutory land-related laws, beginning with the Constitution, was that the customary inhabitant of Liberia was subject to statutory laws, while not being able to participate in them —meaning they possessed little in the way of constitutional rights, resulting in an inability to hold land under statutory law. At the same time Americo-Liberians were not subject to customary laws. This set the formal tenure system against the customary system, which the government attempted to resolve by the delimitation of 'state sponsored customary law', but which instead created a third tenure system." (Unruh 2008: 5)

Another problematic aspect has been a lack of clarity in definitions of basic terms and consequent ambiguity, leading to insecurity and leaving room for "manoeuvring" and deliberate interpretation. For example, the notion

---

the land has an exclusive right to dispose with the land, sell it, or bequeath: "A holder in fee simple has the right to possess the land in perpetuity; the right to exclude others from it; the right to use the land and retain the fruits of its use; the right to devise land to heirs by will and to have such land pass to heirs according to rules of intestacy where there is no will; and the right to sell, mortgage, lease or otherwise alienate rights over the land, temporarily or permanently" (World Bank 2008: viii).

161 Such practices vary among different ethnic groups and have not been systematically documented (World Bank 2008).

of "public land" has not been specified in any legal document. The rights of the communities were vague, since the customary law was non-codified. This has become especially troublesome in the context of a weak justice system and rule of law. Courts (be they customary or statutory) have been perceived as corrupt and delivering justice only to the rich (Isser et al. 2009, Interview #34, GIZ officer, 1 June 2012, Monrovia) and especially in the postwar period suffered from a lack of qualified professionals and basic equipment, which led to extremely long cases.[162] This volatile environment, limited access to justice and enforceability of law, has further strengthened the legal pluralism, as people resorted to alternative mechanisms of dispute resolution, such as palava hut, or presenting the dispute to a trusted authority (e.g., traditional leaders, elders). Seeking justice has taken also more extreme forms, such as using violence as a means of acquiring land and defending one's claims. People also turned to traditional mechanisms, such as the practice of "trial by ordeal".[163]

Unlike in other countries, there is not a fundamental scarcity of land in Liberia. The trouble with land issues in Liberia lies in their complexity. There are several levels of the problem. One is related to belonging, autochthony, and citizenship (Bøås 2009, Chabal 2009).[164] Another level reflects the unequal relationship between the Americo-Liberian settlers

---

162 To file a case is also quite expensive and requires a high level of literacy (Interviews #32, #35, #37, cf. Unruh 2008). Another factor is the geographical distance of the courts; to reach them can be a major logistical challenge, linked to additional costs.

163 A process, also often referred to as "sassywood", where an accused person is supposed to drink a poisonous concoction (there are also alternative methods, such as applying hot oil or a hot machete against the skin of the suspects, see Iser et al. 2009). If the person survives the exposure, he or she is claimed innocent. The poison is extracted from the bark of the sassywood tree (*Erythrophleum suaveolens*).

164 The Mandingo, an ethnic group of Guinean origin, and Lebanese are typical examples in this respect. The Mandingo, despite the fact that they arrived centuries ago, are still seen as newcomers, "strangers", and are therefore required to accept a subordinate position in a "stranger-father" relationship, where a respected member of the community acts as a warrantor, ensuring that the "newcomer" complies with local culture and social norms (Norton 2011). Lebanese, with roughly 4000 people (Paye-Layleh 2005), who dominate the Liberian business community, are excluded from land ownership by virtue of not being Liberian citizens. According to the so-called "negro clause" in the Liberian constitution, only people of black African origin, "a Negro or of Negro descent" (Republic of Liberia 1986), can be citizens of Liberia, and own land in the country.

and native people, and the way the country has been governed, including discriminatory and unspecific laws related to land tenure. Then, there is a tension within communities, with roots in gerontocracy and exploitative marital and labour practices.[165] At a different level, not so closely related to the particular cultural context, there are tensions between the communities and foreign companies, granted large areas of land in concessions for commercial use by the government, without prior consent of the communities.

The underlying problem, making all the cases mentioned here even more difficult to manage is an absence of a cadastre or a similar system, where one can check on the ownership of a certain piece of land. Especially in the hinterland, the demarcation remains a problem, leaving tradition and custom as the main sources of verification.[166] At the individual level, the non-existence of a cadastre makes the very justification of one's claim to a piece of land complicated. In the case of concessions, the consequence is an absence of reliable statistics, so it is actually unclear how much land is taken in concessions. Estimates vary between 25% and 50%, which is one of the highest concession rates in Africa (Kaba and Madan 2014: 5). The contention grows from different perspectives of the government (which claims to legally dispose of the land) and the communities, which perceive the land as theirs. Forests and natural resources, wildly exploited during the civil war and used for financing the conflict (as well as for private enrichment of leading political figures), have been further targeted by foreign companies through the opportunistic use of the Private Use Permits (PUPs).[167] Because of this underlying complexity and the fact

---

165 The problem is the availability of labour for farming the land. Various authors (Richards 2005 as the most notorious one, but also others, e.g., World Bank 2008, Unruh 2008) pointed to the fact that the scarcity of labour led to exploitation of young members of the communities (especially young men) by local chiefs. A common practice was charging fines that were paid off by labour on the chief's farm and that effectively prevented young men from working on their own land. This (together with other factors, such as traditional marital practices) made it difficult to marry and set up families. Another common institution, abused in this context was to claim a "woman damage", where a woman of the chief was urged to "call a name" of an alleged lover, which resulted in charging the indicated man a fine (e.g., Unruh 2008). Such practices, obsolete as they might sound, were still common before the war broke out, and constituted a part of the tensions that led to conflict.

166 Of course, boundaries are also marked by trees or other natural features.

167 Unlike concessions, which are agreements between the government and companies, PUPs are arrangements, where the owner of the privately deeded land

that land issues cross-cut a wide range of fields, from agriculture, natural resources management, rule of law and access to justice, to gender issues, it is difficult to file them neatly into one of the common peacebuilding categories.

In addition to these factors, there have been numbers of refugees and IDPs returning after the war, often facing the fact that their land has been occupied by squatters, or sold on the "black market".[168] The "right to return", as a principle generally promoted by international agencies, clashes with the traditional approach that links the right to land to its use and cultivation (Corriveau-Bourque 2010, Norton 2011).

In post-conflict settings, issues and disputes related to land are quite common. They often turn up as a side-effect of large movements of population, returning after periods of displacement, and trying to re-settle in their original communities, or to find new places to stay. The postwar context with its low level of law enforcement, weak to non-existent rule of law, debilitated justice systems, missing documents proving land ownership, or psychosocial factors, such as traumatised population prone to violent ways of dealing with conflict, aggravates the situation and facilitates the spill-over of conflicts to violence. In some cases, however, land issues can be also one of the factors leading to or sustaining the conflict. Although different authors' opinions vary with regard to the importance and role of land in triggering and maintaining the war in Liberia (Levitt 2205, cf. Tarr 2007, Richards 2005, GRC 2007, World Bank 2008, Sawyer 2005, World Bank 2017), various stakeholders during my field research, experts dealing with the issue, and also the way land reform as such has actually been handled, indicate very clearly the importance of land and its conflict potential in Liberia. As one of the interviewees put it: "If we are to go back to war, and I pray not to, it would be because of land. The conflict over land is huge and it can spark violence in any moment" (Interview #33, Liberia Democracy Watch employee, 30 May 2012, Monrovia). The

---

enters directly into a contract with a company. The PUP area is not limited in size, nor are there restrictions or specifications about how the logging operations should be carried out (e.g., in terms of sustainability or protection of environment). Since late 2012, when it became clear that the tool was being abused by logging companies to bypass more strictly regulated forest concessions, and that PUPs cover almost a quarter of the country, there has been a moratorium on the issue of the permits (Global Witness 2012, De Wit 2012).

168 In the postwar context, documents and records proving land ownership have often been missing and, frequently, it came to cases of their falsification or even multiple sales of the same piece of land (World Bank 2008).

regions with the highest incidence of land conflict in Liberia are the remote counties in hinterland, as well as Monrovia and its surroundings.[169] Although there are inter-ethnic conflicts, ethnicity is usually not at the core of the dispute.[170]

The PRS lists land conflicts among the six key cross-cutting issues that "remain problematic" and "require focused attention (...) to mitigate their potential to mobilize groups for violent action" (PRS 2008: 171). The PRS also acknowledges that issues linked to land and property ownership "continue to pose security threats" (PRS 2008: 55) and stresses the importance of clear policies with regard to land tenure and ownership for investment and general economic revitalisation of the country (PRS 2008). There is a unanimous agreement (World Bank 2008, Unruh and Williams 2013) that beyond conflict-related aspects, land tenure is crucial for the economic growth and political stability of any country. Security of land tenure or respectively a sound land policy ensuring the latter, leads to an increased food security, and possibility of long-term investments into land, which can further increase revenues, ensure higher efficiency in land use and access to land, and therefore reduce polarisation. To provide poor people with land is considered central for reducing poverty (World Bank 2008).

Issues around land touch not only one of the fundamental aspects of traditional state sovereignty (in terms of state's control over its territory), but also issues of identity, belonging, and citizenship (Chabal 2009: 27ff., 57ff., 96ff., Bøås 2009, Unruh 2008). As such, policy development in this field is perceived as a highly sensitive process, that should be firmly in the hands of Liberians. Land policy is considered "one of the most sensitive and important policies" (PRS 2008: 67) for both economic growth and security consolidation.

8.2 After the war: Path to the Land Commission

As already briefly mentioned, the insecurity of land tenure in Liberia after the war has increased as a consequence of illegal occupation and

---

169 Nimba, Lofa, Maryland, and Grand Gedeh have a particularly high level of land-related conflicts. See the map in Annex 5.

170 An exception in this regard is Lofa county, with tensions between Mandingo and Loma. The conflicts revolve around claims of autochthony.

displacements, missing records and documentation[171], dysfunctionality of land-related agencies and courts, and organised fraud in the land sector, with involvement of governmental surveyors or archive staff.

Based on recommendations of the Governance Reform Commission and a baseline analysis by John Bruce[172] (World Bank 2008), summarising what needs to be done in the land sector, it was decided to create a single independent institution, that would deal with land issues in a comprehensive manner. The conditions for the land reform in Liberia were extremely favourable at that time. There was an explicit commitment from the highest political level, with President Ellen Johnson Sirleaf acknowledging the crucial importance of the land reform for immediate and future security of the country, and affirming the "high priority" (World Bank 2008: iii) of the issue, as a "key to the full recovery of Liberia" (World Bank 2008: 8). At the same time, there was a high level of popular support for the reform across various segments of the population, together with good timing in the postwar "window of opportunity" (Sawyer 2009).

Bruce has outlined the major features of the envisaged institution, based on lessons learnt and experience with similar bodies from elsewhere:

- diverse and non-partisan membership (including both official and civil society members);
- strong, respected chair and high-capacity, full-time secretariat as crucial assets;
- broad public consultations with stakeholders as a critical aspect for quality and ownership of decisions; strong focus on process and transparency;
- public as the primary stakeholder to be consulted, not officials;
- participatory methods as tools for fact-finding;
- consultations should not only be a forum for complaints, but an opportunity to get feedback on suggested solutions;
- funds should be channelled through a multilateral donor organisation to avoid excessive reporting duties to different donors (World Bank 2008: 47).

---

171 Some of the records have been lost during the conflict, others have been kept in deplorable conditions, exposed to humidity and found in various stages of decomposition. A sad anecdote goes that during the worst times of conflict, people "bought seeds and nuts from street vendors in paper spills that on closer examination proved to be deeds or pages from deed registries." (World Bank 2008: 37)

172 John Bruce is an international consultant with extensive experience with land sector from different countries around the world.

And indeed, these recommendations were reflected in the establishment of the Land Commission, created in 2009, as a free-standing, independent body with a five-year mandate (Land Commission Act 2009).[173] One of the reasons to create a new institution was the need to overcome the context of fragmentation, where almost a dozen governmental agencies were in charge of land issues.[174] Other reasons that favoured the creation of an *ad hoc* body over the normal decision-making process, was the experience from elsewhere, which showed that such an arrangement can reduce competition between different governmental agencies, limit the influence of vested interests of the government and of political influence over the outputs in general, or offer space for compromise and, subsequently, for a higher political durability of the suggested solutions (World Bank 2008). In other words, "the decision to have a Land Commission was as obvious to any Liberian who knew what they were talking about, as to any international consultant" (Interview #23, international consultant, 3 May 2012, Monrovia).

8.3 The Land Commission

The Land Commission (LC) became operational in March 2010. It consisted of seven commissioners, including a chairman and a vice-chairman, appointed by the president with the consent of the Senate and the "Technical and Administrative Secretariat", supposed to support the Commission. In the act establishing the LC, there is no reference to expertise or experience in land issues the commissioners should possess, apart from their "integrity and impartiality" (Land Commission Act 2009: section 4.1). Gender aspect and geographical representation ("No two Commissioners shall come from the same county", LC Act 2009: section 4.1) were also listed as factors to be considered.[175]

---

173 Similar to the GC, the Land Commission also represents an agency in Skelcher's (2005) sense.

174 They were the Ministry of Land, Mines, and Energy; Ministry of Agriculture (for agricultural concessions); Ministry of Internal Affairs; Ministry of Public Works; Ministry of Finance (taxes and fees); Ministry of Justice; Ministry of Foreign Affairs (deed register from early times of the Republic); National Center for Documents and Records/National Archives (recent deeds register); Forestry Development Authority; and Environmental Protection Agency.

175 All the commissioners actually had experience with the land sector. The same aspect was initially criticised by civil society organisations in the draft act estab-

In 2012, there were about 30 people working for the LC, Liberian nationals, as well as short- and long-term international consultants (Interview #23, international consultant, 3 May 2012, Monrovia). Over time, the number of personnel has grown to 155 (LC 2015: 18), with 94 employees in the headquarters and 61 deployed in the six Land Coordination Centers around the country. The chairman, Dr. Cecil Brandy, is a respected figure, and had a very good working relationship with President Sirleaf. He was praised for his leadership qualities, where he combined an academic viewpoint with practical skills and strong motivation to finish the task the LC has been given. He was also perceived as politically astute and well-connected to different ministries (Interview #31, employee of an international NGO, 28 May 2012, #61, 30 November 2012, USAID employee, Monrovia, Liberia).

The Commission enjoyed solid financial support. The budget for 2014 amounted to 2,67 million USD. The Swedish Development Agency (SIDA) was the largest donor with 936,301 USD, followed by the UN Peacebuilding Fund (channelled through the UN-HABITAT) with 907,239 USD, and the GoL with 827,140 USD. Two-thirds of the budget were spent on personnel costs (1,79 million USD). In this sub-category, the government was the largest contributor with 780,000 USD (amounting to 43% of the personnel budget), followed by SIDA with 540,000 USD, and the UN-HABITAT with 480,000 USD (LC 2015: 28-29). In previous years, the financial allotment to the LC ranged from 1,1 million USD in 2010 (LC 2011) to 1,58 million USD in 2011 (LC 2012).[176]

Apart from the statistics, the good financial backing was reflected in details one could observe: the building of the Commission that had been renovated, conference rooms with an air-conditioning system and a projector, offices equipped with functioning computers and printers. Thanks to strong IT support, financed by USAID, the website of the LC was informative and regularly updated.[177] In 2012, there were even plans to

---

lishing the successor body of the LC, the Land Authority. In the end, relevant expertise was included among the explicit prerequisites for the candidates for commissioners (Land Authority Act 2016).

176 The 2012 Annual Report does not provide any detailed information on the budget. However, it lists the "inadequate budgetary allotment from the Government of Liberia for implementing programs and project activities" (p. 16) as one of the "major constraints" (ibid.) the Commission faced and claimed that it would not be able to fulfil its mandate without donor support.

177 After the end of the LC's mandate, the website has been suspended and is not accessible any more.

create a computer network within the Commission to facilitate document sharing (Interview #23, international consultant, 3 May 2012, Monrovia). Taken-for-granted as they might be, these amenities are far from being common in the public sector in Liberia. During my fieldwork, some of the ministries and governmental institutions were struggling with basic office supplies, lacking internet connection and facing unsuitable facilities and housing conditions.

8.4 The Land Commission: Projects and outcomes

The scope and range of LC's activities and areas of interest was quite broad: land rights policy, land dispute resolution, land use and management, administration, and outreach and education.

8.4.1 Land Rights Policy

Drafting the land rights policy was a crucial project for the Commission. After an "in-house" formulation, the draft went through a consultative process at the regional level, with participation from community leaders, traditional authorities (elders, chiefs), women, and youth.[178] After a validation conference in May 2013, the draft was presented to the president in October 2013. After the review by the president, the cabinet, and legislature, it was reformulated for adoption into law[179], and went through another round of input by ministries, civil society organisations, and the public in 2015.

The development of Land Rights Policy was perceived as a major landmark in the history of the country's dealing with land issues. The document provides the much-needed definitions of four types of land ownership:

(1) *private land*: owned or otherwise held by private persons protected by a legal document referred to as a deed under the laws of Liberia;

---

178 Each consultation brought together representatives from three to four counties. Some civil society organisations pointed to the fact that despite the broad spectre of voices included, the majority of participants was not familiar with the document, which limited the possibility of relevant input from their side (Kaba and Madan 2014).

179 The Land Rights Act, presented to the president in July 2014.

(2) *public land*: acquired by the government through purchase, seizure, gift, or otherwise which is not presently used by the government for it facilities or operations;

(3) *government land*: used by the government for its buildings, projects, or activities that concern the government;

(4) *customary land*: owned by a community and used or managed in accordance with customary practices and standards (Land Rights Act 2014).

For the first time in the history of Liberia, the law would grant customary land the same level of protection that private land enjoys, which means that communities are given an opportunity to manage their land and natural resources according to their own benefit. In addition to the "equal protection", the Act states that a proof of customary land ownership does not have to be a written document. It can be "any competent evidence including oral testimony showing a verifiable longstanding relationship" (Land Rights Act 2014: Chapter 3, Article 9). These and other provisions have far-reaching consequences in the current context, where communities have close to zero protection against the companies granted concessions or extracting mineral resources, and encroaching the lands of the communities, including sacred areas with shrines and burial sites (Maclean 2016).[180]

The Act has been approved by the House of Representatives in August 2017, following coordinated pressure, mainly from the side of Liberian CSOs, on passing the law before the parliamentary break in August 2017:

> "If the legislature does not pass the 2014 version of the Land Rights Act before its recess in August, it will likely be delayed until after the elections; a new government takes office in 2018, leaving the legislation in limbo indefinitely." (Maclean 2016)

The CSOs have expressed concerns not only about the passage of the bill as such, but also about the content of the adopted version, so that the act is to be passed with all the crucial provisions and not in an "unboned" version. A few days after the passage through the House of Representatives, the Senate did not accept the bill and returned it to the committees of the lower House for "additional work to be done on the document" (Senah 2017).[181] Among the senators calling for review was the head of the Senate committee in charge of the issue, Varney Sherman, a lawyer, who has

---

180 The rights of communities do not include the right to extraction of resources under the surface of the soil; these are considered the property of the state (Interview #38, Land Commission, 8 June 2012, Monrovia).

181 Two-thirds of the senators voted against the passage of the bill.

been accused of being involved in a corruption scandal linked to mining concessions.[182] According to a Global Witness report (2016), he bribed influential members of the legislature and other political figures, so that they would pass specific legislation on concessions in 2010. This "friendly version" of the Procurement and Concession Act allowed Sable Minings (a commercial mining company on whose payroll Sherman was) to get access to an iron ore reserve in the north of Liberia without the need to go through a tender (Global Witness 2016, Maclean 2016). It is indeed striking that a person with such a record was chairing a committee in charge of the immensely sensitive law with direct impact on the regulation of the whole land sector. The bill was finally approved by the Senate on 23 August 2018 and signed into law by President Weah in September 2018, together with the Local Government Act (Executive Mansion 2018).

8.4.2 Tribal certificates

Tribal certificates (TCs) are legal documents, issued by customary authorities that certified the consent of the latter to sell customary land. They represented one of the steps in a rather long and complicated process of acquiring a deed and on their own, and according to the statutory law, they had no legal bearings (Corriveau-Bourque 2010). However, there was a different understanding of the certificates at the local level, where they were perceived and issued as a guarantee of the security of land tenure for community members (World Bank 2017). The LC started a collecting exercise with the objective of finding out how much land they actually covered. This is an important step in the process of defining "public land", that is, the land that is not encumbered by any kind of tenure. It also has a major importance for a clear delineation of "customary areas"; "To see what is left and can be used for concessions or other purposes" (Interview #39, LC Commissioner, 8 June 2012, Monrovia).[183]

A comprehensive understanding, including the clarification of legal implications of the TCs, represents the first step for the formulation of a tribal land policy, which will be a prerequisite for the establishment of a comprehensive land administration system. As of 2017, the LC has

---

182 Others were Senators Jim Tornonlah, Daniel Naatehn, Henry Yallah, and Alphonso Gate (Senah 2017).

183 The remaining public land will belong to the state, i.e., the government will manage and dispose of it.

completed inventories of tribal certificates in four counties, and pilot surveys have been started in three others (World Bank 2017).[184] The newly established Land Authority is supposed to finish the exercise.

8.4.3 Land Coordination Centers

The third major project of the Commission are the Land Coordination Centers (LCCs). The LCCs are regional "branches" of the LC, intended to provide information and practical knowledge about options for the resolution of land-related disputes. They also assist the LC in developing a basis for the drafting of Land Dispute Resolution Policy, by coordinating pilot exercises of alternative dispute resolution applied to customary, non-document-based land disputes. Currently, there are six LCCs operational throughout the country, in Bong, Maryland, Margibi, Lofa, Nimba, and Montserrado counties, that were identified as areas of high incidence of land disputes (Dixon 2015).

Apart from these major projects, the LC was engaged in a range of other activities, in the field of land administration, management, as well as in outreach, information, and awareness-raising.[185]

8.5 Taskforces of the Land Commission

Besides quarterly meetings of the Board of Commissioners, there used to be monthly (in some cases bi-monthly) meetings of different taskforces of the Commission. My fieldwork focused on two major lines of LC's activities, one related to policy development, and another one focused on land dispute resolution. For both areas, there were operational taskforces established, holding regular monthly coordination meetings that served as primary arenas of interaction with other stakeholders. One of the fundamental features of the taskforces was the emphasis on Liberian ownership of the latter. To be sure, there were some of the international partners represented, based on the merit of their engagement in land dispute resolution and land issues in general, but they were seen as observers with no right to lead the process:

---

184 USAID and SIDA were the main donors supporting the project (World Bank 2017).

185 For details about other projects, see the Annual Reports of the LC.

"The NRC and the Carter Center are important partners, so we allow them to sit in these meetings. But we do not want them to drive the process and they don't." (Interview #23, international consultant, 3 May 2012, Monrovia)

The Land Commission was, to my initial surprise, one of the most bureaucratic institutions in terms of negotiating access as a researcher. The very first entry point was an informal contact to an international consultant, working for the Commission, who provided a link to a Liberian Program Officer of the LC. The consultant insisted on confidentiality for our meeting, pointing to the potentially problematic impression that a "meeting of two expats, discussing purely Liberian issues" would convey (Interview #23, international consultant, 3 May 2012, Monrovia). The program officer I contacted with a request for an interview first consulted the issue with her commissioner, who demanded my letter of reference[186] and areas of research interest. Upon a positive result of the examination, I was granted an appointment for an interview with the Commissioner. Once "inside" the LC, I was offered the possibility to attend the meetings of the taskforces and to reach out to other potentially relevant interviewees from the Commission. The level of rigour in the vetting process reflects the sensitivity of the whole issue of land and an extraordinary emphasis on the Liberian ownership of the reform.

Meetings of both taskforces showed a high level of professionalism. The Policy Taskforce hosted around 20 people, and the meetings were chaired by a Liberian Program Officer. The participants included the staff of the LC, representatives from ministries and NCDR/National Archives, and a representative of the Carter Center. During the time of my fieldwork, issues on the agenda of the Policy Taskforce revolved around definitions of public land, as one of the key categories in the future Land Rights Policy. An international consultant presented a version of the draft document being written by the LC[187], explained the principles behind certain formu-

---

186 It was the first and only occasion during my field research when I was asked to present my credentials. Also the entire vetting process before getting an appointment was by far the most rigorous, compared to other institutions, including, e.g., the UN or the US Embassy, where I expected a much higher level of "obstructions".

187 The text was projected on the wall. At the beginning of the first meeting I attended, there was a technical problem with the projector. IT support was called upon, who promptly showed up and fixed the device. This anecdote illustrates not only an unusual level of technical equipment of the LC (the very presence of a projector), but also the level of professionalism of the employees

lations, and solicited feedback from others. The participants asked for clarifications, suggested specifications (such as adding an explicit gender dimension to the text), and voiced concerns about certain formulations, such as in the case of definition of public and government land, where a strong wording was appealed for:

> "Everything that government does can be declared a public purpose. Let's be explicit: it's about corruption, abuse." (Meeting of the LC Policy Taskforce, participant, 29 May 2012, Monrovia)

The points raised by attendees were noted by the consultant and later considered in the draft text. The whole meeting was held in a calm, professional atmosphere. In the end, the chair wrapped up the most important points. Later in an interview, the consultant who guided the meeting pointed to the problematic issues related to ownership of the whole process:

> "You know, keeping it Liberian-driven is slow-going. The point of these taskforces is that they are Liberian-owned. So it's [the policy] gonna be a Liberian product. But it is hard to keep the attention of some of the ministries and agencies. There's meeting fatigue. If you wanna meet once a week on a kind of arcane land issues no one knows anything about, it is kind of hard to keep interest. (...) And then you try to educate people, but the ability to absorb the education you are providing is limited, in a lot of cases. There are all sorts of obstacles. The thing is, on the policy reform side of stuff, we need a high participation rate, we need to at least invite people to the table, we need to keep them informed, we need to keep that door open. They might not, you know, because of laziness, or just lack of interest, they might not walk through it, but in order to produce a policy statement, we can say, you were offered to sit at the table, it's your choice whether you take it or not. But don't try to abstract or criticise our policy reform proposals." (Interview #42, international consultant, 13 June 2012, Monrovia)

(the IT person coming immediately and solving the problem). Another example was the quality of its annual reports and their availability on the website of the LC. The Commission was said to be "probably the only governmental agency to have the report on time" (Interview #23, international consultant, 3 May 2012, Monrovia).

Many of these characteristics apply to the meetings of the LDRT as well—the high level of professionalism (with an emphasis on efficient facilitation and timekeeping on the side of the chair), a calm working atmosphere, and a familiarity among the participants, stemming from the long-term engagement.[188] There were comparatively more participants at the LDRT meetings, with the "core members" (around 15 people from the LC, UN-HABITAT, Ministry of Internal Affairs, Carter Center, and Norwegian Refugee Council) seated around the table, and more than 20 others, mainly from civil society, but also a few representatives of governmental agencies, observing the meeting from a small auditorium on the side of the conference room.

The main topics on the agenda of the taskforce were, at the time of my research, the establishment of the first Land Coordination Center in Zorzor, Lofa county, discussions around the use of alternative dispute resolution (ADR), and the collection of Tribal Certificates. Updates about some actual issues and recent developments in member organisations were also brought to the fore. The most outspoken participants were the representatives of the LC, the UN-HABITAT, and the NRC.

Apart from the formal interaction within taskforces, there was an informal group called "Land Partners Group" (also referred to as "Land Donors Group"), where the donors and implementing partners used to meet and discuss the ongoing projects and plans, to see if "someone can benefit from something someone else does, to inform each other in order not to step on each other's toes" (Interview #31, employee of an international NGO, 28 May 2012, Monrovia). A person from the UN-HABITAT used to call the meetings. The practice was interrupted when that person left her position and the country, but later resumed. Another interruption was brought about by the outbreak of Ebola in 2014 and 2015 (LC 2015).

The Ebola epidemics meant a serious impediment for the activities of the Commission. The UN-HABITAT, as the major partner, as well as the international consultants, left the country, which led to a significant delay in progress of the activities of the LC. Due to the delay, the Commission asked the president to extend the tenure of the body (originally foreseen until March 2015), not only to finish the planned tasks, but also to facilitate the establishment and transition of tasks to the successor institution. The mandate of the Commission was extended by the president to 9 January 2016.

---

188 The LDRT was established in 2010, at the very start of the LC operation.

In the meantime, a draft establishment act of a new agency that should replace the LC after the end of its mandate, overcome the fragmentation in land administration and management, and remove the issue of land from other ministries and agencies, was prepared by the LC and presented to the president in early 2015, following several rounds of reviews and stakeholders' consultations. The Liberia Land Authority Act was approved in October 2016, after a prolonged ratification process and a number of critical comments, especially from the side of civil society. The Land Authority, as the new entity is called, is an independent body of "perpetual existence" (LLA Act 2016: 7), in charge of developing and implementing programs, developing policies, and proposing laws "in support of land governance, including land administration and management" (LLA Act 2016: 8). Currently, the transformation process is underway and the Transitional Committee, that should ensure a smooth transition and uninterrupted implementation of the programs of the former LC and services provided by other agencies, such as NCDR/NA or Ministry of Lands, Mines, and Energy (MLME), has been appointed by the president.[189]

8.6 Actors in focus

8.6.1 The Government of Liberia

From the very beginning of the discussion about land issues, the president has explicitly declared her full support for the reform and establishment of the LC (World Bank 2008, interview #39, Land Commission, 8 June 2012, Monrovia). Given the importance of clear land tenure relations for general macroeconomic stability, growth, and investment, this was not a surprising attitude. The executive branch of the government was not directly involved in the work of the Commission. It received the outputs of its work, such as policies and draft bills, for a further validation in the legislative process. Similar to a number of other governmental agencies, the president has the right to recall the leadership of the Commission.

---

189 There are also provisions to establish decentralised offices of the Land Authority in the counties and a Community Land Management and Development Associations in charge of community land. There has been criticism from civil society about an overly bureaucratic structure of the new body and about a lack of checks-and-balances in the internal decision-making process (Tokpah 2016). The CSOs working in the land sector also complained that they were not sufficiently consulted in the process of drafting the act (Yarsiah 2016).

Despite that, no pressure in this respect was mentioned by the staff of the Commission, nor were there any signs evident for an outside observer.

In spite of the complaints about the scope of financial support from the government and the fact that the government contribution to the budget did not extend to the projects and programs of the Commission, voiced in the Annual Reports, there was stable, substantial financial support of personnel and operational costs of the body during the five years of its operations (LC 2015).

Ministries (such as MLME, MIA, and Ministry of Public Works), as well as other agencies (mainly NCDR) were participating at the meetings of the taskforces (Policy Taskforce and LDRT). However, from the Commission's side, there was a perceived lack of interest in the process of policy formulation. One of the reasons could have been meeting fatigue or reservations about the reform process in general (Interview #23, international consultant, 3 May 2012, Monrovia). This is, of course, a problematic aspect with regard to the ownership of the process. Among the ministerial staff, scepticism prevails with regard to the long-term impact of the LC's work (Informal conversations #64, #65, MLME and MIA employees, 30 November 2012, Monrovia). Firstly, the adoption of policies and recommendations of the Commission depends entirely on the approval of the parliament and the president. It is evident, from the case of the Land Rights Act for example, that even a sound policy is not resistant to interventions from the legislature and the final law runs the risk of being tampered with, approved in an unsatisfactory form, or simply put aside, leaving major concerns that led to its creation unaddressed.[190] Secondly, there is a "bit of a negative feeling" (Interview #23, international consultant, 3 May 2012, Monrovia) with regard to the international presence from the side of the ministries: "People think: 'You do not care. Your contract is over in a few months. But we have to live here'" (ibid).

8.6.2 International actors

Despite the proclaimed sensitivity of land issues and an emphasis on local ownership, there is a high level of international presence in the Commission, as well as of interest from the side of donors, for example,

---

190 In the case of the Land Rights Act, there were concerns from the civil society organisations that especially the provisions related to the protection of customary rights might be tampered with by the legislature (Yarsiah 2016).

in comparison with the Governance Commission. The bulk of the LC's project work has been financed by the international partners: the WB, the UN Peacebuilding Fund (channelled through the UN-HABITAT), and SIDA.[191] There was initial in-kind support from the UN-HABITAT (renovations of the premises of the LC), the NRC (basic equipment of the LCCs), the American Bar Association (vehicles), and other partners.

There is a great deal of donor interest in land issues in Liberia, even to the extent that "it is easy to have conflicts between the donors" (Interview #31, employee of an international NGO, 28 May 2012, Monrovia). In this respect, the negotiation skills of Dr. Brandy, chairman of the Commission, have been praised:

> "He is very good in mediating the thing, keeping the line: here is the role of the LC. This is the way to do it. He also has the luxury, he can also afford to say 'No, I want to do this.' Because there is enough money." (Interview #31, employee of an international NGO, 28 May 2012, Monrovia)

Apart from generous donor support, there is also a high level of international presence at the Commission in a very physical, tangible way. Firstly, the UN-HABITAT has been located in the same compound as the LC, in Sinkor. All other UN agencies reside in the Mamba Point area in central Monrovia.

There was also a special arrangement, called "Land and Policy Institutional Support Project", funded by USAID. In this project, foreign consultants were working one-to-one along with Liberians and providing basic policy and institutional support:

> "There is almost like a shadow LC, consisting of foreigners. It's very clever. The commissioners are all Liberians, as their program officers. And then there's the Land and Policy Institutional Support Project (...) They're all foreign consultants. They're there to help along the process, to work along with Liberians, to respond to their needs, to point out some other things that should be taken into consideration, things like that. I think it's probably a pretty special arrangement, if you go to the other ministries, you won't see that level of cooperation, that level of foreign presence. I don't think, if you go to the Ministry of Justice,

---

191 For some time, even the salaries of the program officers were provided by SIDA (Interview #23, international consultant, 3 May 2012, Monrovia).

there is a shadow Ministry of Justice." (Interview #23, international consultant, 3 May 2012, Monrovia)

Several external actors have been participating at the taskforce meetings, despite the emphasis on Liberian ownership. This was more the case of the LDRT[192], where the UN-HABITAT played a coordinating role in the activities, a representative of USAID was present at the meetings, and the Carter Center and the Norwegian Refugee Council were granted "observers' status" based on the merits of their work in the field of land dispute resolution.[193] Both of them adhered to the observer's role, offering advice or sharing experience during the meetings, but not attempting to drive the decision-making process.

8.6.3 Civil society

In both taskforces, a number of NGOs were participating regularly and actively. In the Policy Taskforce, they were giving input and voicing their concerns about formulations and wording of the policy. In the LDRT, due to the general character of the taskforce meetings, they were sharing information about their current projects and engagement in the dispute resolution. The LC worked in close collaboration with NGOs, which supported the work of the Commission in a practical sense; for example, by providing knowledge of local context and dynamics and doing baseline studies. As in the case of the Early Warning Working Group, the taskforces offered opportunities for networking and means of staying informed about the projects of bigger players, as well as about potential funding opportunities.

Similar to the Governance Commission, civil society has been a crucial partner of the LC, but the Land Commission did not rely on them for the implementation of its projects, as it often has been the case for govern-

---

192 In the Policy Taskforce, the majority of participants were Liberian, with the exception of one international consultant (who was working for the LC), and a representative of the Carter Center.

193 The Carter Center has been involved in alternative dispute resolution projects at the local level. The NRC, although originally a humanitarian actor with a primary focus on work with refugees, has built a sound reputation of being a non-partisan mediator in the field of land disputes. The staff has been working at the grassroots level all over the country, using interest-based mediation as the main tool for dispute resolution.

ment- or UN-led programs. The LC put emphasis on the fact that it did the outreach work on its own, rather than delegating it to anyone else. This approach then translated to a positive perception of the LC among the citizens, reinforced by the presence of the LCCs as "branch offices" on the ground, signalling the proximity and accessibility of the LC to citizens. (Interview #41, Norwegian Refugee Council employee, 11 June 2012, informal conversations #61, #63, #64, November 2012, Monrovia).

Liberian NGOs also represented an important source of input for the drafts and policies the LC produced. The Land Rights Act, as well as other outcomes, have been consulted with the CSOs[194] and other stakeholders in order to gain feedback. In some cases, such as the Sustainable Development Institute (an NGO involved in advocacy for the protection of customary land rights), the engagement was at times so intense that it led to tensions in the working relations with the LC (Kaba and Madan 2014). The NGOs involved in land issues even formed a platform[195], the Civil Society Working Group on Land Rights Reform, performing advocacy and raising awareness about the reform. They campaigned with the legislature for the swift passage of the Land Rights Act in its 2014 version, providing full protection of customary land rights. In Liberian context, the latter represents a not-so-common phenomenon, where the civil society actually performs monitoring and advocacy and, by that, fulfils one of its key functions, ascribed, for example, by Paffenholz (2010), to be found beyond the post-conflict context, in established, stable political environments.

8.7 General Analysis

The Land Commission represents an example of a sound application of a post-conflict peacebuilding strategy in practice. It was a body established to address an issue with a high conflict potential, essential for peace, long-term stability, and economic growth in the country. The importance of a solution for land-related problems has been acknowledged from the highest political level and at the same time consistently supported by bi- and multilateral donors. The institution was designed based on best practices from other countries; got a strong, respected chairman; and was staffed

---

194 The overwhelming majority of the civil society actors in the field of land reform (as well as in other areas) are actually Liberian NGOs. Despite that, my interviewees, various reports, and media always used the term "civil society".

195 After the draft of the Land Right Policy was presented in 2014.

with qualified Liberian employees. The presence of land specialists in the country (e.g., Dr. Jeanette Carter at the University of Liberia) represented an additional support for the endeavour.

One clear and fundamental challenge the LC faced was the daunting scope of the work it was supposed to accomplish in the limited time of its original five-year mandate. Some tasks in the field of land administration and management are projects that take decades to finish (such as building a cadastre), and experts in the field were unanimous in the opinion that it is hardly possible to accomplish everything in such a short time. especially true given the state of disarray of the whole system of land administration, and the absence of basic structures, institutions, and policies in the field. However, as the discrepancy between the scope of the work and limited time span of the Commission was evident from the beginning, plans for a successor body were envisaged early on.

A more serious challenge is the implementation and sustainability of the results of the LC's work. The LC was, similar to the Governance Commission, only a think-tank, supposed to produce recommendations and policies that have to be approved in a standard legislative process. And this is where the value of the LC's work can be jeopardised. As the case of the Land Rights Act shows, there is no guarantee that a sound policy, addressing contentious issues and aiming for protecting rights and groups that had been marginalised, will be approved in its original, substantial form—or approved at all. In other words, there is no guarantee that an elaborated peacebuilding measure survives a clash with "politics as usual".

Another similarity with the GC is the same emphasis on an inclusive, consultative process and strong outreach to the local level, which contributes to the positive image and perception of the body among the citizens. In contrast to the Governance Commission, which is a body that generates a lot of tensions and tacit resentment *vis-à-vis* other domestic political institutions, the LC is on good terms, with the executive branch, as well as with the ministries and agencies involved in land issues. Even the new Land Authority, which is supposed to centralise and take over the duties of other institutions, does not seem to generate much resentment from their side, mainly due to the provision that foresees a takeover of the personnel, touched by the measure, to the new authority (LAA Act 2016).

Some of the international staff perceived a slightly negative feeling about the international presence in the sense of the temporary engagement of the international consultants. On the other hand, the working relationship of the LC's employees to the international personnel seemed generally friendly and positive (Interview #39, LC Commissioner, 8 June

2012, informal conversations #61, #63, November 2012, Monrovia). The comparatively high level of international presence in the LC, especially in the cases of everyday "institutional support", makes it hard to assess the actual impact of the foreign element on the process. It is, for sure, very much dependent on a particular approach of each employee or consultant. In the context of a close, one-to-one collaboration, it is quite easy to exercise considerable influence. Such an impact was not visible at the meetings of the taskforces, but could well take place in the processes of the everyday functioning of the body.

With regard to the financial constraints of the Commission, a topic that was repeatedly mentioned in the Annual Reports, opinions vary (cf. interviews #23, #31, #61, May–November 2012, Monrovia). On the one hand, the premises and equipment of the institution, the level of professionalism and quality of the outcomes of its work, as well as the simple comparison of budgets with other governmental agencies, show that the LC was relatively well catered to. On the other hand, the fact that the government did not provide adequate support for the projects and programs of the Commission, rendering it dependent on international donors if its mandate was to be accomplished, was repeatedly raised as an issue. Compared with the GC again, the LC received a relatively similar level of support from the GoL (around 1 million USD for the GC vs. 870,000 USD for the LC). However, it is important to bear in mind that the LC exceeded the GC in the number of personnel several times over.

8.8 Conclusion

Land issues are not a topic that commonly features in the top positions of peacebuilding checklists. In Liberia, however, land has been acknowledged to have high conflict potential, and solving land issues is crucial for peace and stability, as well as for the future political and economic development of the country. As such, it has been promptly included among the priority topics of postwar reconstruction. The conditions for the reform have been very much favourable in Liberia: the support from the highest political level and popular demand have met the interest of major donors and external actors. The reform has been further facilitated by the fact that major donors (both bi- and multilateral) have experience from implementation of similar projects elsewhere, as well as a number of expert personnel available for short- or long-term consultancies.

Land reform has been treated as a sensitive issue, and there has been a great deal of emphasis on Liberian ownership of the process and results. As in the case of the Governance Commission, strong leadership, professionalism and dedication of the employees, and the focus on an inclusive, consultative process, have been crucial factors facilitating the impact of the LC, very much in line with Skelcher's (2005) point about the performance of agencies in contexts with a low level of institutionalisation. Unlike the GC, the Land Commission enjoyed more support from the side of donors. With regard to the unprecedented level of an international presence and its role in the everyday operations of the Commission, especially in the framework of Policy and Institutional Support Project administered by USAID, it is difficult to assess the actual influence of the foreign consultants over the process of policy formulation and overall functioning of the body. It depends, after all, to a large extent on the personal attitude of particular individuals. However, both the international personnel and their Liberian counterparts were unanimous in the opinion that the process has been steered by Liberians.

A particularly sensitive aspect in this regard is the interconnectedness of land with commercial interests, such as logging, mining, or large-scale agricultural concessions, where there is a lot of money at stake. Plans to regulate a hitherto "grey area", which in the past gave a great deal of room to manoeuvre to low-cost operations and high profit rates, go directly against the interests of the companies involved. There was no presence, nor were there any signs of influence of commercial actors at the work of the Commission. The attention of the companies has been instead strategically focused on the legislature, as the pivotal actor in the process (Maclean 2016).

The interests and objectives of particular actors are quite similar, as in the field of the governance reform. The institution in charge of a reform (the LC or the GC, respectively) is devoted to a clear goal to bring about change and create policies that underpin it. This "reform spirit", however, clashes with the position of the ministries and other governmental bodies. These are rather sceptical with regard to the reforms and "conservative" in resisting them, despite the obvious dysfunctionality of the system. In some ways, the envisioned change brings uncomfortable disruption to the ways things used to be so far. The parliament plays a key role of a gatekeeper in the reform process, determining the fate of the reform by allowing a policy to become a law. Taking this into consideration, it is indeed striking, that there is no concentrated attention given to the structured work with the legislature, be it in a form of informal preliminary talks or simple communication and securing future support for the policy approval neither growing organically from the domestic side, nor suggested from the international one. For the international actors, land represents an attractive field with a lot of potential for peacebuilding and with clearly defined tasks, bringing easily presentable results. Liberian NGOs have been active and outspoken, especially with regard to the passage of the Land Rights Bill through the legislature. Apart from the usual "information, support, and implementation" function, to be found in other fields of engagement in the reconstruction process, here they perform the monitoring and advocacy functions. Triggered by the importance of the issue at stake, their engagement can be considered the first step in the direction of strengthening civil society as an actor in the political process.

The national government has been consistently supportive *vis-à-vis* the work of the Commission. On the other hand, the legislature turned out to be obstructive with regard to the approval of the Land Rights Policy. This represents a frustrating example of the peacebuilding practice, where the fate of a very much needed measure (the Land Rights Policy), locally produced by an appropriate institutional structure (the LC), is put into jeopardy by the common political process and vested interests of powerful local or international actors.

Land issues, after all, mirror major societal cleavages in Liberia: the tensions between Americo-Liberians and natives, between youth and elders, strangers and autochthons. The contention around land reflects discriminatory, unequal, and unjust relationships and practices that are deeply interwoven in the social fabric and therefore hard to change. In this regard, a recently introduced approach to dealing with land disputes based on the alternative dispute resolution (ADR) techniques, used by the actors involved in the field, can also indirectly contribute to the transformation of the way conflicts in general are being dealt with. As such, the ADR can support non-violent ways of conflict resolution on an everyday basis, which would have an undoubtedly positive effect on the sustainability of peace in the country.[196]

Land reform in Liberia shows that it is possible to generate a substantial external support even for an issue, that is normally not part of the peacebuilding packages, if the field is attractive for the potential donors. With

---

196 Cf. the results of a study by the Innovation for Poverty Action and Yale University that found out that peacebuilding, dialogue, and civic education programs actually increase the incidence of land conflict, but the conflicts are less likely to be violent (Blattman, Hartman and Blair 2011).

regard to the lack of progress in the field, the reasons are partly linked to the scope of the task that requires considerable time (e.g., putting up a functional cadastre), but the decisive factor remains the obstructions in the legislative process, which is influenced by the interests of powerful actors behind the scenes.

Chapter 9 Gender in peacebuilding: Addressing gender-based violence in Liberia

"Gender makes the world go round."
Cynthia Enloe: Bananas, Beaches and Bases (2014)

9.1 Gender and conflict

It has been gradually recognised that gender[197] has its place in the design of peacebuilding strategies. There is a consensus about violent conflicts being an ultimately gendered experience, one that affects women in different ways than men. Initially, when gender was acknowledged as a relevant category, there was an exclusive focus on women and emphasis on inclusion of measures that take women specifically into consideration in the process of peace talks, in the design of the peace agreement, and in the postwar phase. Later, men were "included" in the gender lens as well.[198]

9.2 Women in conflict

There are many clichés linked to the role women play in violent conflicts. For a long time, women were perceived and presented (by scholars and practitioners, but also in the popular narratives) primarily as victims. This image has been linked to the conception of war as a predominantly masculine field of activity, related to particular norms and behaviours, practices and values, regarded as purely masculine: bravery, endurance, honour, and

---

197 The concept "refers not to *essential/biological* differences between women and men but to *asymmetrical social constructions* of masculinity and femininity" (True 2001: 236). As such, it is reinforced (some authors would argue that even created) by our actions and as such, "it exists only so far as it is ritualistically and repetitively performed" (O'Reilly 2013: 59, see also Butler 1990).

198 Inclusion sounds rather ironic in this respect, since generally, men's presence has always been taken for granted in conflict resolution approaches and women represented the new, specific category introduced. However, gender scholarship had focused predominantly on women for a considerable time and men have been included only in the "second step".

rationality (O'Reilly 2013, Goldstein 2006, Barrett 1996). A long-prevalent popular "gender cleavage" preserved the image of male fighters and female non-combatants, which led to the general masculinisation of combat and feminisation of peace and "normal life" (Elshtain 1995).

To be sure, women are often victims. This is not to downplay that fact. During conflict, men are often forced to hide, as they are targeted by the armed factions. Women, on the other hand, have to leave homes to care for the basic needs of the family, to search for food, water, supplies, etc. They also engage in commerce. Often, women enjoy more free movement than men during conflicts, since they are regarded as non-dangerous. This, on the other hand, contributes to their increased exposure (El Jack 2003, Utas 2003).

Despite the stereotypes about "peaceful women and violent men", women also take up arms and join their male counterparts in combat.[199] Often, they act as logistic experts, spies, munition workers, prostitutes, or camp followers.[200] An aspect often brought up with regard to child soldiers, namely that they transgressed the hitherto clear division between victims and perpetrators of violence, can be equally applied to women. They are often both (Wessels 2009, Rosen 2005, Honwana 2007). Besides all that, they also stay mothers, sisters, wives, and girlfriends (Enloe 1983). In Liberia, there were a number of women engaged in combat during the civil war. There were some well-known, distinguished fighters (such as the Black Diamond, Julia Rambo, Martina Johnson, Ruth "Attila" Milton), and NPFL and INPFL even had all-female units (Utas 2003). There was also a special unit of female bodyguards assigned to Taylor, dubbed "Charlie's Angels" (Reno 2004).

9.3 Change of the gender roles

The change of the external conditions that violent conflicts bring leads inevitably to a transformation of gender identities and roles, with a transfor-

---

199 There are different reasons why, the main one being to ensure their own security. They can join by choice, but many women are being abducted as "bush wives", and then accompany their boyfriends to the warfront. The majority, however, does not receive any formal training (e.g., Utas 2003).

200 To encompass all these possible roles, the term of "women associated with fighting forces" (WAFF) has been established and used as an alternative to a "female combatant", to reflect the fact that most women do not actually engage in combat as such.

mation of economic and social roles accompanying the latter shift (Moser and Clark 2001, Meintjes et al. 2002).[201] The phenomenon was noticed during WWI and WWII. Men were absent, so women had to take up some of their roles and enter fields and professions hitherto reserved to men. On the one hand, this change can be used as an opportunity for a transformation and reconfiguration of gender roles and relations in the postwar phase (Meintjes et al. 2002). On the other hand, it often becomes a point of contention after the conflict, when everything is expected to be "normalised" again. O'Reilly (2013) speaks of the return of "domestic patriarchy", often reinforced by the arrival of "international patriarchy", with peacekeepers refusing to take gender into account in the design and implementation of post-conflict strategies.

In fact, the whole concept of "post-conflict" is being put into question by some authors.[202] Meintjes et al. (2002) argues that there is "no aftermath" for women. After the official cessation of hostilities, the level of violence and insecurity for women stays the same as before (Porter 2007), and can be so prevalent, that it becomes "normalised" (Handrahan 2004). In addition, there is often an increase in trafficking, prostitution, domestic violence, rape, and other forms of gendered violence (Aoláin et al. 2011, Cohen and Nordås 2014, Handrahan 2004, Pankhurst 2008, Rehn and Johnson Sirleaf 2002). Some potential explanations for the phenomenon are the long-term effects of "combatant socialization during wartime" (Krause: 109), and of trauma and brutality experienced during the conflict (Skjelsbaek 2013, Liebling Kalifani 2011). The postwar period is characterised by fluidity and changing of social norms and orders in all spheres of life (Abramowitz 2014). This transformation only adds to the widespread feeling of insecurity and of being "lost" in the new phase of "the aftermath".

9.4 Gender-based violence in conflict

In the 90s, with a number of conflicts deliberately targeting civilian populations as a means of intimidation, instilling fear, and forcing displacement, rape started to be used as a weapon of war on a mass scale, and women came forward again as victims (Baaz and Stern 2009, Enloe 2000,

---

201 Gender roles are generally in a constant flux, but during wartime, the change is much more intensive.
202 See the theoretical chapter for more details about the argument.

Goldstein 2006, Hansen 2000, Stiglmayer 1994). The conflicts in former Yugoslavia, the DRC, and the genocide in Rwanda come to mind as first-hand examples. But the label of rape as a "weapon of war" covers a complex, multi-causal phenomenon. It is important to bear in mind that "violence against women in war is not necessarily a reflection of exceptional circumstances, but rather a reflection of a broader phenomenon of female insecurity and victimization in 'war' and 'peace'" (DeRouen and Newman 2015: 238).

There are several interpretations trying to explain this phenomenon. An essentialist perspective, based on biologically driven sexual aggression (e.g., by Brownmiller 1975), claims that "all women in war zones are potential victims of sexual violence because war increases men's opportunities for rape" (Krause 2015: 104), and that "rape happens during war for the same reasons it happens during peace"—because it stems from "inequality, discrimination, male domination and aggression, misogyny and the entrenched socialization of sexual myth" (Tompkins 1994: 851). This approach, however, offers no explanation for men as targets of GBV in conflicts, nor for different patterns of sexual violence in wars.

The structuralist perspective emphasises the socio-cultural group identity, arguing that women are targeted because they belong to a certain ethnic, religious, political, or social group and their humiliation shames their male relatives for not being able to provide adequate protection (Bastick, Grimm and Kunz 2007). In the paternalistic context, women are regarded as property, and as such, they are part of the fighters' bounty just as any other looted "goods". However, this argument does not explain the targeting of men either. In addition, it does not sufficiently take into consideration the fact that there are conflicts where sexual violence is largely absent (Cohen 2013, Wood 2009).

In fact, even in cases where it occurs, the phenomenon is far from being uniform. There is not a universal purpose, nor a single pattern of the violence. It might vary in many respects; there can be different forms of sexual violence (mass rape in Bosnia as a means of ethnic cleansing and diluting the bloodlines of an ethnicity, vs. sexual torture in Liberia, e.g., Cohen et al. 2013, or "comfort women" in Japan during World War II). There are also different motives on both the individual and group levels: opportunistic, strategic, and private (Wood 2012, Eriksson Baaz and Stern 2009). It can serve as a tactic to terrify the population and a means of "clearing out" a territory (as in eastern DRC or Libya).[203] Sexual violence can serve as a strategy of combatant socialisation and strengthening the group cohesion (Cohen 2013, Goldstein 2006). There is also a differing approach to the phenomenon by commanders and the leadership of armed factions, ranging from encouragement and tolerance[204] to suppression.[205] In this respect, the level of obedience and command enforcement remains a crucial variable.

9.5 Conventions and international documents

There is a range of international conventions and "soft-law" instruments, dealing with the role of women in the field of peace and security and trying to address the particular challenges they face.

In 1979, CEDAW (Convention on the Elimination of All Forms of Discrimination Against Women) was adopted by the UN General Assembly, and has since been ratified by 189 states.[206] A blueprint for advancing women's rights, the Beijing Declaration and Platform for Action were signed in 1995 during the 4th UN Conference on Women—a culmination point of two decades of women's activism, starting in 1975.[207]

In 2000, UN SC Resolution 1325 was adopted. This is the most common reference with regard to gender at the international level, which led to the establishment of gender action plans at the level of national states in a number of countries.[208] The resolution recognises that women are disproportionately affected by violent conflict and calls for "special measures to protect women and girls from gender-based violence" in armed conflicts. Apart from the protection, it also reiterates their roles in peace processes and calls for increasing women's participation in all stages of

---

203 The territorial aspect came to the fore, for example, during the partition of states (India and Pakistan in 1947, Pakistan and Bangladesh 1971), where women from particular ethnic groups were targeted to ensure that they would never return and the separation becomes irreversible (Hayden 2000).

204 With sexual violence as a "social practice", there are cases where the cost of suppression is perceived as too high (Wood 2009).

205 RUF in Sierra Leone prohibited rape as "counter-revolutionary", see Marks 2014.

206 As of August 2017 (https://treaties.un.org/Pages/ViewDetails.aspx?src=TREATY &mtdsg_no=IV-8&chapter=4&lang=en).

207 The year was declared to be the "Year of Women" by the UN.

208 In 67 out of 192 signatory countries, as of August 2017 (http://www.peacewome n.org/member-states).

peace processes, as well as in the conflict prevention, resolution, and post-conflict reconstruction. It calls for the promotion of women's rights and the mainstreaming of gender into all aspects of peacekeeping operations. However, feminist scholars criticised the resolution as overly focusing on protection, portraying women mainly as victims and not recognising their agency (Shepherd 2011).

The resolutions that followed focused more on the issue of gender-based violence in conflict situations and women's engagement in peace processes. In 2008, adopted as a response to widespread sexual violence in the eastern DRC[209], UN SC Resolution 1820 for the first time ever recognised that conflict-related sexual violence "can constitute, a war crime, a crime against humanity, or a constitutive act with respect to genocide" (UN SCR 2008) and represent a threat to world peace and security. The resolution called for "the immediate and complete cessation by all parties to armed conflict of all acts of sexual violence against civilians with immediate effect" (ibid.) and upon development of mechanisms that could provide protection against it. In 2009, UN SCR 1888 aimed to support 1820 by calling for the establishment of effective implementation mechanisms, such as the appointment of a Special Representative of the Secretary General (SRSG) for addressing the issue of SGBV[210] and the inclusion of the latter on the agenda of peace negotiations. The agency of women was further emphasised in UN SC Resolution 1889, which called for a greater focus on the empowerment of women, in addition to their protection. It urged "the Member States, international and regional organizations to take further measures to improve women's participation during all stages of peace processes, particularly in conflict resolution, post-conflict planning and peacebuilding" (UN SCR 2009). It also demanded creation of indicators measuring the progress of 1325's implementation.

In December 2010, UN SC Resolution 1960 called upon the Secretary General to "establish monitoring, analysis and reporting arrangements on conflict-related sexual violence" (UN SCR 2010). In 2013, UN SC Resolution 2106 acknowledged that "women's political, social and economic empowerment, gender equality and the enlistment of men and boys in the effort to combat all forms of violence against women are central to long-

---

209 Contrary to 1325, which was perceived as a result of the pressure "from below", 1820 is an example of a top-down initiative brought about by US Secretary of State Condoleezza Rice (Gunda Werner Institute 2018).

210 The office was established in February 2010.

term efforts to prevent sexual violence in armed conflict and post-conflict situations" (UN SCR 2013).

The same year, UN SC Resolution 2122 was adopted and discussed the critical contribution of civil society in conflict prevention, resolution, and peacebuilding, as well as the importance of the interaction of the Security Council with civil society (both in the headquarters and during field visits). In addition, it names the economic empowerment of women as crucial for postwar stabilisation of societies, promises to devote more attention to women, peace, and security in all areas of the UN work, and encourages the inclusion of provisions on gender equality and women's empowerment in peacekeeping operation mandates, including the appointment of gender advisors (UN SCR 2013).

The Global Summit to End Sexual Violence in Conflict in 2014 can be seen as a climax of the aforementioned activism, with 140 UN member states signing the Declaration of Commitment to End Sexual Violence in Conflict. Despite all these efforts and a well-deserved attention the issue has been granted, the commitments listed have not translated into tangible changes.

9.6 Women in peace negotiation processes[211]

Peace negotiation tables are one of the arenas where the lack of women's presence is visible at the first sight. Despite their indisputably active involvement in conflicts around the globe and the fact that they are being severely affected by war, women have not been commonly included and invited to peace negotiations. As the UNIFEM report from 2012 states, from 1992, women have accounted for 2,4% of signatories on peace agreements, less than 10% of peace negotiators, and until now, there was not a single case of a women appointed as a chief negotiator (cited in Ellerby 2013). There is a significant body of research on the importance of wom-

---

211 Feminist scholars argue that peace processes have to be considered more broadly than just the talks happening around the negotiation table (Porter 2007, de Alwis et al. 2013) and should take into account not only the informal processes, a range of actors who are not covered by the media, but also the origins of the conflict, their broader social, political, economic, and historical contexts, as well as the political stakes involved. The subsequent implementation of the peace agreement is also part of the process. Although acknowledging this perspective, the following section will limit itself to the narrow understanding of peace processes.

en's inclusion in peace processes (Aoláin et al. 2011, Hudson 2009, Hunt 2002). In fact, women are present and involved in all stages of broadly conceived peace processes, which include long-term engagement beyond the formal "Track 1" negotiations. On the other hand, they are still underrepresented in the latter. Despite the fact that they are often paving the way to peace by informally engaging warring parties, or putting pressure on them, women are often not "high enough" in the hierarchy to be included in the official peace negotiation processes. This has been slowly changing. After all, they represent half of the population of the affected countries. To exclude them would mean that half of the population is being excluded. In the past, there was a generally accepted assumption that peace agreements are "gender neutral". However, in reality, seemingly gender neutral agreement is very often discriminatory, since it does not take women into consideration at all (de Alwis et al. 2013).

There are several arguments used by practitioners, and female peace activists themselves, as to why women should be involved in formal peace processes: because they are more peaceful, based on their moral legitimacy as mothers, or because they were victims of the war. The question, however, might be very well the opposite—why should not they be included? Feminist scholars offer several reasons for women's inclusion, such as the right to represent their specific interests, assuming that their needs and concerns might be different from men's, or because they can bring up issues that are crucial for the transformation of post-conflict societies as a whole (de Alwis et al. 2013). What they have in common is the "paradox of sexual difference" (Scott 1996), where they seek to emphasise the difference and to reject it at the same time—an approach characteristic to the whole feminist political movement. The most comprehensive argument for women's inclusion remains, however, the right to be represented simply as political subjects.

Sometimes, even if included, women's participation is rather tokenised, showcasing inclusiveness and the "democratic character" of the negotiations, while the real decision-making takes place elsewhere. Another question is, once at the table, whom and which interests do those women represent (de Alwis et al. 2013). Edita Tahiri, the only woman participating in the negotiation with Serbia on the Albanian side, who has acknowledged that she pushed an Albanian nationalist agenda rather than women's interests (Villellas Arino 2010: 35-36), can serve as an apt counter-example of the simplistic view that women always represent other women.[212]

9.7 Peace negotiations in Liberia

During the long series of peace talks throughout the 1990s, Liberian women were not invited to the table. In the course of the conflict, many suffered from the armed violence, displacement, and diseases, and were exposed to sexual violence of an unprecedented scale and brutality. Their discontent rose. They organised themselves for peaceful protests. In a mass action for peace, they mobilised a broad spectrum of women across ethnic and religious lines, dividing Liberian society. Dressed in white[213], they "sat for peace", marched through the streets of Monrovia to the Capitol and Executive Mansion, and even went on a sex strike (Gbowee 2011, Lederach 2015).[214]

Later, in the early 2000s, a delegation of women went to Accra, where the peace talks were held. Their engagement gained international attention and media coverage. They were not invited to the table, but they made their presence felt by blocking the hall of the hotel, where negotiations took place, to put pressure on the leaders to come to a conclusion.[215] Women's engagement went beyond the borders of the states and took a regional dimension, with cross-national networks, such as MARWOPNET (Mano River Women in Peace Network) or WIPNET (Women in Peacebuilding Network), created in 2002 as a program within WANEP (West Africa Network for Peacebuilding) taking the lead. Leymah Gbowee, a

---

212 Other examples include instances where women are present as family members of influential men. Some well-known cases of this phenomenon are India, Indonesia, and the Philippines (Porter 2007).

213 In the protests, they raised their voices as women, but more importantly, they referred to their identities as mothers (Lederach 2015). The whole movement was deeply embedded in local context and tradition, with white as a colour traditionally associated with childbirth and the mass-aspect of the protest, with a collective action being a traditional way of women's political engagement and means of protest (Moran 2006).

214 A measure that might seem amusing (cf. Gbowee 2011), but is in fact very serious, since it entails a risk of a violent reaction from their spouses.

215 A notorious anecdote has often been evoked how Leymah Gbowee threatened to undress herself—a measure used by mothers to shame their sons and believed to bring a "terrible curse" (Gbowee 2011: 162) on the men who would see the naked woman.

Nobel Peace Prize laureate[216] from 2011, was a leading figure in this movement.

After the war, although the "official" fighting stopped, there was a period of high insecurity and uncertainty for everyone, but for women in particular (Abramowitz 2014). Apart from the almost non-existent rule of law and inefficient police forces, there was the "post-bellum" reaction of men. There is a general tendency for a "backlash", where "violent masculinities" often gain prominence in postwar times (Specht 2013). The level of domestic violence and sexual gender-based violence (SGBV) was particularly high at that time. The presence of international peacekeepers added to the momentum, with prostitution and transactional sex being widespread (Beber et al. 2017, Liebling-Kalifani 2011).[217] Various authors also talk about the economisation of intimate relationships as one of the consequences of war (Schäfer 2008, Utas 2003, cf. Oldenburg 2014 for DRC).

9.8 Gender and post-conflict peacebuilding: theoretical aspects

As already mentioned in the theoretical chapter, the whole concept of post-conflict reconstruction has often been questioned by feminist scholars. The currently prevalent peacebuilding approaches, based on the notion of liberal peace, have been criticised from the feminist positions because, although they seem to be gender-neutral, they often fail to take gender into consideration.[218] The values that the liberal approach to peace is built upon (e.g., democracy, human rights, rule of law) do not automatically ensure that both women and men benefit equally, mainly due to the fact that women are still often excluded from the high level of decision-making, starting with the peace negotiations (Reilly 2007: 159, Lister 1997, Pateman 1988, Phillips 1991).

---

216 Gbowee was awarded the prize together with Ellen Johnson Sirleaf and a Yemeni journalist Tawakkol Karman.

217 Liberia is far from being an exception in this respect. Similar developments have been observed in a number of countries emerging from a civil conflict. See, e.g., Higate and Henry (2004) for evidence from Sierra Leone and DRC, Withworth (2004) for Somalia, or Jennings and Nikolić-Ristanović (2009) for Kosovo.

218 Alternatively, they include women in a mechanical, "add-women-and-stir" manner.

Feminist scholars often criticise the fact that "mainstream" peacebuilding does not recognise women's engagement in peacebuilding, and is focused predominantly on formal activities after the peace agreement is reached. The whole scope of peacebuilding work at the grassroots level, taking place during all stages of conflict, where women are actively involved, therefore falls off the scope (Porter 2007). Another stream of critique is related to the fact that gender has been adopted and "mainstreamed" to the peacebuilding discourse by the UN and leading international donors, but more fundamental critiques voiced by feminist scholars remain unaddressed (O'Reilly 2013).

9.9 Postwar phase in Liberia

The CPA itself does not take gender perspective into much consideration, apart from mentioning women as a vulnerable group, worth "particular attention" of the NTGL, and ensuring gender balance in the membership of particular institutions (e.g., NTGL or Governance Reform Commission). There were some measures mainstreamed in the design and implementation of the DDR, but specific needs of female ex-combatants, including exposure to SGBV, were not adequately addressed (Basini 2013). Shortly after the peace conference, the first structured post-conflict processes took place—DDR, SSR, and reconciliation.

The DDR process in Liberia did consider female ex-combatants as a group with specific needs, which was already an improvement in comparison to earlier DDRs in other countries. However, there were still a number of obstacles for women's participation, including the fear of being stigmatised, inadequate facilities, and absence of services at cantonment sites (Basini 2013).[219]

The Security System Reform (SSR) included some gender-specific measures[220] and specifically targeted women for recruitment into security

---

219 Very limited medical services were available; there were no separate hygienic facilities for women, which increased the risk of sexual harassment, etc. For more details see Basini 2013.

220 Gender was included in the curricula and training for the police and army, and special units for the protection of women and children within the LNP were created. However, general policies or guidelines on gender or sexual harassment have not been developed (DCAF 2011).

forces.[221] Gender-based violence (GBV) was an issue that was granted special attention by the Truth and Reconciliation Commission (TRC), which established a special committee tasked with oversight of the gender aspect of the reconciliation process. And although women provided about half of the statements the Commission collected, former fighters' testimonies were almost completely missing, due to the related danger of stigmatisation and ostracism, which resulted in a prevailing representation of women as victims in the conflict (Pietsch 2010).[222] The abuse and violence men suffered during the conflict was largely left out in the public hearings and the overall truth-telling discourse. All these aspects contributed to the reproduction of the already existing gender stereotypes related to the conflict (Pietsch 2010).

Gender was also included in the Poverty Reduction Strategy as one of the cross-cutting issues to be mainstreamed into all policies and decisions in the postwar era. GBV was mentioned in the section on "Strengthening Human and Personal Security" as a "major problem" (PRS 2008: 54), ranking "among the most common crimes reported nationwide" (ibid.). Challenges, such as limited human and financial resources, weak protection and legal support, and gaps in medical and psychosocial services, were acknowledged as serious impediments to attempts for change. The Agenda for Transformation lists gender among the cross-cutting issues as well and focuses more extensively on the options and possible strategies for the economic empowerment of women, their increased enrolment at school, and availability of adequate health care (Agenda for Transformation 2012).[223]

In 2009, a National Gender Policy (NGP) was developed by the Ministry of Gender and Development (MoGD), as a result of a participatory process involving a wide range of stakeholders, from ministries and governmental agencies, civil society, media practitioners, and cultural and traditional leaders. The document called for "integration of gender perspectives in all policies and programs" (NGP 2009: 5) and set a broad goal to "promote gender equitable, socio-economic development and improve national capacities for enhanced gender mainstreaming in the national development

---

221 There was a 20% quota for women in the armed forces set by the GoL and UNMIL, and a special Female Recruitment Program was created within the LNP. As of 2009, women formed 12,6% of the Liberian police force (DCAF 2011), increasing to 17,4% by 2013 (Bacon 2015).

222 Apart from the fear of stigmatisation, there were also other issues linked to logistics, mobility, etc., that prevented women from giving their testimonies.

223 All the documents mentioned in this section focus predominantly on *women* in their objectives and recommendations.

processes" (NGP 2009: 7). Although it defines the roles of different stake-holders in broad terms, the policy remains a general outline that does not include specific measures or implementation strategies.

9.10 Gender-based violence in Liberia

It is important to bear in mind that the statistics are very inaccurate. They catch only the ratio of GBV cases that were reported, so the real scope of the phenomenon is hard to assess.[224] At the same time, different actors might have different motivations to manipulate them (DeLargy 2013). Still, the numbers indicate that GBV in Liberia is widespread.[225] In 2014, there were 1392 incidents of GBV reported, with 626 of them being rape (UN SRSG for Sexual violence in conflict 2015).[226] An SGBV report from 2016 speaks of 1511 cases of SGBV in 2014 (with 708 rapes) and 1555 cases in 2015 (with 803 rapes) reported to various recipients: health care providers, law enforcement agencies, and NGOs (UN OHCHR and UNMIL 2016). Twenty-four cases in 2014 and 34 in 2015 resulted in a conviction. Despite the questionable level of the statistics' accuracy, the numbers give an idea of the scope of the phenomenon and the discrepancy between the occurrence of the GBV and the extremely low rates of conviction (UN OHCHR and UNMIL 2016). In the long term, there is a steady, increasing trend in the number of reported cases of GBV, with a particular increase in child rape.[227]

Violence against women is a phenomenon rooted in Liberia's history well before the civil war broke out. Liberia has a legacy of inequality of social relations in all spheres of economic and social life, and women were no exception in these general settings. Their position was volatile mainly due to the lack of rights they had in customary marriages and to their sub-ordinate position in gender relations. Sexual and domestic violence were not uncommon before the war, but the conflict shifted the phenomenon

---

224 Most of the statistics come from a single data set collected by the MoGD.

225 There are also potentially harmful "traditional" beliefs that might indirectly contribute to GBV, such as the belief that children's blood can bring power and wealth (GoL-UN 2011).

226 Among them, 606 victims were minors under 18 years of age (UN SRSG for Sexual violence in conflict 2015).

227 In 2012, the percentage of total rapes that were reported against children under 12 years of age reached 44%. One year later, it was 52,7% (GBV Prevention Report 2013).

to a deliberate strategy of instilling fear and humiliating the population. Statistics estimate that by the end of the war, 40% of the total population, with an estimated 61%–77% of women, were subjected to sexual violence (GoL-UN 2011). With regard to violence against men, about one-third of men associated with fighting forces and 7% of civilians are estimated to have been subjected to sexual violence, with many more forced to commit or witness it (GoL-UN 2011). Contrary to women, who could at least to some extent take advantage of psychosocial and trauma-healing services after the war, men's traumatic experiences went largely unaddressed. In addition to that, men were confronted with the change of gender roles the conflict brought with it, which were often bitter pills to swallow.[228] However, the changes in gender relations occurring during the conflict did not translate into durable changes in gender roles in the aftermath. Perpetrators of GBV were no longer fighters, but civilian men, in most cases from the immediate vicinity of the victim. There are still major gender inequalities rooted in socio-cultural institutions.

Poverty represents a crucial structural problem, creating "the conditions in which the problem of gender based violence thrives" (GoL-UN 2011: 62). Men have been confronted with a perceived loss of power and authority stemming from their inability to provide for their families and to fulfil their expected social roles by doing so. There have been many initiatives focusing on improving women's status and economic empowerment, but the NGOs hardly ever target men, which leads to feelings of resentment and marginalisation from the side of the latter. This, in combination with distress and traumatic experiences from the war, makes men prone to violent behaviour (GoL-UN 2011). In addition, the high level of unemployment leads to a situation where children also engage in income-generating activities, in order to contribute to the family budget, which makes them an easy target of sexual violence.[229]

Various measures have been adopted in order to improve the situation, to address GBV and gender inequality. The first of them was an amendment of the Customary Marriages Law in 2003, granting women, among other provisions, the right to inherit one-third of the property acquired in the marriage. In 2005, the national transitional government approved a new law, broadening the definition of rape and making it gender-neutral,

---

228 E.g., women often engaged in extra-marital affairs with fighters to provide for their families.

229 Children engaged in "street-selling business" are particularly vulnerable in this respect.

and also including gang rape as a specific case. In October 2017, however, there was an initiative in the legislature to amend the rape law again, making it a bailable offense, which unleashed a wave of protests from women's organisations in the country (Karmo 2017).[230]

In 2006, a National GBV Plan of Action was developed in consultation with relevant stakeholders, with a goal of reducing the occurrence of GBV by 30% in five years. The plan aims to strengthen the capacities of health care providers in prevention and response to GBV, to empower the justice system, and to develop an integrated protection system nationwide.[231]

There is a lot of engagement and financial support for programs in the field of gender and, more specifically, in the fight against gender-based violence. There is a Joint Government-UN Program on GBV, and a number of donors and international NGOs that engage in women empowerment. International NGOs brought the human rights and gender equality discourse, spread through workshops and awareness-raising campaigns, but in practice, the situation of women has not changed much, especially in rural areas.

9.11 *"Factor Ellen"*

At the end of 2005, Ellen Johnson Sirleaf was elected president—the first elected female head of state in Africa, as she is often referred in the media. During her campaign, she presented herself as an alternative to other (male) candidates in terms of her education and experience, but she also played the "maternal" card, presenting herself as a "mother of the nation".[232] In her election campaign, she specifically targeted women[233], with promises to improve their lives, and succeeded in mobilising robust

---

230 The rationale behind this move was to improve the situation in crowded prisons, where the vast majority of detainees are being held in pre-trial detention. This "added value" is, however, questionable, compared to the consequences for the victims, both psychological ones and in terms of security.

231 The Plan of Action covers the period between 2006 and 2011. To my knowledge, there is no successive document to the plan.

232 Liberians often refer to their president as "Ma Ellen" ("ma" is a colloquial expression in Liberian English for "mama"), or simply as "Ellen".

233 Especially market women. The Liberian Women Initiative (an NGO) actively campaigned for women's vote registration and were said to have an impact on Sirleaf's election. See, e.g., Pailey 2014.

support from women throughout the country.[234] After her inauguration, she appointed a number of women to the administration, from the local and county level up to the national one.[235] She supported the implementation of the 2005 rape law and the related establishment of a special court (Criminal Court E) designed to focus on cases of GBV.[236] In 2011, she was awarded a Nobel Peace Prize for her engagement in the field of women's and girls' rights. However, her legacy in this regard has been relativised by corruption and nepotism scandals.[237] At the same time, despite her declared commitment to women's issues, Ellen's overall engagement in gender equity is perceived as lukewarm (Pailey and Williams 2017). It is fair to note that she had to face a number of challenges during her 10 years in office and has contributed substantially to the stabilisation of the country in many respects. However, in spite of her initial proclamation of support for women, she did not subscribe to a program of radical reform in the field of gender relation, only confirming that "women can replace men in economic and political positions without necessarily transforming structural inequalities embedded in society" (Steady 2006: 2).

---

234 She also reached out to the traditional women secret societies for mobilisation of support. Ironically, in her second term, she decided to ban the Sande secret societies, which has been interpreted both positively, as a measure supporting gender equality and women's rights (with reference to female genital cutting as a part of initiation rituals), and in a negative way as a step that "effectively entrenched patriarchy in rural communities" (Pailey 2014: 182), depriving women of their traditional base of support, protection, and power.

235 Some authors denounce the appointments of women in her administration as insufficient. However, with five female-headed ministries and governmental agencies for each term, and five out of 15 superintendents (chief administrative positions at the county level), taking into account the general scarcity of educated and capable professionals in the postwar Liberia, the criticism is slightly exaggerated.

236 The court started to operate in 2009 and was supposed to provide a fast-track option for cases of GBV. The actual record of the court, however, has been rather disappointing. Limited human resources and structural conditions, such as the absence of forensic expertise, limited capacities of the LNP, and the location of the court in the capital, among others, are the major factors hindering its performance.

237 E.g., the notorious appointments of her three sons into strategic positions in the central bank, National Oil Company, and the National Security Agency. In 2012, Leymah Gbowee, the co-laureate of the Nobel Peace Prize, publicly expressed her disappointment with the president's corrupt and nepotistic practices.

9.12 Ministry of Gender and Development

The Ministry of Gender and Development (MoGD) was established in 2001 and between 2013 and 2015 renamed the Ministry of Gender and Social Welfare, and later the Ministry of Gender, Children, and Social Protection.[238] The building of the ministry is located in Mamba Point in central Monrovia, alongside the majority of other ministries. The building looked rather shabby in 2011 and 2012. In comparison to the beginning of its operations, when there was no equipment at all, there has been some improvement; the first minister recounted in an interview that at the very beginning in 2001, the whole ministry resided in one office and the facilities and equipment were close to zero:

> "The office did not have a roof; it had an easily removable flat top. I had to sit on a chair that had three legs and was about to break [...] They gave us Coca-Cola crates to sit on. The office was a shell. People could see me from outside, the doors were open, you could see into the building, birds could fly in, and there were no bathrooms. When it started to rain all we had were barrels, we had to move everything to avoid damages from the rain." (Interview with Vabah Gayflor, the first Minister of Gender, iknowpolitics.org 2008)

Even in 2012, more than 10 years later, the facilities were not impressive. The GBV unit resided in a small office with a computer and a desk. My second appointment in the ministry had to be cancelled because the building was partly flooded as a consequence of a heavy rain. Features such as air conditioning, to be seen in the Land Commission or at the Ministry of Justice, were not there. Computers were far from common in all the offices, and the internet connection was not stable. The website of the ministry was created in 2011; however, it has not been always functional. The ministry has a page on Facebook, featuring pictures from events and official visits. Between 2012 and 2017, there were no documents available online, nor information about the projects, structure, or annual reports. Most of the records, such as the minutes of the GBV Taskforce, statistics, etc., have been stored in hard copies:

---

238 The exact point of change of the name is difficult to track, since it has not been addressed by the media, nor by a specific legislative act. The lack of coverage hints to the rather "cosmetic" nature of the renaming.

"We used to keep minutes on the computer, but sometimes it broke down, so we started to make hard copies. Most of them [the data files] were missing, so we decided to make hard copies instead." (Interview MoGD, GBV Unit, 1 May 2012, Monrovia)

There were 164 employees in the ministry in 2011 (105 in the headquarters, 59 in the county offices), and 96 in 2012 (with 66 in the headquarters). The budget rose from the appropriation of over 700,000 USD in 2011 to 1,131,125 USD in 2012. This places the MoGD at the lower end of the budget spectrum. By comparison, the Ministry of Justice had a budget of 11 million USD for the same year, the Ministry of Health over 40 million USD, and the Ministry of Youth 4,5 million USD (Liberia National Budget for Fiscal Year 2012–2013).

The MoGD has been the main actor coordinating the UN-Government Joint Program of GBV, established in 2008. The program consists of five pillars: coordination, security, protection, health, and legal, and has been designed to address the issue of GBV in a comprehensive, integrated manner.[239] The UN provides the necessary financial and technical support for the projects. The first phase of the program was focused on raising awareness about GBV; later, after an evaluation in 2013, the focus shifted to prevention and addressing the "root causes" of the phenomenon (GBV Prevention Report 2013).

In 2006, a special unit—the GBV Unit—was established at the MoGD to provide complex services (in terms of mediation, counselling, and referral) to the survivors of GBV. It collects and analyses data about GBV, works on prevention, networking, and supporting survivors in various ways, including financial ones, to access medical, legal, or psychosocial services.[240] At the same time, the Unit serves as a secretariat to the GBV Taskforce, a body tasked with the implementation of the GBV National Action Plan from 2006, whose drafting it has also initiated.

9.13 GBV Taskforce

The Taskforce used to meet once a month in the building of the Gender Ministry. There were over 20 participants in a room arranged in the theatre

---

239 As of August 2018, there is no information about a continuation of the Joint Program available online.
240 An Endowment Fund has been established for the sake of financial support of the survivors.

style, with a desk for the chairpersons in front and rows of chairs for the audience. The meetings were co-chaired by the Gender Minister (or the Deputy Minister, if the former was absent), and the coordinator of the Joint Government-UN Program on GBV. Members of the Taskforce belonged to the line ministries (Ministry of Health and Ministry of Justice were the crucial ones), service-providing organisations (mainly NGOs, local as well as international), gender focal points, representatives from the Liberia National Police (LNP), UNPOL, UN Women, and UNMIL. The local and international personnel was represented roughly half-and-half. Around two-thirds of the audience were female.

At the beginning, after an opening prayer, the chair asked the new members of the Taskforce to introduce themselves. There were always some of them, for example, seven new members at the meeting in May 2012. This indicates a relatively high level of fluctuation within the member organisations. The issue was also frequently mentioned as one of the challenges for an effective work of the taskforce, leading to an unstable connection to the member organisations and to the need to build the links again and again.

Updates from the "chairing table" were given, about projects throughout the country, about challenges, and upcoming tasks. Although the taskforce was referred to as the decision-making body by the desk officer at the ministry, there was no decision-making during the sessions. It was a purely coordination meeting with updates about the state-of-the-art of different projects and issues. The question comes to mind, if not here, where have the decisions then being made? Given the context, it is likely that the strategic decisions were taken on high-level meetings at the ministerial level, e.g., at the GoL-UN Joint Program meetings.[241]

There were also regional GBV taskforces on the county level, meeting once a month in each county. The issues discussed on the county level were brought to the national level, where the decisions were supposed to be made. There was, however, a general problem with low participation on the county level meetings, with crucial partners, such as Women and Children Protection Unit of the LNP, not taking part (GBV Taskforce meeting, 31 May 2012, MoGD, Monrovia).

Apart from the monthly meetings, there was also an annual retreat, where the plan of action for the upcoming year was discussed and drafted.

---

241 No meetings of the Joint Program took place during the time of my field research.

Generally, the yearly plan was always designed to be in line with the National GBV Plan of Action from 2006.[242]

9.14 Projects of the GBV Unit

The GBV Unit has initiated the creation of networks involved in awareness raising[243] and established several safe homes for survivors of GBV.[244] Later, with the support of international partners, nine "one-stop centers" providing complex services to survivors were established, mainly at the premises of health facilities to ensure confidential treatment. Unfortunately, many of them were closed during the Ebola outbreak and their re-opening has not been at the order of the day (UN OHCHR and UNMIL 2016).

"Gender Focal Points" is a project foreseen by the National Gender Policy as one of the few specific measures the document contained. Gender Focal Points are individuals appointed in all ministries, governmental agencies, and public institutions with the task of mainstreaming gender, drawing attention to the topic, and to the specific needs of women. The general challenge people in these positions often encountered was that their status in the respective institutions did not allow them to enforce the proposed reforms and changes. In other words, they were too low in the hierarchy, not only to push through the changes, but usually even to access the decision-makers for a discussion about gender-related issues (Interview MoGD, GBV Unit, 1 May 2012, Monrovia). The MoGD was often approached and asked for mediation in this regard:

> "They [the Gender Focal Points] ask us: 'So how can you as the Gender Ministry help us reach our bosses so that they are aware of this issue [gender], that it is important?' So we try to see whether our minister could speak with the defence minister, for example, to explain, what it's all about, why it is important." (Interview MoGD, SGBV Unit, 1 May 2012, Monrovia)

---

242 The annual retreat scheduled for May 2012 did not take place as planned for, due to a lack of financial resources (GBV Taskforce meeting, 31 May 2012, MoGD, Monrovia).

243 One of them is the Journalists against SGBV, another one The Christians and Muslims United against GBV.

244 In 2012, there were five safe homes in operation.

In 2012, the Domestic Violence Law started to be drafted in cooperation with MoJ and other stakeholders, to be passed through the legislature five years later, in July 2017.[245] Another achievement of the Gender Ministry was the listing of sexual harassment at the workplace as a criminal offense, codified in the Code of Conduct for public servants from 2012 (Bernath 2015).

9.15 Actor interaction

The meetings of the GBV Taskforce, as mentioned above, were more a place of coordination and information-sharing than decision-making. The interaction and communication was overwhelmingly one-directional, with only modest input from the audience. In fact, the very existence of division between "speakers" and "audience", reflected in the setting of the room, was a major factor determining the patterns of interaction. The GBV Task-force was the largest in terms of number of participants, compared to other meetings I attended during my research. However, nowhere else was the difference between the chairpersons and the rest so visible and audible. Apart from the short introductory round, the contributions from the audience were close to zero. As a result, the meetings resembled debriefings. Apparently, the decision-making was located at the side of the chairs—the MoGD and UN-GoL Joint Program.

9.15.1 Government of Liberia

The GoL is a major actor engaged in the initiatives against GBV, with the MoGD as a flag-bearer institution. However, the ministry faces fundamental financial constraints to fulfil its tasks. The Sirleaf administration presented GBV as a major issue, but the real support was rather symbolic, with the president attending various opening meetings and launches of different initiatives. On the other hand, several important legal instruments were pushed through by the administration, such as the amended

---

245 A point of contention delaying the passage through the parliament in the summer of 2017 was the topic of female genital cutting, seen as a harmful practice in conflict with human rights by some, while being defended as a part of Liberian culture and tradition by some others, e.g., the former minister of health, Senator Peter Coleman (Worzi 2017).

Rape Law and the establishment of the Criminal Court E for prosecution of GBV cases.

Within the Taskforce, attendance of the representatives from the line ministries (i.e., Ministry of Justice, Ministry of Health) was not regular, partly due to a high fluctuation of personnel (Informal conversations #29, #36). The experience of Gender Focal Points, seconded to other ministries and governmental agencies, showed that gender was not considered a relevant issue on the agenda of the public institutions.

In the framework of the Joint UN-Government Program on GBV, MoGD represented the governmental side, with the GBV Unit as a coordination centre. Due to the lack of access to meetings of the Joint Program, it was not possible to assess the interaction in this framework.

9.15.2 International actors

The UN family has been a crucial actor in the field of actions against GBV, with its Joint UN-GoL Program. It has been providing technical and financial assistance to the programs focused on GBV and, more generally, on women's empowerment. The projects within the UN-GoL Joint GBV Program show that the initiatives do not follow the often criticised top-down approach, but rather have been based on cooperation with local partners, taking into consideration the particular context and local realities.[246]

UNMIL closely collaborated with other UN agencies on the issue. The mission had an Office of Senior Gender Adviser, supposed to provide general support for the mission in terms of advocacy, policy advice, training for the personnel, and monitoring and analysis of gender-related issues. More specifically, it has aimed to mainstream gender into the security sector reform, programs in rule of law, and to contribute to the design and implementation of the UN-GoL Joint Program (UNMIL Website). Despite that, the training and sensitisation of the mission personnel did not seem to bear much fruit, as transactional sex between the peacekeepers and

---

246 E.g., the campaigns against GBV have used popular musicians, sensitisation through radio talks, work with traditional and religious leaders, etc. See, e.g., GBV Prevention report 2013.

local population, or, more generally, SEA (sexual exploitation and abuse) occurred in an alarming scope.[247]

Apart from the UN, there has been a number of international organisations providing funding for projects. SIDA (Swedish Development Agency) has been one of the stable bilateral supporters in this respect. Besides that, there has been a large number of other international NGOs, faith-based organisations and other contributors bringing the financial resources in. This high level of donor interest can be explained by the "popularity" of the issue. GBV was, together with pictures of child soldiers, one of the aspects of the Liberian civil war that garnered attention around the world. At the same time, the importance of gender in development has been on the rise in the development aid industry, and aptly met the demand side, represented by the initiatives on the ground.

The general availability of funding is certainly a positive thing. Much less could have been done without it.[248] However, there are also less positive aspects. One of them is the over-emphasis of donors on the fight against rape, leaving other forms of GBV, such as domestic violence, equally widespread in Liberia, unaddressed (Medie 2013). This is not to say that there is no demand and need for action against rape—quite the contrary. The approach, however, illustrates how donors can shift the agenda of the actors on the ground by offering funding opportunities.

9.15.3 Civil society

Civil society forms the backbone of the initiatives against GBV in Liberia. It started to work at the local level already during the war, as a reaction to the widespread atrocities perpetrated by the armed factions, and gained significant support in the postwar period, thanks to massive awareness-raising campaigns and funding made available by the international actors. Local NGOs are the main service providers for survivors of GBV and for the external actors, they represent an easy-to-tap-upon means of outreach to the local communities, even up-country. Their grassroots work is appre-

---

247 A random sample of over 470 women (between 18 and 30 years old) from Monrovia showed that over half of them have engaged in transactional sex and 75% of the cases involved UN personnel (Beber et al. 2016).

248 Although there are examples of women's initiatives that do completely without external funding, e.g., Westpoint Women, a community-based organization in one of the slums in Monrovia (Kaufmann 2011).

ciated and acknowledged by the "big players", such as the UN: "We know we cannot do anything without CSO participation" (Interview with the Coordinator of the UN-GoL Joint Program on GBV, GBV Taskforce meeting, 31 May 2012, Monrovia). There are some organisations active nationwide (such as WIPNET – Women in Peacebuilding Network); however, most of the NGOs are still concentrated in the capital and several bigger towns in the hinterland counties and face substantial (mainly financial) constraints in their work. The services they provide range from offering shelter and protection in safe homes, to legal counselling and acting as liaisons between the survivors and police officers. As such, they effectively substitute the state and other service providers, who fail to deliver such kind of services.[249]

Apart from service provision, women's organisations were influential in pushing for the adoption of some policy documents on women's rights, such as the amendment of the Rape Law in 2005, creation of the Criminal Court E, and sensitisation and production of training materials for the police in the matters of GBV. AFELL (Association of Female Lawyers of Liberia)[250] or THINK (Touching Humanity in Need of Kindness) are examples of the more influential players, able to generate substantial impact thanks to their expertise and ability to offer specialised services to the survivors. The GBV Taskforce also represents an important platform for smaller civil society organisations, providing the leverage of a large group, whose demands cannot be easily overlooked (Interview #21, MoGD desk officer, 1 May 2012, Monrovia, cf. Medie 2013). The network of Journalists against GBV has been actively engaged in an awareness raising campaign. Also, religious leaders across the Christian-Muslim divide are tapped upon for support.[251]

Despite being united by a common cause, dissent exists within the civil society organisations. There is a scarcity of resources, as well as feelings of competition among some institutions and personalities (Informal conversations #56, #59, May 2012, Monrovia). The MoGD is sometimes accused

---

249 Often, the NGOs provide transportation to the police officers to investigate or follow up on the cases, or telephone airtime to facilitate communication. The LNP is largely underfunded and lacks even basic equipment for effective work.

250 Among others, AFELL was a crucial actor contributing to the creation of a specialised SGBV Crimes Unit within the Ministry of Justice in 2009, designed to function as a complementary to the Criminal Court E and Women and Children Protection Unit of the LNP in investigation and prosecution of the GBV and to provide holistic counselling to the victims (Medie 2013).

251 The Inter-Religious Council of Liberia is a key actor in this regard.

of silencing the opposition (UN OHCHR and UNMIL 2016), which leads to resentments and hinders the coordinated, unified action.

9.16 Conclusion

Gender-based violence represents a phenomenon with a low conflict potential, and as such, it does not fit the strictly "technocratic" definitions and approaches to peacebuilding, not representing a direct challenge to peace *per se*. On the other hand, seen from an individual-oriented, human security perspective, initiatives addressing GBV are decisive for attaining the positive peace in Galtung's sense. The security, empowerment, and general well-being of women are factors unanimously accepted as indispensable for development.

GBV cannot be included on the list of conflict drivers or factors fuelling the civil war in Liberia. The phenomenon was prevalent in pre-war times but muted to a large extent. During the conflict, it went out of scale in number and brutality. After the end of the war, the issue became more exposed, publicly discussed, and thematised, partly from the human rights perspective, but also with regard to the development of the country, and, on a more general level, as a problem of marginalisation of a substantial segment of Liberian population. Despite a number of important achievements, such as the adoption of a revised rape law, the establishment of a special tribunal for cases of GBV, a range of services for survivors of GBV, and a prevention and awareness-raising campaign, GBV is still prevalent in Liberia. Firstly, the phenomenon is a manifestation of gender inequality, rooted in the socio-cultural institutions and values behind them. Beside the atrocities committed by different armed groups during the civil war, there was also a "postwar reaction" of traumatised men within the context of highly unstable and polarised social and economic realities. As such, efforts to address the phenomenon have to tackle some deeply entrenched cultural and traditional convictions.

In addition to that, the effective prosecution of perpetrators clashes with the weak judiciary, limited access to justice for both men and women, and the insufficient performance of the police as the main law enforcement agency. The medical, as well as psychosocial, support for survivors, despite significant efforts from the local NGOs, remains inadequate. The implementation of structural measures, such as the adoption of new legislation or a general change of attitude with regard to GBV, is further complicated in the context of a male-dominated culture across the bureaucracy, political institutions, and peacekeeping environment. On the other hand, an obvious weakness of the approach is the lack of men's inclusion in the focus of the initiatives. Most of the work that is being done in the GBV field focuses on assistance to the survivors and targets women. In order to transcend this and achieve a change in the general mindset, it is crucial to look at the other side as well and include men, so that the feelings of marginalisation from their side can be overcome.

The initiatives against GBV are implemented in a synergetic manner: Liberian NGOs do the bulk of the work on the ground, stepping in as service-providers in areas, where the services of the state are missing. External actors provide the necessary financial backing, sometimes supplemented by specific expertise. Despite their undeniable positive contribution, donors tend to prioritise the fight against rape, which leads to a situation, where the agenda of many NGOs is supply-driven, and other forms of GBV are being pushed aside as "less important". The UN, as the main international actor in the field, coordinates the efforts with the government in the framework of the Government-UN Joint Program. On the governmental side, the Ministry of Gender is the main institution in charge, with a special GBV Unit and Taskforce. The ministry, however, faces substantial constraints in terms of human and material resources. The GBV Taskforce, although presented as the decision-making body, only fulfils coordination functions. The actual decision-making takes part at the higher level—at the ministry and within the Joint Program. On the other hand, the taskforce certainly provides a platform for unified action, and as such, it can work as leverage *vis-à-vis* other actors, such as the LNP. Despite the impossibility to access meetings of the Joint Program, based on the reports, campaigns, and programs implemented within the program, it is obvious that the measures have been developed in close cooperation with Liberian counterparts, and the local context has been taken into consideration.

Actions against GBV had been on the agenda of President Sirleaf since the beginning of her first term, at least nominally. Her record in this regard is, however, considered lukewarm. She supported all the important legal developments and has been present at various events. However, gender is far from being at the top of her agenda.

Taking these points into consideration, we can conclude by saying that measures against GBV comply with the "best practices" standards in peace-building. The issue is important for long-term peace and development, and acknowledged as such not only by the international actors, but by the domestic actors as well. This acknowledgement, however, does not translate into adequate material support. The bulk of the actions has been implemented by the local civil society organisations, which have been assisted and funded by the external actors. The MoGD faces substantial financial, material, and capacity constraints. As such, actions against GBV hit the two common problems that confront peacebuilding in many other post-conflict contexts: firstly, it aims to change some deeply entrenched attitudes and social practices. And secondly, it is not considered a priority on the postwar peacebuilding agenda. In the competition with other issues, GBV tends to be pushed aside by more pressing concerns. Both of these factors also explain the lack of progress in the field.

Chapter 10 Early warning in Liberia

"Cui bono?"

Early warning systems are not an issue that commonly figures on peace-building checklists in post-conflict countries. However, in Liberia, early warning offers a very interesting insight into the nature of everyday political business and into the reality of the exercise of peacebuilding. The Early Warning Working Group (EWWG) provides a platform, where all three groups in the focus of this study (external actors, the government of Liberia, and civil society actors) meet. As such, it represents a microcosmos of their interaction, where issues like a lack of coordination, a multitude of actors whose activities do not intersect, a regional dimension of the initiative, and a lack of interconnectedness with the policy-making level come to the fore.

10.1 The concept of early warning

The first early warning projects started in the 1950s in the field of military intelligence and, later, in prediction of natural or humanitarian disasters, human rights violations, diseases, or economic crises (Wulf and Debiel 2009). Nowadays, there are a number of databases and EW systems monitoring places all around the world, administered by NGOs, research institutes, and regional intergovernmental organisations. Some of these are focused on places of ongoing, protracted conflict, or fragile, conflict-prone areas, some are being created *ad hoc,* with a specific purpose (such as election) in mind. Some have even been established as research projects (e.g., the Voix des Kivus in eastern DRC, see van der Windt 2014). In Liberia, the system of early warning, created in the context of monitoring election process in 2011, has been transformed into a longer-term project.

There are a number of definitions of early warning systems, as well as of their classifications, according to methodology they use.[252] Austin

---

252 For a discussion about the merits of different methodological approaches, see, e.g., Austin 2004, Wulf and Debiel 2009, or Rupesinghe 2009. For an overview

defines early warning as "any initiative that focuses on systematic data collection, analysis and/or formulation of recommendations, including risk assessment and information sharing, regardless of the topic, whether they are quantitative, qualitative or a blend of both" (Austin 2004: 2). The term often refers to a broader range of activities than warning as such. It can also include conflict analysis and monitoring, data analysis, or advocacy, with the aim to "a) identify the causes of conflict, (b) predict the outbreak of conflict and, what is more, (c) mitigate that conflict" (Austin 2004: 17).

A UN definition, slightly less universal and drawing attention to the beneficiaries and their agency, defines early warning as "the set of capacities needed to generate and disseminate timely and meaningful warning information to enable individuals, communities and organisations threatened by a hazard to prepare and to act appropriately and in sufficient time to reduce the possibility of harm or loss" (UN/ISDR 2009).

The early response (also called early action) is a counterpart of the latter concept, standing for "any initiative that occurs in the latent stages of a perceived potential armed conflict with the aim at reduction, resolution or transformation" (Austin 2004: 2). Diller (1997) defines early action more specifically as "processes of consultation, policy making, planning, and action to reduce or avoid armed conflict. These processes include i) diplomatic/political; ii) military/security; iii) humanitarian; and iv) development/economic activity" (Diller 1997: 7).

The ideal relationship between the two concepts would be a dynamic, two-way flow of information between the warning and response actors, where the measures adopted for the mitigation of a conflict are fed back to the warning system, and further assessed in a spiral-like process. This is, however, a rare thing to be seen. Not even a simpler version of the ideal, where the information sent out from the "warning" side generates an effective response, is a rule. On the contrary, it is widely acknowledged that the gap between the early warning and early response represents the main hurdle for early warning systems (Austin 2004, Wulf and Debiel 2009, Rupesinghe 2009, Nathan 2007). To anticipate that a response occurs, once the information is conveyed to the right places and right people, would be exaggerated. It does not, due to a number of reasons. The common denominator of many of them is the limited rationality of decision-making actors and the nature of the state and of the everyday political business (Rogers 2011, Nathan 2007).

---

of existing models and their classification, see, e.g., Barton and von Hippel 2008, Nyheim 2008, or Marshall 2008.

Nathan (2007) provides a list of more specific examples in this regard. It includes the difference in seniority on both sides of the barrier, relying on trusted sources of information from diplomatic and other channels (similar to decision-makers' "illusion of understanding" mentioned in section 10.5), overload of decision-makers, and confidential character of some information. Apart from the political will and interest in the information as such, a pertinent factor is whether, or, in how far, the provided information matches the needs of the decision-makers. Ideally, there should be "a high level of collaboration between the designers and the intended users" (Nathan 2007: 53) in the process of building up of the system. However, the reality is again different and the involvement of the response side is mostly quite limited. In this regard Austin rightly notes that "until there is a better understanding of the conditions, motivations and reasons for response, as well as the relationship between early warning and early response, there will be little utility in focusing on improving the accuracy and methodology of the specific early warning system" (Austin 2004: 12). In this regard, Nathan (2007) reminds us of an aspect that is often overlooked, but is very pertinent—namely that conflict early warning is an utmost political mechanism, not a technical one, as it might seem. In this respect, it is very similar to the concept of good governance, which is also presented as a purely technical exercise but is, in reality, profoundly political.[253]

Rupesinghe (2009) offers a useful theoretical lens, distinguishing three generations of early warning systems. In the first one, data obtained from secondary sources are collected and analysed outside the conflict region. The response actors belong to the "Track 1": the UN, regional governments, and national governments. Systems of the second generation collect data on the ground, but the analysis still takes place outside the conflict area. Despite some progress in methodology, response actors are largely the same as in the first generation and the response gap remains a major challenge. The third generation, on the other hand, represents a fundamental shift in the approach. In contrast to the former ones, the third generation of early warning is created "by citizens and for citizens" (Rupesinghe 2009: 11). The data collection and analysis take place in the conflict area and the proximity to conflict facilitates effective and rapid intervention. Response actors include national governments from the given region, locally based NGOs, or, such as in the Liberian case, the

---

253 The "real face" of good governance is, however, better known, since the topic is more prominent and more widely discussed than early warning.

community-level response, based on mediation or other conflict resolution techniques. It is obvious that the evolution of early warning approaches mirrors the changes in the nature of conflict in the last few decades and also a shift in the security paradigm, reflected in a move towards human security, with individuals replacing states as points of reference.

One of the features that marks a fundamental change in the third-generation approach is the acknowledgement of agency of people who are threatened by conflict, an aspect largely absent in the former ones. Wulf and Debiel remind us that the "question of *who* is going to be warned and *who* is supposed to act upon this warning" (Wulf and Debiel 2009: 3, emphasis in original) has not yet been sufficiently examined. And indeed, in the literature, the term "response actors" usually refers to the traditional security providers—be it the security forces of a state or external actors (the UN, individual governments of foreign countries,…), who are supposed to be warned in order to protect the people on the ground. In the first two generations of early warning (and in the majority of the literature), the individuals and communities in danger are not considered either as recipients of the warning message, or as actors with potential to act and protect themselves.

10.2 Early warning in Liberia

The system of early warning was set up before the presidential election in 2011. At that time, there was no comprehensive system where security-related information could be gathered, shared, and viewed interactively by those who needed them. The collected information was stored in written reports that were not routinely shared among different actors, not even among different branches of the UN family (Cummings 2012). UNMIL, as the main security provider, stood at the birth of the idea of creating a more interactive approach and a non-profit technology company Ushahidi came in with the technical solution that was already tested in a comparable context.[254] The interactive online platform created as a result of this cooperation substantially improved the hitherto system of information sharing. By adding elements of interactivity, visual representation, and crowdsourcing, it upgraded the security reporting to a completely different level. Not only did the online platform allow UNMIL to view the reports geospatially,

---

254 The system was used for the monitoring of post-election violence in Kenya in 2008.

it also permitted to identify trends that would otherwise, using standard reporting mechanisms (such as written reports), be virtually impossible (Cummings 2012). A partnership with 16 civil society organisations that complemented the work of UNMIL, international observers, and media by the information collected by their respective networks on the ground was another added value of the project (Foster 2012).

It was necessary to find solutions for several technical challenges, caused mainly by an unreliable electricity supply and internet connection. But the system worked very well in the end, providing timely security information to the UN and other interested parties. After the election, the internet platform was maintained to further serve the purposes of early warning. The Peacebuilding Office and Humanity United, an international donor organisation, stepped in with financial backing and the organisations working in the field established a working group, the Early Warning/Early Response Working Group. The Ushahidi platform was transformed into LERN, Liberia's Early Warning and Response Network.

The LERN platform features an interactive map, displaying the instances of instability and violence countrywide. Over time, it has moved from simple reports of "violence" to over 20 categories, such as land issues, socio-economic issues, border issues, violence related to drug or alcohol abuse, etc., with several categories listed as priority topics of interest.[255] At the same time, the primary purpose of the platform has shifted. The initial ambition to become a source of reliable real-time information about instability and conflict in the country, with the state actors (security providers, but also decision-makers) as the intended primary beneficiaries, did not materialise. Instead of providing input on conflict-triggering issues for the purposes of rapid response, but also of strategic planning, LERN has instead become an archive, a source of data for tracking trends and tendencies in conflict issues. This was mainly due to the two-level system of reporting, where the data obtained by the network of reporters on the ground are firstly processed in each member organisation according to its own methodology and objectives, and only then submitted to the LERN platform.

---

255 The priority issues in 2012 were land, border issues, drug abuse, and youth dimension.

10.3 Early Warning Working Group

As mentioned above, the Early Warning Working Group (EWWG) represents a micro-arena of interaction of the international, national, and civil society actors. It is a "loose-knit voluntary group" (Rogers 2011: 8) with around 18 active members (Interview #59, Chairman of the EWWG, 28 November 2012, Monrovia); however, the membership is relatively fluid and not formally regulated.[256] It does not bring any special material benefits to the members. There are representatives of the security forces, the UN, and a number of civil society organisations. Table 3 provides an overview of the membership. Members considered "active" are those who contribute to the LERN platform and participate in the group's coordination meetings.

The membership in EWWG is open due to several reasons. Firstly, in the context of absence of stable bureaucratic structures, the ties to other bodies and their representatives are highly dependent on personal relationships. In the case of high fluctuation of personnel, especially at national ministries and governmental agencies, this means that there is no established, "permanent" link to the new appointees. Therefore, if a representative from a ministry is replaced, there is no guarantee that the new person automatically gets involved in the activities of the EWWG or any other initiative:

"The leadership at the ministries is changing quickly—twice a year, once a year. When there is a change, ministries have to nominate new people to represent them at various bodies. And that is the problem, we have to get in touch with them, there is no stable link to new appointees. In the last three years, there were three police directors appointed." (Interview #59, Chairman of the EWWG, 28 November 2012, Monrovia)

Secondly, certain agencies are reluctant to be publicly associated with the EWWG because of the fear that it could clash with their position of neutrality and their policy of not taking sides:

"Another challenge we sometimes face, not all the time but sometimes, is the issue of [...] maybe neutrality, not taking sides, not taking positions, you know, is sometimes a challenge. For example, we have

---

256 The last conflict analysis report of the EWWG from 2014 listed 31 member organisations (EWER 2014: 29).

an interview with some government official on a particular subject. One group comes and says: 'No, no, no, we are not supposed to be listed on this. Our name is not supposed to appear on this.' Some organisations, they are afraid that the association [with the group] could create problems. It's not a big, big challenge, because the way how we work, we have government actors on, in the working group, there are representatives from the National Police, from the Ministry of Justice, from the Bureau of Immigration, so from the very beginning, they are understanding what we are trying to achieve. Sometimes, there is a view of early warning like spies, who are reporting, but once they are at the table, they see it differently. But there are some organisations that do not want to be put on the front page." (Interview #22, PBO employee/Chairman of the EWWG, 1 May 2012, Monrovia)

During the time of my fieldwork in 2012, the group met twice a month at the premises of one of the member organisations, since it did not have its own "place". One of the monthly meetings was focused predominantly on planning, information-sharing, and updates about what is going on in the member organisations. Another one was reserved for the strategic analysis of various early warning and conflict issues, often in a form of debriefing.

Apart from the main, "full-group" level, there were *ad hoc* taskforces set up as operative, flexible structures to deal with particular issues. In 2012, one taskforce worked on the standardisation of indicators for data collection and the second one was in charge of developing a two-year action plan.[257] They provided an opportunity for members, willing to engage in a particular area of activities, to take the lead. The taskforces reported to the group as a whole. The activities of the EWWG have been coordinated by a chairman, a long-term international consultant, who was, at the same time, an employee of the Liberia Peacebuilding Office (PBO).[258]

Until autumn 2012, the EWWG had no budget of its own and had to rely on its members when financial support was needed. The most important actor, sponsoring a number of organisations involved in early

---

257 Later in 2014, a Special Taskforce on Ebola was established.
258 The PBO serves as a secretariat of the EWWG. The chairman of the EWWG is a Liberian national, living in the US, but based in Monrovia for the duration of his contract.

warning in Liberia[259], was Humanity United (HU).[260] UN agencies occasionally provided funding for particular projects, but the bulk part of money in the early warning field came from the HU through individual organisations. Originally, the grants in early warning, although coming from a single donor, did not have integration as a requirement. Only later, with the establishment of the EWWG, it turned out that the fragmentation and isolation of the organisations involved can represent an obstacle in creating a single, integrated system of early warning.[261] For the EWWG, as a new player on the ground, it meant that they had to convince other organisations to get on board:

"They [the HU] give out grants to different organisations but do not require them to integrate or collaborate [...] We realised later on that there is a need to bring all the actors together, into a formation of an early warning ecosystem. By then, there was no requirement for those organisations to collaborate [...] It was an afterthought. If they [the HU] thought about it before, they would integrate it into proposals. So that was a challenge—trying to get those organisations to buy in. There are some organisations that have different priorities, answering more to the headquarters, their home offices, especially international organisations. But the grant we have with Humanity United requires us to do this. But we have no force [to make them take part]. Along the way, we've managed to overcome it, because as the grant expires, and it has to be renewed, HU will insist that the programs align with the priorities of the working group and they will be required to collaborate." (Interview #22, PBO employee/Chairman of the EWWG, 1 May 2012, Monrovia)

---

259 The Liberia Democracy Watch, Ushahidi, Peacebuilding Office, and the Norwegian Refugee Council are some of them.

260 Humanity United is a foundation engaged in initiatives in the field of peacebuilding and conflict transformation, the fight against human trafficking and modern slavery, and public policy issues in a number of countries around the world. For more information, see https://humanityunited.org/.

261 Different methodologies and approaches of particular organisations are another factor that complicates the integration. At the beginning, they were not perceived as a problem by the members (Rogers 2011), but this attitude has changed over time, especially after the issue started to complicate the analysis of data (cf. EWER 2014).

10.4 Meetings of the EWWG

The meetings of the group were taking place at the premises of different member organisations, since the group did not have its own workspace. The atmosphere of the meetings was largely informal and there were no signs of competition or conflict among the members. Members of the group were familiar with each other and with the work of the respective member organisations. Due to its informal character, it was relatively easy (in comparison to other institutions) to get access to the meetings for observation, as well as for interviews with the members.

At the beginning, the chairman of the group distributed the agenda and the meeting started with each representative giving a brief update about her respective organisation, on the issues relevant for the group. Some of the issues discussed during the time of my fieldwork were the possible impact of the announcement of the verdict in process with Charles Taylor on the security in the city, an update on research conducted by the Justice and Peace Commission and Landmine Action in Westpoint (a large informal settlement close to the city centre)[262], and a discussion on the new categories of incidents for the LERN platform. The chairman gave updates on the drafting process of the National Reconciliation Roadmap[263], and on plans for a meeting where a new long-term action plan for the group would be prepared. Logistics, especially, were discussed: possible dates, venue, and, most importantly, the availability of funding for the event. The representative of Ushahidi, the NGO maintaining the LERN platform, reported on statistics, such as the number of displays of the platform, their geographical location, and the latest trends in reported cases. After going through the points on the agenda, some of the participants engaged in short, informal conversations with the chairman or with each other.

There were no special decision-making arrangements. The chairman facilitated the course of the meeting, and when a decision was to be made,

---

262 The two NGOs initiated a participatory baseline study, where the members of the Westpoint community were first trained and afterwards conducted the research in a participatory manner. The aim was to map the security concerns of the people living in the area and subsequently, to use the study for advocacy. Despite the fact that the neighbourhood is located in central Monrovia, and in spite of having a "bad reputation" as a dangerous place, at that time, there was no source of reliable data on the area with regard to security—and, in fact, on any other aspect of life in the neighbourhood.

263 As mentioned, the chairman of the group was also an employee of the PBO, a body involved in drafting the Reconciliation Roadmap.

it came as a consensual result of the discussion. Not all the attendants took an active part in the discussions—some stayed silent, while others seemed uninterested, checking their mobile phones frequently.

Despite the effort to bring all the relevant early warning actors on board, the majority of the participants at the meetings belonged to civil society. From the UN side, there was an UNMIL representative; the governmental level was represented by an officer of the Liberia National Police (LNP) and a representative from the Bureau of Immigration and Naturalization (BIN). The outreach to the governmental actors, or to "response" actors in more general terms, was frequently mentioned as the biggest challenge in the functioning of the group (Interview #59, Chairman of the EWWG, 28 November 2012, #43, Liberia Democracy Watch employee, 13 June 2012, #28, Foundation for Peace and Development, 24 May 2012, Monrovia).

10.5 The response side of the coin

"To effectively link with response actors" (EWER 2013: 4) has been listed as one of the key objectives of the working group, together with giving policy recommendations, driving advocacy, and "getting the information from the ground, supported by sound research, to the decision-makers" (Interview #22, PBO staff/Chairman of the EWWG, 1 May 2012, Monrovia). In this regard, however, there has been little success. The lack of interconnectedness with the decision-making level shows that, in Liberia, as well as in many other cases, the gap between the warning and the response side is there across several different levels. At the most general level, the capacities of the traditional security providers are still limited, even more than a decade after the end of the civil war. The police presence does not effectively stretch beyond the capital. In the counties, the number of police forces is quite low and officers face the absence of basic equipment and logistical challenges, such as lack of vehicles, that makes performing their duties extremely difficult.[264] The army is comparatively better off, and the regional security hubs, despite all the relevant criticism around the project, represent a certain improvement in terms of reaching out to remote areas.

---

264 The salaries are also very low. A security guard working for a private company can earn several times more than a police officer (Enca.com: 2014). In addition, the police are not adequately equipped and allowed to carry arms, which renders them powerless, such as in the cases of assaults or armed robberies.

However, UNMIL is still the main security provider, and the only one able to respond to situations of a more serious character.

As the second aspect of the "response gap", there is an issue of disinterest by the decision-making level, that is, the executive branch, the main actor able to leverage any kind of meaningful change and action in terms of addressing the security issues identified by the EWWG. One of the reasons behind it could be the "illusion of understanding"—a situation, particularly common among people in a position of authority, where people are convinced that they are sufficiently informed about all relevant issues:

> "Information is power and power has unusual access to information and analytical insights. The result is that there is little demand or support for external analysis. The thinking goes, 'What could anyone tell me that I don't already know by virtue of my position?'" (Rogers 2011: 41)

Another reason, somehow similar to the latter one, is the "seniority mismatch" (cf. Nathan 2007). EWWG has been perceived as an initiative predominantly driven by civil society. Taking into consideration the general relationship of CSOs with the government, as well as the historically rooted lack of cordiality of the former *vis-à-vis* the security forces, it is not surprising that the EWWG is not seen as important enough a player to be taken seriously by the "highest level". Connected to this is the issue of individual contacts. The EWWG does not have the right personal networks that would facilitate the access to the targeted decision-makers. Last but not least, the cases presented by the group are often uncomfortable for the government.[265]

The range of actors that can engage in an early response is quite broad, as the literature suggests (see especially Rupesinghe 2009). In this respect, it is interesting to see how the response is defined by the EWWG. Whether as a result of the realities on the ground and the impossibility to effectively connect with the traditional response actors, or from whatever other reason, the group's definition of response is very much in line with Rupesinghe's "third generation" approach:

> "We do not believe in early warning as a fire-brigade—something happens, so let's call the police to calm the things—but as the capacity

---

265 E.g., the conflicts between local communities and companies granted agricultural or other concessions. Sime Darby plantation has been one such case, identified by the EWWG. For more details about the case, see, e.g., Ford 2012.

to deal with it on the low level, in the community, through mediation for example. We do not have to involve the higher level, because it is not necessary." (Interview #59, Chairman of the EWWG, 28 November 2012, Monrovia)

This community-based, bottom-up response is an approach promoted by the majority of the group members. The EWWG has been involved in the project of County Peace Committees (CPCs)[266] that act as the first instance of the early warning system and, at the same time, the first stage of the early warning intervention. There is a network of focal persons, trusted leaders in their respective communities, representing men, women, and youth, who are trained to submit reports to the LERN platform via SMS, but also to resolve disputes through mediation and prevent them from escalation. The Peace Committee members seek to identify instability before the actual conflict erupts and to mitigate the conflict by mediation or other suitable dispute-resolution techniques. By that, they are effectively bridging a part of the "response gap". In the current security situation in the country, community-based response is by far the quickest and most flexible option to deal with disputes. The police, apart from not always being readily available where needed, are often perceived as corrupt and untrustworthy. This perspective also resonates with the community-based, grassroots approach to peacebuilding, adopted by the majority of civil society organisations in Liberia.

The range of "interventions" where the CPCs are involved is broad, from family disputes, through fights and motorbike accidents, to land-related conflicts. They are connected to local security providers, such as the police, courts, and security hubs, and can give advice to the parties of the conflict, including where to go:

> "So, there is a car accident, for example. People, the witnesses, call the CPC members to calm the situation. Things can escalate very quickly. So the Peace Committee members come and talk to the people involved in the accident. They are respected in their community, so people listen to them. They try to find a solution, and if it's necessary, they can also point to other instances, they can advise people on where to go—to the police, or to the hub. But usually, it is not even necessary. [...] And they also report on the incident to the [LERN]

---

266 County Peace Committees are a project of conflict prevention and mediation at the community level supported by UNMIL and PBO.

platform later." (Interview #30, Inter-religious Council of Liberia, 28 May 2012, Monrovia)

10.6 Too many cooks?

Another feature of early warning in Liberia worth noting is the number of organisations involved in the field at different levels, beyond the scope of the EWWG itself. It has already been mentioned that some members of the group (e.g., Liberia Democracy Watch, or WANEP) have their own methodologies for data collection and analysis, and process the data in the framework of their own projects. As such, the activities in the framework of the Working Group represent an additional layer of engagement for them. The purpose of the EWWG was to overcome this fragmentation by bringing all the actors in the field together and integrating the information coming from different sources in one platform.

A surprising aspect in this regard is the initial lack of coordination, absent as a requirement from the donor's side. Originally, Humanity United supported various organisations in the field of early warning, but they were not required to cooperate. This, however, changed in the second half of 2012, with the new batch of grants from HU:

> "Next year, the EWWG will have to expand, because one of the new requirements of the new phase of the grant is that every NGO doing early warning should be involved. This will attract new organisations, who just change their hats and say, 'Yes, yes, we are doing early warning and peacebuilding!' And it might have even bad consequences for the group in terms of operationality." (Interview #59, Chairman of the EWWG, 28 November 2012, Monrovia)

10.7 Regional dimension: ECOWARN

Apart from the NGOs active in the EWWG, there is a separate early warning program reaching out to the regional level: the ECOWARN, linked to and supported by ECOWAS. The system has been in place since 2004 (Interview #55, ECOWAS Official, 26 November 2012, Monrovia) and in contrast to LERN, the information collected is intended for the internal use of ECOWAS, not accessible for wider public. The Monrovia office covers, apart from Liberia, three other countries: Ghana, Guinea, and Sierra Leone. The office relies on secondary sources of information from the media and two focal points: one from the Ministry of Planning, representing the government, and one from WANEP, representing the civil society and based on the information from their own network of reporters throughout the country.[267] The data are further analysed and submitted to the level of the ECOWAS Commission, which also represents the response actor. The combination of two independent sources of information, and in particular the involvement of civil society as one of them, actually represents quite an innovative approach, in comparison to other early warning projects in Africa. As such, ECOWARN often serves as an exemplary model for other similar initiatives (Wulf and Debiel 2009).

The ECOWAS representative confirmed that her work has been very much based on personal relations and admitted that there are a number of initiatives in the field of early warning. However, somehow surprisingly, she was not aware of the existence of the EWWG (Interview #49, ECOWAS Office, 26 November 2012, Monrovia). This demonstrates a feature common with many peacebuilding initiatives at the "Track 1" level. They are focused very much on certain levels and certain actors who are not necessarily the most relevant ones.[268] Other actors inevitably fall off the scope. Although the "peacebuilding community" in Liberia is very small, and, generally, people working in the same field know each other, this is apparently not the case here. There were some efforts from the EWWG side to cooperate and network with the ECOWAS office, but these efforts were not realised.[269]

One of the reasons behind this lack of networking and cooperation might be the fact that both systems use different sources of data and have different intended end users. Unlike the EWWG, ECOWAS relies on secondary sources of data, mainly from the news, and from stable focal points. It falls into the category of the second generation of early warning,

---

267　The two focal points submit their reports separately and are not able to see each other's reports. In the case of an incident, the ECOWAS representative complements this information with additional sources, including informal ones, e.g., rumours (Interview #55, ECOWAS Official, 26 November 2012, Monrovia).

268　WANEP, for example, is considered "not so strong in Liberia" by other early warning organisations, but is still chosen and kept as the civil society focal point, since the ECOWAS system cooperates with WANEP as the information provider in other countries in the region (Interview #59, Chairman of the EWWG, 28 November 2012, Monrovia, cf. Bombande 2016).

269　The coordinator of the EWWG claimed to have tried to establish contact with the ECOWARN, inviting a representative to join the group; however, this was met with no success; the ECOWARN representative did not appear at the meeting. (Interview #59, Chairman of the EWWG, 28 November 2012, Monrovia).

with information collected in the given region, but analysed elsewhere—in this particular case in the Abuja headquarters (cf. Rupesinghe 2009). The EWWG, on the other hand, can be considered a third-generation project, especially taking into account the involvement of the local level on the response side and generally the fact that the system targets and serves other actors rather than just the traditional, first-track ones.

ECOWARN and LERN are obviously quite different at first sight: LERN is based on first-hand information from the ground, builds on civil society organisations as the base of membership, and, although to a large extent it is disconnected from the national level, the collected data are, at least potentially, accessible to the wider public. ECOWARN relies on secondary sources of information, includes the governmental level, but the results of analysis are submitted to the intergovernmental, regional body. An interesting aspect that these systems have in common is that they both effectively single out the national, governmental level as the primary response actor. LERN by pragmatically relying on the community-driven, bottom-up response; ECOWARN by engaging the supranational level of international intergovernmental organisation.[270] The common denominator of both systems is then an effective omission of the national level as a response actor.

Another aspect, related to the one sketched here but more general, is the relationship to the beneficiaries of the system. The role of beneficiaries (i.e., of the intended users of the system) is underthematised in the literature (cf. Wulf and Debiel 2009). In fact, apart from the lack of attention, the more problematic aspect with regard to this category is the fact that it is not sufficiently elaborated. To be sure, it is useful to acknowledge the conceptual difference between the actors to be warned and those, who intervene. These categories certainly do not have to (and in many cases in practice they do not) overlap. However, the term "beneficiary" encompasses an even broader scope, including actors and individuals who are not directly involved in the conflict area, such as researchers, academics, international NGOs, and donor organisations. Much of the literature in the field of early warning focuses on nuances of methodology and theoretical discourse. There is a solid body of analysis of particular systems of early warning (for Africa, see e.g., Affa'a-Mindzie 2012, Aseto 2013, Cilliers 2005, Etyang et al. 2016, or Nathan 2007), but only rarely are the systems

---

270 To be sure, potential response measures are directed towards the national government. The latter, however, takes up a passive role in the schema—not an active one.

assessed in terms of who are their real beneficiaries and what the systems offer them.

Beneficiaries of the LERN project are by far the most problematic element in the whole system. The original intended beneficiaries were mainly governmental agencies. For the purposes of rapid response, but also for the sake of more strategic planning and project implementation. However, they are not interested. The community-level response is certainly an innovative approach that effectively bypasses the response gap. However, the actors who are likely to intervene in an early stage of a conflict at the community level do not get their warning from the LERN platform. They see the threat by virtue of their presence, by being around the location of the conflict, or through their personal networks. The LERN platform is by and large redundant for them. In Liberia, with only about 8% of the population having access to the internet[271], the majority of the population, especially in the rural areas, is almost entirely excluded from access to the platform. The added value of the early warning system for the population is rather in capacity building, in training the reporters and members of the County Peace Committees in techniques of conflict transformation or mitigation strategies.

There are a number of entities within Liberia that could benefit from the system—members of the UN family and other, predominantly foreign organisations or NGOs are most likely to consult the platform. It can also be useful for researchers, peacebuilding practitioners, students, or the like, both based in Monrovia and abroad. However, it is exactly this aspect that leaves the whole project somehow open-ended. The local population is virtually excluded, and national authorities are uninterested. Those who remain are mainly external actors, based in the country, but even more likely elsewhere, whose number is, in addition, quite limited. As a result, the whole project, however elaborate, is floating in the air—the proverbial white elephant.[272] Well rooted in the ground, dispersing water from the trunk all around, without a specific target. Such an image can be, for sure, simply beautiful. But beauty alone is sometimes not enough.

---

271 Estimates from 2016 are 8,6% (http://www.internetlivestats.com/internet-users /liberia/), resp. 8,4% for 2017 (http://www.internetworldstats.com/africa.htm# lr). The number of internet users almost quadrupled in comparison with 2012, where there were only about 2,6% of population with internet access (http://ww w.internetlivestats.com/internet-users/liberia).

272 *Elephant blanc*, or white elephant, is a term used to describe huge, expensive development projects that are, however, inefficient, useless, and can even have a negative social or environmental impact (Robinson and Torvik 2004).

10.8 Interaction

10.8.1 Government of Liberia and "traditional" response actors

As already indicated in the previous sections, the decision-making level (i.e., mainly the executive branch) is not particularly interested in the data or information provided by the EWWG project, although it would be the first entity that comes to mind as a recipient of the information. Some security-related agencies, such as the Liberia National Police (LNP) or Bureau of Immigration and Naturalization (BIN), are members of the working group and regularly attend meetings, despite the original reluctance to work with civil society actors. In spite of this, liaison officers from governmental agencies still belong to the technical, mid-level bureaucrats and often do not have access to the decision-making level within their respective institutions either. The situation is further complicated by the already mentioned high fluctuation of personnel in governmental agencies and the historically rooted lack of cordiality between security agencies and civil society.

For the executive branch of the government, early warning is one of the many initiatives, supported from outside. It does not stand out in any respect (Informal conversations #30, #45, #50, May–November 2012, Monrovia). The chairman of the group does not have contact with the people at the highest level, nor a rank "high enough", so it is not surprising that the recommendations and cases presented by the group are not treated with a great portion of attention. The perception of the working group is very much similar to other civil society actors and activities—they are there, they make cases, they demand action. But there is no sanction for the government if they do not react. The demand side is not strong enough.

10.8.2 External actors

External actors stood at the cradle of the whole project. First UNMIL, triggering the upgrade of the system, together with Ushahidi, who provided the technical backing. Humanity United has been supporting early warning financially. Apart from being the conveners, international actors are also in the position of the primary beneficiaries of the outputs, as they are potentially interested and dispose of the technical prerequisites to access the information on the online platform (in contrast to some governmental agencies).[273] UNMIL comes to mind as the first one, be it for the analysis of the conflict trends, for a swift response to outbreaks of violence, or for the purposes of planning and strategic decision-making. External actors (especially members of the UN family) also represent potential sources of funding for specific projects of the working group, and can disseminate the information about the early warning project in their own organisations and broader networks.

Bilateral partners based in Liberia, be it development agencies or diplomatic representations, can access and use the LERN platform and other products of the EWWG as a source of data for project planning or advocacy purposes.[274] The platform can serve as an entry point for potential donors as well. There is, however, a weak point in the fact that the platform's website is not easily found, unless one knows the exact URL. Search engines do not find it even after entering the exact name of the platform.[275]

For Humanity United, the main donor, the platform is a tangible, easily accessible output of the EWWG's work. The overall relationship and communication between HU and the group was perceived as good; HU was praised for listening to feedback from the EWWG, which is not a commonplace thing in this kind of relation[276], and for being very supportive in the process of grant applications (Interview #25, member of the EWWG, 16 May 2012, Monrovia). Such a relationship, based on open communication, support, and genuine personal engagement, represents an ideal case of a partnership between a donor and a recipient.

All in all, international actors are the primary beneficiaries of the project. According to the statistics, an overwhelming majority of access-

---

273 BIN, for example, has disposed of its limited internet access and preferred to receive the reports of the EWWG in the form of hard copies (Rogers 2011).

274 It is, however, hard to assess in how far the information actually influences their decisions.

275 Recently, the platform domain changed, and I was not able to find it online anymore, despite knowing what I am looking for, until I got the new link (www.ewerliberia.net) from the coordinator of the EWWG in June 2017. A year later (at the beginning of September 2018), however, the new link was non-functional again. As of October 2021, the platform could be found under https://pboliberiaewer.org/.

276 For example, the EWWG suggested the required coordination of organisations working in the field of early warning as one of the conditions for the second batch of funding (Interview #59, Chairman of the EWWG, 28 November 2012, Monrovia).

es to the LERN platform came from outside of Liberia.[277] Even on the displays of the platform from within the country, it is obvious that they were coming from the organisations equipped with stable internet access and interest in the topic, that is, most likely, the UN family, or other international organisations and NGOs.

Except for this latter point, early warning could represent an exemplary case of peacebuilding cooperation—the system is fed at the grassroots level, maintained and administered by local counterparts with heavy involvement from civil society actors. The "outsiders" provide funds and necessary guidance (e.g., the technical know-how). The only missing part of an otherwise perfect picture is the connection to the "right" beneficiaries, be it the state and the traditional security providers, or the general population. Although with regard to the citizens, it would be wrong to say that there is no added value for them. There is a pertinent aspect of capacity-building, where citizens are trained in mediation and conflict resolution techniques to better deal with conflicts at the local level. They are also familiarised with using mobile phones for texting. Most importantly, they are offered a form of participation. In the Liberian context, where the information flow has been always from the capital towards the hinterland, the whole system of information flow is turned upside down. For the first time, it is the periphery that takes over, even though it is only in one particular, small field. People get the signal that what is going on in the counties is important, and certain people in the capital do care about what is going on at the local level.

10.8.3 Civil society

Civil society organisations are the pillars of the whole early warning initiative, doing the everyday work, supplying the system with information, and implementing projects. Each organisation follows its own framework, methodology, and processing of data for its own purposes. The participation in the working group represents another level of engagement that enables them to stay informed about what is going on in other organisations, and facilitates cooperation and coordination in a horizontal fashion.

Although there are a number of members who do not belong to civil society, the group as a whole is perceived from the outside as a corporate civil society actor (e.g., by the government) and treated accordingly. The

---

277 Around 85% (Meeting of the EWWG, 24 May 2012, Monrovia).

EWWG by its nature as a voluntary, informal platform and a meeting point, fosters coordination among CSOs engaged in the field of early warning and mitigates the effect of the settings in which civil society commonly operates—a competitive landscape, driven by the logic of a zero-sum game, where resources are scarce and players are many. The group also offers networking possibilities beyond the CSOs, an avenue for informal access to UN representatives, or for improvement in the relationship with the security agencies.

10.9 Conclusion

Despite looking like a purely technical mechanism, the system of early warning in Liberia, maintained by the EWWG, offers a number of lessons about the nature of the political landscape in Liberia, as well as about the reality of peacebuilding processes.

The system, using an internet platform for displaying instances of violence, based on the data collected by a network of reporters on the ground, was established in order to monitor the presidential election in Liberia in 2011. The project continued after the election and developed into a long-term initiative, bringing together a number of actors from civil society, governmental and international agencies, and NGOs. Despite all the merits, the system faces a number of challenges, typical for projects of its kind: a lack of connection to the response actors, or to the decision-making level, respectively, being the most fundamental ones.

The functioning of the group is complicated by factors related to the nature of the political environment in postwar Liberia—high fluctuation of personnel, emphasis on the "rank" or the level of seniority in the bureaucracy, and the historically problematic relationship between security agencies (and governmental agencies in general) and civil society. At the same time, the interaction within the EWWG helps to overcome some of them; by virtue of long-term cooperation, the group contributes to building trust, not only between civil society and the security providers, but also to an improvement of the relations and cooperation among the CSOs themselves, shaped by the competitive, and sometimes tacitly conflicting, context in which civil society in Liberia operates.

Some other aspects that the experience of the EWWG indicates to be crucial are good relations with donors, responsiveness to the feedback of the partners on the ground, and commitment to a long-term engagement. Another one is the importance of personal networks, as a means of reaching the "right places". With regard to the broader context of early warning, the multitude of actors and initiatives, whose activities are overlapping, uncoordinated, and sometimes even going on without being aware of the existence of the others, is an issue worth attention.

In many respects, LERN represents an exemplary case of a peacebuilding initiative. It is well-rooted and supported from the grassroots level, contributing to capacity development of local actors. There is a robust involvement of civil society actors and stable support from donor's side. External actors are involved in the system, bringing support and know-how where necessary, but not taking up too much initiative. The field of early warning also clearly shows the multi-level character of peacebuilding and the constraints represented by actors' particular mandates coming from their headquarters. However, all the positive aspects are undermined by the complete lack of practical utility and impact of the system on its beneficiaries. The LERN system falls in the third generation of early warning approaches, with the focus on citizens as both contributors and beneficiaries. However, in Liberia's case, the population is virtually excluded from the benefits of the project. As a consequence, the information in the system flows in one way only, very much mimicking the relationship of LERN with the second group of intended beneficiaries—governmental response actors. There, the communication also goes only in one way, not in a circular fashion, as a well-functioning system should work. However, the engagement of response actors represents a problem with early warning systems in general. The access to other potential beneficiaries, defined beyond the usual categories of the actors to be warned, respectively of those to act upon a warning, be it within or outside the country, is complicated by the fact that unless one knows the URL, it is almost impossible to find the LERN platform using internet search engines.

The lack of involvement of traditional response actors is, in the case of LERN, bridged by an innovative conception of response coming from the local level. The focus on grassroots also conveys a message of relevance to the latter, signalling the importance of local communities as active participants in the system of early warning. Another interesting phenomenon in this regard is an effective bypassing, or singling out, of the state as a primary response actor—be it from LERN, as a pragmatic acceptance of political realities, or from ECOWARN, which emphasises the regional dimension of the response.

Despite the fact that early warning systems do not feature the usual peacebuilding checklists, they are beyond all doubt a useful tool for conflict prevention and management, or even for the purpose of strategic planning. In addition, as profoundly political mechanisms, they offer a space, where phenomena otherwise hidden can be observed, such as the relationships between different actors on the political scene, or the practice of peacebuilding reality, where the initiatives coming from the "Track 2" are often overlooked by the actors from the "Track 1", and are therefore relegated to the role of redundant white elephants.

Table 3: EWWG members 2013-2014

Governmental Actors		
	Liberia National Police	
	Bureau of Immigration and Naturalization	
	Ministry of Justice	
	Ministry of Internal Affairs/National Disaster Relief Commission	
Sub-total	4	
International Actors		
	UNMIL (Civil Affairs)	
	UNICEF	
	UNHCR	
	Innovation for Poverty Action Liberia (IPAL)	International NGO
	Norwegian Refugee Council (NRC)	International NGO
	Trust Africa, only until 2013	Donor organisation
	Ushahidi/iLab Liberia	International NGO
Sub-total	7	
Civil society		
	Accountability Lab	
	Center for Democratic Empowerment	
	Center for Media Studies and Peacebuilding	
	Citizen Bureau for Development and Productivity	
	Flomo Theater	
	Foundation for Peace and Development	

	Global Alliance for Peace and Sustainability	
	Inter-Religious Council of Liberia	
	Justice and Peace Commission	
	Landmine Action/Action on Armed Violence	
	Liberia Democracy Watch	
	Liberia Media Center	
	Lutheran Trauma Healing and Reconciliation Program	
	Messengers of Peace	
	Peacebuilding Resource Center	
	Platform for Dialogue and Peacebuilding	
	Rice and Rights Foundation	
	West Africa Network for Peacebuilding (WANEP) Liberia	
	Youth Crime Watch Liberia	
Sub-total	19	
Members total	30	

Chapter 11 Cross-case analysis

The analysis in this section is guided by the research questions, focusing first on the roles of actors and their interaction, and subsequently on the explanations of the lack of progress in the postwar reform process. Apart from explanations related to the four specific cases, the latter part of the chapter features several variables that crystallised along the way, in a bottom-up process of data analysis as factors worth attention: the category of support, operationalised in terms of rhetorical and material backing, the nature of the issue at stake, with conflict potential as a specific sub-category, and aspects linked to the individual level of the reform process. The last part analyses contextual and external factors relevant for the progress of peacebuilding exercise in Liberia.

11.1 Roles of the actors across the cases

11.1.1 International actors

In the case of governance, the role of international actors is rather tacit; they set the broader context and general objectives of the reforms, in the direction of good governance, democracy, decentralisation, and rule of law. Most of the aims overlap with the goals pursued by the Governance Commission, that is, the objectives set by Liberians. The physical presence of international actors in the GC is negligible. The reasons behind this might be manifold, ranging from the obvious argument of a "Liberian solution to a Liberian problem", to the perception of the reforms as a lip service and therefore as something not worth the effort, or to the absence of material incentives for the engagement. In the broader context of governance, beyond the GC itself, international actors implement various programs supporting good governance (be it the UN or individual governments through their development agencies), and some external actors are present in the political institutions (ministries, governmental agencies,....), doing capacity building and sharing know-how.

In the case of the Land Commission, the situation is exactly the opposite. The agenda and objectives are also set by Liberians, but the Commission is full of foreigners. Some of them occupy positions as international consultants, some work as seconded experts for the LC itself. There is a prominent role of the US, through the USAID program of institutional and policy support, where the expatriates form a "shadow Land Commission", mirroring the structure of the real Commission and being involved in the day-to-day operation of the body. There is also a close cooperation between the LC and UN-HABITAT, which resides in the same building—a unique feature, not to be found in similar institutions in Liberia. External actors are involved in the legislative processes around law reform as well, albeit in an indirect and ambiguous manner, through efforts to manipulate and influence the results of the legislative process to their own benefit.

In the Gender Ministry and the respective Taskforce, the UN represents the leading actor of the initiatives, bringing financial support and being very much involved in the planning and strategic decision-making process. The UN-Government Joint Program on GBV is the main initiative in the field. In the GBV Taskforce, the presence of international actors is prominent (about half of the participants in the Taskforce were expatriates). External donors have a major impact on setting the agenda in the field, with a priority on initiatives against rape, despite the voices from the domestic side, advocating for the support of other issues as well.

In the case of the Early Warning Group, external actors (e.g., UNMIL with an international non-profit Ushahidi) facilitated the creation of the project, but later stepped back into the role of technical support and maintenance (in the case of Ushahidi), or beneficiary of the information provided by the group, as in the case of UNMIL and other UN agencies. Humanity United, the main donor supporting the project, seems to fulfil an exemplary role as a supportive, yet unobtrusive partner, devoted to a long-term support of the project.

In all the four cases, international actors bring financial support that is vital to the implementation of the programs and the reform agenda. The contributions of external partners represent a major portion of the Liberian national budget.[278] In this respect, the steady decline of the external support definitely impacts on the pace and progress of the reforms.[279]

---

278 In 2012, the amount of off-budget contributions from the donors slightly exceeded the domestic revenues and in-budget contributions amounted to almost 10% (see chapter five and annex 3 for details). Over time, the ratio of external contributions decreased from over 500 million USD in 2012 to about 13 million USD projected for the fiscal year 2017/18.

279 Although, given the generally slow pace of progress and few results in terms of policies, it is questionable how much difference the weakening of the commissions caused by diminished financial support really make.

UNMIL and the UN agencies are by far the most important external actors on the ground. Individual states are present through their diplomatic missions or through their development agencies. On the supranational level, they are involved in the mobilisation of political and financial support through the Liberia Country-Specific Configuration. At the "high level" of peacebuilding decision-making, some bilateral partners are members of the Joint Steering Committee. However, they were not involved at the "working level", that is, in any of the institutions in focus of this study. Regional organisations, or the regional dimension of peacebuilding was not prominent either.

11.1.2 Government of Liberia

The role of the government in the four cases is slightly more difficult to assess. After all, three out of four institutions in our focus *were* actually parts of governmental structures. The Governance Commission has a difficult relationship with governmental actors. It is perceived as an unwanted reformer, "stepping on people's toes" and trying to change the status quo. Its unpopularity is also reflected in the long time spans for approval of its policies by the Parliament. The executive branch provides limited support to the reform, mainly at the rhetorical level.

The LC has a relatively better position. The chairman was on good terms with President Johnson Sirleaf and the land reform was, apart from formal support, well backed financially. However, the land rights policy got stuck in the parliament for several years and the decision-making process was influenced by various vested interests. Representatives of several ministries were formally members of the two taskforces in our focus; however, they were often absent and their general level of participation was rather low. Both commissions were handicapped by their positions as advisory bodies with no implementation power that rendered the results of their work dependent on the legislature and other actors in the political process.

With regard to the Gender Ministry and actions against GBV, the government provided rather formal support. Ellen Johnson Sirleaf did not follow a specific, women-related agenda, and her engagement in this regard was perceived as insufficient by many, especially by women's groups. Gender issues in general have not been treated as a priority political topic.

Early warning is an issue with the lowest level of interest for governmental actors. Despite the ambition of the project to provide information to the decision-makers, the latter are not interested. A few governmental agencies have been members of the group; however, some of them did not want to be associated with the working group and preferred to stay out of the spotlights.

11.1.3 Civil society

In the case of governance, civil society represents a crucial partner of the Governance Commission, especially in outreach work and consultations. Their cooperation is based on mutual support, strengthened by good inter-personal relations.

In the taskforces of the Land Commission, civil society representatives were actively engaged. The meetings also served as an opportunity for information sharing and networking. In the subsequent legislative process, civil society organisations were campaigning for a fast adoption of the land rights bill in the parliament.

With regard to gender issues, their presence was even more prominent. Civil society representatives formed a majority of the participants in the GBV Taskforce, and constituted the major implementation partners and information providers on the ground. However, they were sometimes donor-driven in their agenda.

In the case of early warning, civil society was the alpha and omega of the whole initiative.

11.2 Actors' roles

Generally, there seems to be a clear division of labour between the actors in focus based on their strengths and particular capacities. Liberian case indicates that external actors' principal role is to provide material resources, in some cases the know-how and human resources as well. They set broad priorities of the postwar reforms, currently in the neo-liberal direction and in line with a more or less uncontested "checklists", including DDR, SSR, economic reforms, rebuilding state institutions, and infrastructure. They also set more specific objectives, usually in cooperation with the domestic government. In this case, the extent of external vs. internal influence in the process is case-specific and depends on various factors. It is also difficult to assess, due to a lack of evidence and primary data. In Liberia, according to some interviews, the government was quite outspoken and assertive in putting through their priorities.

The UN, as the most influential actor in this group operates as a "manager", able to break the broad objectives into smaller parts and to translate them into programs and projects. For the implementation of the latter, civil society and at times governmental agencies are called upon. More often, however, governmental structures are subjects of reforms, with external actors providing training and know-how for the institution-building. At the same time, there is a lot of emphasis on not being overly intrusive and "not doing everything" (Interview #29, UNMIL official, 25 May 2012, Monrovia), engaging only in fields, where the UN provides an added value in terms of knowledge or technical expertise.

An often-overlooked factor, not paid much attention in the scholarly literature, is the groups and institutions at the supranational level, such as the Liberia Country-Specific Configuration (LCSC), with a substantial impact on calling for funds and mobilising international support. The focus of the LCSC is diplomatic work, rather than presence on the ground.

The role of the Liberian government is crucial in terms of providing support to the particular reforms, both in a material and in a rhetorical way. Being on good terms with the government matters (the example of governance reform, being a problematic issue *per se* shows it quite clearly). Apart from this "allowing capacity", essential for making things happen at all, there is also a substantial "blocking capacity", visible in the legislative, rather than in the executive branch. This manifests, for example, in the long time (often years) it takes to approve some policies or bills, and the manoeuvring and playing around with the content of the bills. Often, there are specific vested interests present.

Civil society mainly plays the role of an implementation partner in a chain, where the broad goals are portioned into manageable pieces by the UN. Civil society is also used as a service or information provider from the local level, or from the areas with limited accessibility, where other actors do not reach out. In many cases, they are used as a substitute for international consultants for the work on the ground, operating with far lower costs (cf. Neubert 1997). Increasingly, civil society engages in advocacy and monitoring functions; other areas, as suggested by Paffenholz (2010) are not so much pronounced. *Vis-à-vis* the government, civil society tries to strengthen its position by "speaking with a unified voice". This seems to follow a logic presented by Moran (2006) in the case of women, where the collective character of a demand compensates a generally lower political weight of the particular subject. A problematic aspect is the high level of dependency of civil society on external funding, which often has an impact on the agenda. The focus of activities tends to follow financial opportunities offered by the donors. This is also complicated by the generally low level of development of the sector.

11.3 *Interaction*

The very existence of the institutions in focus in this study has contributed to the interaction between different actors by virtue of providing a "place of encounter" for them. The relatively small size of the "peacebuilding community" in the country further facilitated coordination and planning by opening the door for easy, informal networking and communication. The interaction between the three groups of actors is shaped by the specific circumstances of each case, determined mainly by the nature and political character of the particular issue at stake, ranging from complete disconnectedness to close cooperation. Generally, despite some underlying tensions, there has been no open rivalry or conflict. There seems to be a tacit understanding on a division of labour, based on the strengths of each particular actor. With regard to decision-making, if it took place at all, it was based on consensus, not on any voting procedures.

A factor worth mentioning was the general low level of participation of the governmental actors. It can be explained by "meeting fatigue", or by the lack of "buy-in" of the reform agenda. In any case, the mode of interaction and strategies of the Liberian domestic political actors are strongly reminiscent of Bayart's concept of extraversion (Bayart and Ellis 2000), reaching out to external resources and actors and using them (at least to some extent) for achieving their own goals and pursuing their own agenda.

11.4 *Ownership*

National ownership, as an aspect closely related to the issue of interaction, is analysed from two perspectives in this section: as setting the *agenda* in a respective field of reform, and secondly, as the ownership of the reform *process*. Early warning scores high on both fronts. The project is a genuine product of Liberian engagement. The middle, Track 2 level, represented mainly by civil society, forms the backbone of the initiative. External involvement is, apart from funding, limited to the representation of the UN and international NGOs, but the process, including choosing priorities, is not driven by them. Governance occupies the second place.

Here, priorities are set by the Governance Commission (i.e., by Liberians) and the external involvement in the implementation process is limited. However, the agenda is very much in line with the general principles of good governance already, so a pertinent question comes to mind of the extent in how far the national priorities have actually been influenced by the ruling good governance paradigm.

In the field of gender, national actors, especially civil society, are prominent at the level of engagement and implementation. External actors play a more pronounced role in agenda setting, often defining the priorities and direction of action, especially by the means of allocating financial support. The previously mentioned focus on rape in donor support represents an example of this phenomenon.

Land is a field with the highest international presence and donor interest of all the cases in focus. However, this high level of external interest and involvement is deliberately limited from the Liberian side. Land is treated as a highly sensitive issue that should stay entirely in Liberian hands. In this respect, a strong, charismatic leader of the Land Commission plays a decisive role. Dr. Brandy, the chairman of the LC, is regarded as someone who can resist pressures from different sides, counterbalancing the tendencies of external actors to be overly dominant (be it in the agenda-setting or ways "how to get there"), and, at the same time, is well-connected to the highest executive level. In other words, there is a high degree of national ownership and control of setting priorities.[280] On the other hand, the level of national ownership in the processes, in the everyday work and functioning of the LC, is more difficult to assess. As chapter eight has shown, due to a high level of international presence (the highest across the four cases) there might be much more influence of the external actors in this regard. In addition, there is a hidden pressure from the external actors coming into the process, once it reaches the legislature.

The perceived sensitivity of the issue, regarded as such by Liberians, seems to be a factor that determines the importance of ownership across the four cases. Governance and land are considered sensitive, highly political issues closely linked to the sovereignty of the state. Therefore, there is a lot of emphasis on national ownership of the reforms. In the case of gender, the "political sensitivity" and an approach of "Liberian solution to Liberian problems" is not so crucial. Universal measures and a "blueprint"

---

280 Although in the particular case of land reform, there are no substantial differences between the "external" and "domestic" agenda priorities. There is broad agreement about what needs to be done.

approach designed in the global North are considered fine. Early warn-ing is not perceived as sensitive either, but in this case, firstly, Liberian ownership of the initiative is obvious. Secondly—and more importantly—regarding the decision-making level, no one really cares, since the project is not a part of the peacebuilding package, where the issue of ownership is discussed and assessed as important.

11.5 The progress conundrum

The explanatory factors behind the lack of progress in the reform process vary across cases; however, some common traits can be identified. In gover-nance and land sectors, the main factor is the dependency of the reforms on other actors in the political process. The policies have to be approved by the legislature, which, due to different reasons, is not always favourable. In the case of governance, it is mainly due to the inherently problematic nature of the reforms, trying to bring change into the muddy waters of old political practices. With regard to land reform, vested interests of powerful individuals and companies come into play as well. It would have been useful to include these perspectives and actors in order to get a more comprehensive picture. However, their importance became evident only after my field research, as it manifested in the protracted legislative process. Fortunately, it was possible to follow the developments from the news, which covered the interests of different actors quite well. Although it would have been good to include primary data and conduct interviews with the politicians or businessmen, it is quite unlikely that they would disclose much more about their real motives and objectives than was already covered by the media.[281]

In both cases, it is also the scope of the reforms, requiring a considerable amount of time for their actual implementation that has to be taken into consideration.

The nature of the issue at stake seems to be the main factor hindering progress in the fight against GBV—this time combined with the problem's

---

281 The motives are no big secret for anyone familiar with politics. Apart from more noble goals, both politicians and companies are driven by profit. Polit-icians are used as brokers in this regard, influencing the decision-making ac-cording to the interests of the companies, or of their own. These, of course, are principles to be found beyond Liberia, and beyond the context of African politics.

low level of importance on the list of peacebuilding priorities, leading to relatively low financial support. There is little conflict potential in GBV; the issue is not directly linked to economic interests. In addition, a genuine reform would have to go beyond treating the symptoms and address the underlying causes of the phenomenon, rooted in socio-cultural norms and values. In this respect, the issue is similar to governance reform, which also tries to change the mindset of people, this time with regard to the functioning of the political institutions.

Early warning seems not to fit the research question at first sight, but, in fact, it offers a different perspective, one of progress "off record", out of the spotlights. The EWER initiative works, but it is irrelevant. The issue is not part of the official, mainstream reform package designed by the Track 1 actors. It comes from an alternative direction, growing from the bottom up, and has been maintained thanks to the engagement of civil society. It offers potentially relevant information to the decision-makers, but they are not interested. It works; it has results and impact at the grassroots level. But no one cares about the small early warning micro-world. This is kind of a paradox—a progress no one calls for counts as no progress at all, since it is largely ignored by the actors, who plan the broad reform framework.

At a general level, a factor that proved to be crucial for the progress of the reforms was the somehow abstract category of support for and interest in the particular issue, mainly from the side of international and governmental actors. The following paragraphs reflect on this category.

11.6 *"The support"*

Not all peacebuilding issues are created equal. They differ by their position on the imaginary ladder of peacebuilding priorities, manifested by its presence in the documents framing the reconstruction process, and by the promotion from the side of the involved domestic and international agencies.

Apart from this formal, rhetorical support, what matters even more is the material backing for the work of a specific institution. When we look across our four cases, land enjoys both —the declared support from the international and domestic political actors (as well as from the population), and the material support. Governance and gender are at a similar level— the rhetorical support is relatively high, but does not transform into an adequate level of material support. In the case of governance reform, the reasons for the lack of domestic political support lie in an inherent danger of change that would mean a potential limitation of power and benefits for the elites. For the external actors, explanations are more difficult to identify and can be more diversified as well. They can include fear of being overly intrusive in the domestic affairs of a foreign state, and the difficulties of changing the system in place, as it is closely connected to the political culture and socio-economic context, with a consequent perception of the reforms as a mere lip service. The lack of benefits from engagement in the field could be another factor; contrary to, for example, land, where there is a clear link to economic profit. For gender, the last two points apply as well. In the case of domestic support, gender is simply not considered high enough on the list of priorities, despite being featured as a crucial cross-cutting issue in the frameworks documents. For the international side, there is a good deal of financial support for projects related to gender-based violence and gender in general, but the problem is that most of the programs focus on symptoms rather than on the core of the phenomenon, which is, after all, deeply embedded in the socio-cultural context and, as such, is difficult to influence. Early warning is the least-well-off case, with its importance neither acknowledged by the framework documents, nor domestic or international actors. As a consequence, there is little material support, apart from funding from a single donor, for the issue.

An interesting positive correlation is the direct proportion of the level of financial support and the level of international presence. The more external actors are present in an institution, the more money the latter tends to have in our four selected cases.

11.6.1 Nature of the issue

Nature of the issue at stake is an important factor, determining the feasibility and implementation of reforms, but also linked to the attractivity of the field for potential engagement. A crucial factor in this regard is the conflict potential of the issue in question, either as a factor that contributed to the outbreak of the war, or as a general driver, with a potential to fuel conflicts in the postwar phase.

Two of the issues treated in the case-studies had a clear connection to the origins of the conflict: governance and land. Poor governance has been acknowledged as a problem by most of the authors who have analysed the Liberian case. In the case of land, the opinions vary (see chapter eight). However, in the postwar time, the imminent conflict potential of governance decreased somehow. Issues dealt with by the Governance Commission are important, but they generate little actual tension among the population. Land, however, still remains a clear security risk and a conflict trigger.

Gender-based violence was a phenomenon that came to the fore during the conflict but remained a prominent topic throughout the postwar time as well. From the traditional perspective, it does not pose a substantial threat to the national security and stability of the country. However, from the human security standpoint, it clearly affects the safety of half of the population and is also a decisive factor in the long-term development of the country—not only in terms of well-being of women, but concerning the welfare of whole families and communities.

With regard to early warning, the category of "conflict potential" does not really apply. Early warning is rather a mechanism that monitors conflict-related phenomena and aims to mitigate conflict. As such, it clearly has a link to security, but not in the same sense as the other issues. It was also a project established well after the end of the war, so there is no connection to the origins of the conflict.

The correlation of security-link and support depends on a perspective then. Departing from the traditional conception of security, the correlation is strong. Land, broadly acknowledged as a security risk in the framework documents and by the actors on the ground, receives a great deal of attention and financial resources. The other issues do not. Coming from a human security perspective, however, the correlation of a security risk and support does not apply.

Secondly, the potential for successful reforms is related to the question of how easy it is to influence the issue at stake and in what time-frame. Some phenomena, deeply embedded in social tissue and touching local values or political culture (such as corruption, gender inequality, or marginalisation), are difficult to be subjected to a deliberate change, in the form of a simple "reform". Peacebuilding reforms are generally presented as "technical", despite their profoundly political character. Apart from the hypocrisy, the technocratic perspective runs the risk of staying on the surface and not addressing the core of the problem. Gender-based violence represents an example of such an approach—most of the measures implemented in the frame of the UN-Government Joint Program focus on providing help to the survivors or on the economic empowerment of women. However, the underlying aspects, linked to gender inequality and some cultural norms and beliefs, remain unaddressed. Governance reform is similar; external actors present it as a technical exercise, but in reality, it *is* deeply political. It would take decades to change the legacy of the autocratic history and political culture, shaping the rules of the game. In fact, reforms in all the cases except early warning, are tasks of a considerable scope, where a long-term approach is needed to get results.

Time is indeed a necessary ingredient to achieve results in peacebuilding. Changes need time to take root. National ownership requires time. Keeping the reforms consultative and participative needs time as well. This, however, is in sharp contrast with project frameworks, schedules, and deadlines for most external actors and donors. Few are able and willing to engage extensively in the temporal sense.[282]

At the level of political processes, the slow pace of reforms is determined by the factors linked to the domestic political context. Although it seems to be a matter of common sense, it is not a topic considered in all the framework plans and by the people on the ground—especially by the UN as the main architect of the postwar reform. This could be interpreted as a disregard for the political subjecthood and agency of the Liberian side, in line with Sabaratnam (2017), but also as an acknowledged limitation of scope of the postwar intervention from the external actors. Consultations or other kinds of work that would involve domestic political actors, the legislature in particular, in the earlier stages of the reform process might bring some difference. Or, at least, might be worth considering.

11.6.2 The individual aspect

Leadership and individual engagement turned out to be two additional factors of crucial importance for the way an issue is being treated and for the success of the reform efforts. It is not only the "leadership" skills, such as communication, charisma, efficiency, etc., that matter, but also the rank of the person—who they are and where they stand in the political-institutional hierarchy.

Both the Land and Governance Commissions have well-known leaders, with a clear vision and access to the "right places", whose opinions are respected across the spectrum of all actors and institutions in our focus. Gender does not have a comparable figure. The Gender Minister has never been mentioned as someone who makes a difference in how the gender

---

282 In this respect, early warning stands out again. The main donor supporting the project showed a long-term commitment, both in the case of Liberia, and in other countries where it has been involved.

problematics are being treated, and President Sirleaf did not position herself as an ambassador of women's and gender issues. The "rank" was also thematised as an issue in the Early Warning Working Group that tried to use the director of the Peacebuilding Office for getting access to "high places", but his status and institutional affiliation was not sufficient to reach the goal.

Leadership, however crucial it is from the common-sense perspective, as well as backed by the data from the particular cases presented here, is hardly ever mentioned as an issue in the literature on peacebuilding.[283] The same is true for the "individual engagement" factor. It was clear from many interviews and observations (Interviews #22, #23, #25, #38, #49) that what was going on in the respective institutions and *how*, depends very much on the people who are in charge (cf. Skelcher 2005). Not only in terms of general interest and dedication to the respective issues, or their goal-oriented attitude, but also in terms of the process, involvement, and cooperation with different actors and consideration of their views. A number of examples illustrate this: an international consultant at the Land Commission, keeping the policy drafting process slow in order to solicit and include input from the Liberian counterparts. A UN-HABITAT officer, calling the informal meetings of different actors involved in the land sector. The ECOWAS representative, not knowing about the early warning initiative around LERN. Individual contacts and informal channels are acknowledged by different actors as essential for "getting things done", especially in the context of low institutionalisation. The individual aspect is closely connected to another issue, not so often explicitly mentioned in the interviews, but clearly making a difference—the issue of trust, based (among other things) on long-term contact and cooperation. These, individual-level aspects, as a factor that can influence the whole peacebuilding process, are hardly ever mentioned in the literature either, although the practice shows the crucial role they play. They also point to a limitation of the actor-centered institutionalism, which does not assume particular individuals to play such a significant role in institutions.[284]

At the highest executive level, it was clearly the strong presidential leadership that determined the constellation of domestic and external actors. President Sirleaf was perceived as assertive and outspoken in this regard (Interview #37, foreign embassy, 7 June 2012, Monrovia). As a Har-

---

283 Here again, Autesserre (2017), reminding of the importance of the informal and personal, represents a notable exception.
284 This aspect is more elaborated in the section 11.8.

vard-trained economist, with experience in the WB, she was regarded as a credible partner for the international donors and, indeed, she followed the neo-liberal path of reforms. The question remains, if the latter choice was based on a conviction about this trajectory, or on the simple acceptance of reality, shaped by the neo-liberal paradigm, combined with Liberia's dependence on externally provided financial resources. In this respect, Bayart's concept of extraversion comes to mind again.

11.7 Contextual variables and external factors

Context plays an essential role in peacebuilding at all levels, from the international to the local one. The decisive role of the international context with financial dependency of recipient states and IFIs "calling the tune" mentioned here represents only a part of the story. Another aspect is the situation in the post-conflict countries themselves, with varying degrees of destruction (physical, institutional, and individual), as well as scarce financial and human resources. This fast-changing environment with a low level of institutional stability becomes a landing place for a large number of international personnel with limited knowledge of local realities. Due to this low level of institutional stability, many institutions are inactive or non-functional for various reasons. Apart from a lack of basic equipment, the everyday work is further complicated by unpredictable changes of schedules and unexpected circumstances. Clearly, under such conditions, individual relationships become more important, but the high level of fluctuation on the domestic and international sides makes the cooperation and trust-building in working relations difficult. The temporality of the international presence frames the whole peacebuilding intervention. The tacit knowledge of the limited nature of the former impacts the overall setting and relationships among the actors, and also their position *vis à vis* the reform agenda. The reconstruction and reforms are to a very large extent dependent on external support—in some cases financial, in others on a more encompassing one, including know-how and human resources.

The position of a particular institution in the political context is another crucial determining factor of its success and the viability of the reforms. Not only considering how political the issue at stake is, but also how much political weight the specific institution has and how "un/comfortable" it is for other actors around (e.g., ministries, executive, and legislative branches of government, as well as powerful individuals or companies with specific interests). As the examples of governance and land policies show, the fate of the policies is to a large extent dependent on the decisions of the legislature, which is, in addition, often influenced by the vested interests of powerful actors "behind the scenes". This clash with "politics as usual" has been underthematised in the peacebuilding debates, despite its indisputable importance.

In the same vein, dependency on other parts of the polity in the area of implementation hinders the impact of some reforms. For example, the legislation on GBV remains toothless without an adequate performance of the police and judiciary, both of them currently being unable to ensure any meaningful law enforcement.

11.7.1 External factors

Apart from the factors discussed, there is also a category of structural factors, which are difficult to influence, but can have a major impact on the fate of the reforms and the country in general, especially in a negative sense. A major issue that cast the country off track was the Ebola epidemics. A fight against the strike of a *force majeure* overthrew all the plans and consumed a major portion of financial resources for the sake of emergency measures. Apart from decimating the population, it also dealt a heavy blow to the economy of the country, further affected by the decline in commodity prices on global markets.

From a middle- to long-term perspective, the departure of UNMIL had a considerable impact on the progress of the reforms. It means a transition to a different funding scheme and a subsequent decline in external financial resources on which the progress of the reforms largely depends.

11.8 Aspects linked to theory and literature

There are a number of features our case studies illustrate, which are, despite their obvious importance, insufficiently reflected in the theoretical debate on peacebuilding. Some of them have been already mentioned: the role of strong leadership, individual engagement, and good interpersonal relations, that are, together with time, crucial elements of the process of building trust. The blocking character of the legislature and, more generally, the importance of everyday political processes for the fate of peacebuilding reforms add to the list. Scholarly literature tends to focus on the reforms *an sich*, but not on the processes coming after them, on their implementation and sustainability, both being to a very large extent determined by the local political context. This, according to Sabaratnam (2017) can be explained by a Euro-centric attitude of the interveners and their denial of political subjecthood of the country of intervention. On the other hand, it can also point to the exact opposite – to the acknowledgment of limits of the externally supported reform, *acknowledging* the sovereignty and political agency of the country of intervention, conveying the message "our work here is done, whatever happens with the reforms now is in the hand of the Liberians". A convincing answer would, however, have to be backed by further empirical evidence.

There is a lot of emphasis on formal coherence of the peacebuilding intervention. All action plans, sectional plans, and frameworks are in line with the priorities outlined in the general framework documents. This coherence, however, applies only within the system itself and makes it disconnected from other parts of postwar reality. For one, it creates a mainstream, hegemonic discourse that does not grant space for alternative voices or ways of doing things (such as the early warning initiative). For another, the system is self-referential and does not reach to other parts of the polity that would be useful to include, as they play an important part in the implementation process (e.g., the legislature).

Last but not least, there is a clear detachment from the post-conflict individuals, an absence of an individual, human-centred approach. The ultimate beneficiaries of the peacebuilding reforms and their needs are somehow not at the centre of attention. The focus is rather on institution- and state-building. To be sure, macro-economic stability and institutional reforms are important. But, bearing in mind the uncontested importance of the "peace dividend" for maintaining stability in a postwar context, it is striking that there has been, for example, no employment-generating policy since 2003, or that the health care system is, as the Ebola epidemics exposed, still extremely insufficient. In this respect, different *conceptions* of peacebuilding, representing points of departure of different actors come to light. As our empirical examples show, building peace for international actors means, first and foremost, building well-functioning states and state institutions. Domestic political elites conceive of peacebuilding as a conflict-sensitive "way of doing things", defined in the Poverty Reduction Strategy as the underlying principle of the postwar reconstruction process. Local actors at the middle level, represented, for example, by the Peacebuilding Office or NGOs, take yet a different perspective, one similar to Lederach and the conflict resolution school, building peace from the bottom up and stressing the importance of the grassroots and middle levels.

Although peacebuilding interventions are fields shaped by the multitude of actors and levels involved in the implementation of the reforms, the analysis has so far focused mainly on the dichotomy between the national (or local) and international, the external and domestic levels. Multi-level governance seems to be a much more relevant approach in this respect. It emphasises the impact of actors' internal rules and constraints in the interaction and takes it into consideration as a factor adding to the complexities of the decision-making processes in different institutional settings.

The peacebuilding literature usually does not thematise the crucial role of some actors at the supranational level. A regional level of cooperation in peacebuilding initiatives is often stressed (taking into consideration regional dimension of conflicts: Liberia/West Africa or the Great Lakes being a classic example of regional security complexes), but in reality, there is little done within the regional cooperation framework. The ECOWAS office in Liberia was far from being a place of frenetic activity or a networking hub. Also some projects (e.g., GIZ), promoting the regional dimension of the cooperation, were in fact rather limited in this respect (Interview #34, GIZ employee, 4 June 2012, Monrovia). On the contrary, the "working committees" of some international organisations, such as the Liberia Country Configuration in PBC, or international "clubs of friends", not easily classified, have a crucial impact on generating and sustaining both material and ideal support for the post-conflict countries.

The findings related to the importance of particular individuals for the results of the policy-making also point to the limits of the actor-centered institutionalism. The ACI does not assume that individuals play such an important role, since the approach was developed for a different context, one with a relatively high level of institutionalisation and a prevalence of composite actors. As this study shows, however, in a setting with lower level of institutional stability the individual aspect can be much more pronounced.

Speaking of particular actors, it is interesting to take a step back and see who is usually not included in the common lens of peacebuilding analysis. Firstly, it is economic actors. Representatives of private companies, although powerful players influencing the decision-making processes, were not included in any of the institutions in our focus. The same applies to the representatives of local administration and (neo)-traditional leaders, as well as religious organisations. The exclusion of the former can be ascribed to the still very much centralised character of the Liberian political system. The latter, although having a significant role in bringing the conflict to an end, seemed to be singled out as religious actors in the postwar phase and included only under the label of civil society, as NGOs, such as the Inter-Religious Council of Liberia.

Last but not least, as mentioned in the theoretical overview in chapter two, there is a question of accountability in the current peacebuilding projects. Interestingly, it did not turn out to be an issue mentioned by anyone, in any interview I had done. It could mean that the legitimacy aspect of the reforms is perceived as sufficiently covered by the initial consent of the Liberian political elites and their say in the process of setting priorities. It could also point to the underlying pragmatic attitude to the temporality of international engagement and ephemeral character of the reforms. Following this logic, in the long term, domestic political actors do not have to worry about accountability—things are going to adjust and "go the right way" over time anyway.

Chapter 12 Conclusion

Peacebuilding, especially in post-conflict contexts, is a joint endeavour of a variety of actors. This study looked at the case of Liberia, more particularly at the interaction and the respective roles of the Liberian government, international actors, and civil society in the postwar peacebuilding process. Against the backdrop of four specific institutions, the study analysed their interaction and respective roles in the particular institutional settings. It also looked at the issue of progress, trying to identify the reasons for the slow pace of the reforms, which, after a relatively long time and despite favourable conditions, seem to yield few tangible results. The inquiry was designed as a qualitative case study with Liberia serving as a general case, and the four institutions representing the embedded units of analysis.

The Governance Commission, with its precarious position as a reform actor and a lack of adequate financial support for its work, represented the first case. The Land Commission, featuring a high level of international presence, substantial material support, and a high conflict potential regarding the matter in question, stood for its ultimate opposite. In both cases, the fate of the Commissions' efforts was completely dependent on the legislature. The other two cases were less prominent. The GBV Taskforce is a platform for coordination and information sharing, rather than a policy- and decision-making body. The fact that the issue at stake is difficult to influence represents, together with limited financial backing, the main impediment to the work of the taskforce. The Early Warning Working Group seems to fulfil all the criteria of a good peacebuilding initiative, being built from the bottom up, with robust involvement from civil society, and the support of the international actors. However, the project is completely disconnected from its beneficiaries.

The roles of particular actors in each of the four cases were different, but still, some general characteristics could be identified. With regard to the international actors, they set the broad direction of the reconstruction, and bring material and human resources to support the reforms. The UN is the most prominent actor on the ground and serves as a "manager" of the reconstruction process, breaking the general objectives included in the framework plans into smaller tasks and programs for a subsequent implementation. Bilateral partners are present through their diplomatic representations on the ground, and in the institutions at the supranational and highest decision-making level. They do not participate directly in the institutions in the focus of the study (i.e., at the middle, working level). The individual states are, however, often represented by their development agencies. The regional dimension of the reconstruction process and the presence of regional organisations on the ground was marginal.

Liberian governmental actors do set priorities to some extent, but they are limited by the broader context of the neo-liberal direction of the current peacebuilding discourse. However, they dispose of a substantial blocking potential.

Civil society, as the third actor in our focus, serves mainly as an implementation partner, an information and service provider. Due to the dependency on external funding and a general low level of development, its agenda is often donor-driven. Civil society aspires to become a partner to be consulted in the policy-making process. It is indeed included in all four sub-cases; however, the highest decision-making level takes a reserved stance in this respect and does not reach out for the civil society expertise as for an auxiliary source of information in the decision-making process.

The interaction among the three groups of actors was defined by the multi-level character of the peacebuilding exercise and their respective roles outlined above. These were based on the particular strengths of each actor. Despite some underlying tensions, there were no signs of animosity or antagonism. Decision-making was consensual, with no voting procedures present. The very existence of the "places of encounter" has actually facilitated the interaction of the three groups. Another favourable factor in this respect was the informal personal networks and relations, which, in the context of institutional fragility and low level of institutionalisation, played a crucial role. The relative small size of the country and of the community involved in the peacebuilding reforms rendered coordination along the informal channels easy as well.

The factors hindering the progress of the reforms were different across the cases, but still can be classified into several categories. Firstly, there are external factors that are difficult to influence, such as the outbreak of Ebola or a decrease in stable financial support linked to the departure of UNMIL. Secondly, there are issues related to the nature of the particular peacebuilding issue at stake. Some topics are more difficult to be influenced, due to different reasons, and some need a long time span for completion due to their complexity. Others are deeply embedded in the socio-cultural values and norms. What turned out to be a decisive factor was the impact of the domestic political context. The initial phase of the reforms was usually well-planned. According to a general outline, in a more or less participative process and with the assistance of external actors, a policy was produced. Then, however, in the next step, it had to be approved in the regular legislative process. And it was here that the previous steps were jeopardised or completely blocked. Apart from that, additional factors, such as potential vested interests of influential actors, proved to be crucial as well. A factor with an enabling potential to facilitate progress, on the other hand, was the individual engagement, made manifest, for example, in a capable, well-connected leader with the access to the "right places".

Generally, the analysis of the four institutional cases showed that peacebuilding, despite the substantial progress in the academic debate, to a large extent remains shaped by the ruling neo-liberal paradigm. It is organised in a top-down manner, according to a series of framework plans in a coherent, yet closed-up system, which is rather disconnected from the postwar reality and the needs of post-conflict individuals. Building peace is still carried out as creating well-functioning states and state institutions, and production of policies that provide foundation to the organisation of a post-conflict life. Nevertheless, despite all of the efforts and financial resources invested, the fate of the reforms is ultimately dependent on the legislative processes and, later, in the implementation phase, on the everyday functioning of the political system in the country of intervention. This fundamental reality is, however, ignored by the architects of the reforms. Hidden, yet powerful actors make an impact, but they are not approached in order to be incorporated in the "official" reform processes. The imperative of local ownership is covered by the inclusion of civil society. Yet, too much "local context" is waved aside—after all, it can be clashing with the promoted values of good governance, transparency, accountability, and human rights.

In the literature on peacebuilding, the aforementioned factors (domestic political context, nature of the issue at stake, and influential individuals as both the enabling factor and potential spoilers) are hardly discussed. When progress is debated, it is usually in technocratic terms of efficiency and sequencing of the reforms within the mainstream, top-down approach to peacebuilding, or in terms of the involvement of domestic actors in the "local ownership" stream of thought. However, empirical studies questioning specific impact factors are rare.[285]

---

285 Autessere (2017) with her focus on everyday practices, Sabaratnam (2017) tracing the coloniality of power in Mozambique, Muhire (2017) analysing the

Another interesting feature is the absence of the individual level as an issue to be considered in the mainstream peacebuilding debate. The relevance of individuals is acknowledged by the practitioners (e.g., Lederach 1997), but neo-liberal peacebuilding usually sticks to the dichotomy of international and local actors, however simplified and problematic in terms of real-life applicability this classification is. Charbonneau et al. (2012) take the individual into the centre of analysis, but they focus rather on the post-conflict individuals, with their rights and needs, currently still at the margins of the attention in neo-liberal approaches. The results of this study show the significance of the individuals as *agents within* Liberian postwar reconstruction process (i.e., as potential facilitators or spoilers of the progress).

Some of the issues listed here are reflected in the academic debates, especially in the critical stream of thought. However, they do not translate into a change of the general, international peacebuilding policies and strategies. The perspective of the international actors remains blinkered for issues beyond the institutional and policy reform field, however decisive they might be. As in many other fields, there is a gap between theory and practice, research and policy, academics and practitioners. Both worlds stay closed up to a large extent. Practitioners tend to focus on the hurdles of implementation. Academia, on the other hand, runs the risk of being locked up in too much theorising and normative debates about how things should be. More empirical input, drawing attention to challenges of practical application of the knowledge, and to what is actually possible, would certainly be desirable. The presented study goes exactly in this direction and tries to fill a part of the empirical gap. Apart from the analysis, it offers a rich descriptive component, particularly valuable in the case of Liberia, where a lot of information, reports, and materials can be accessed only on the spot and are not available elsewhere.

Like every piece of research, this study has certain limitations. One of them is its focus on the single case of a post-conflict country. The arguments acknowledging the value of a single-case study design were presented in the methodological section and do not need to be repeated here. In terms of external validity of the results, it is clear that it is not possible to make any broad generalisations, despite the number of similarities Liberia shares with other countries emerging from a violent conflict. Another constraint was a limited approach to meetings of different institutions

---

situation in eastern DR Congo, and to some extent Utas (2008) for Liberia, represent noteworthy exceptions.

for the purpose of data collection. The high-level meetings were impossible to attend, although they would certainly provide interesting material that could be compared with the data from the middle-level institutions. Similarly, it was not possible to attend meetings of the Governance Commission and the data had to be obtained indirectly, through interviews. In the same vein, I could get only secondary information about the informal avenues of interaction. Some of these limitations, however, represent opportunities for future research. An ethnographic study of informal places of interaction could bring interesting insights, complementing the perspective of formal institutions presented here. Inquiry into reasons behind the exclusion of the domestic political institutions from the reform framework could bring valuable insights into different the perspectives on political subjectivity of the countries of intervention. External validity of the results of this study can be strengthened in comparative studies of other countries emerging from conflict. Another interesting avenue would be a longitudinal study of Liberia, tracing the trajectories of the reforms over a longer time span.

The results of this study show quite clearly that in the context of temporary external engagement, the results, sustainability, and the ultimate fate of the reforms depends entirely on the domestic political actors. Taking this into consideration, the question arises, what is the reason for them to buy in and follow the suggested reform path. The reasons are seemingly mainly pragmatic. Firstly, there is broad agreement that everyone is simply better off in peace. The acceptance of the proposed way of reconstruction brings funds, has stabilising effects on political and economic context, and brings opportunities for employment. The general settings and direction of the reforms is given, yet there is always some space for a "bespoke tailoring", to put through some modification, specific priorities, hybridisation, and, not to forget, extraversion.

Taking one more step back, it is also almost impossible to opt out of the current style of postwar reconstruction. In the globalised world of today, there are no alternatives. Countries are tacitly, yet firmly, pushed in the direction of neo-liberal reforms. Those, who refused and decided to pursue their own trajectory do not face an easy task. Some, such as Somaliland, are effectively ignored by the international community. Despite becoming an outcast, being left alone provides the necessary space and time to build peace from within, according to their own values and needs. Others, such as Rwanda, bet on a more moderate version of the independent path, backed up by a strong, authoritarian leadership. This is, however, not possible for every country, as some pre-conditions have to be met. One of them, an essential one, is a certain level of development. It is hard to imagine that a country coming out of a violent conflict, massively destroyed in many respects, has the capacity to draft its own alternative peacebuilding strategy, based mainly on self-help and minimal external assistance.

To what extent are the findings from the Liberian case transferable to other postwar contexts?[286] It was already pointed out that variables shaping the contexts of peacebuilding interventions are in many respects similar in different countries around the globe; not only in terms of the broad international setting with its both tacit and explicit rules and conditions, but also with regard to the goals of specific reforms, and practices of the personnel deployed to implement the programmes (Autesserre 2017).

Most of the peacebuilding interventions have been implemented in the countries of the Global South. It is clear that the latter is not a homogeneous space. First, there are significant differences among regions, especially with regard to the concept of statehood and overall strength and presence of the state – which is a key aspect in the institution-building field. The state in Africa is certainly different than, e.g., in Asia or Latin America. Second, the conditions in each particular country of intervention vary as well. All these factors are also to a large extent determined by the pre-conflict situation in the respective country.

The roles of respective actors in every country are likely to vary to some extent, depending on the particular power constellation in each case, or other factors (e.g., the size of the country, or the level of centralisation). Generally, the room for manoeuvre of the international actors is meted out in interaction with the domestic political representation. In other words, how much space the external actors get is (co)-determined by the political actors in the country of intervention, by their strength and approval of the reform efforts. The role of civil society is even more case- and context-dependent. However, the overall division of labour of different actors in other postwar contexts would probably be more or less in line with the findings from Liberia, since it is influenced by the same broad neo-liberal framework.

Despite the fact that the relationship among the actors is shaped by inequalities, the political representation in Liberia plays a key role in the ultimate result of the reforms. This factor is very likely to be similar in other countries of intervention. More empirical evidence in this regard

---

286 All assumptions about transferability of the findings in the next paragraphs would, of course, have to be backed up by research for a robust and convincing evidence.

would certainly be desirable, since the long-term impact of the political "everyday" is currently being overlooked, both in the scholarly debate and in practice. The role of important individuals is likely to be more pronounced in countries with lower level of institutional stability or contexts, where the role of formal political institutions is not so strong. To speculate about the impact of other factors identified as dependent variables behind the progress in the reform process (nature of the "dossier", conflict potential or the "priority status") is difficult for they would be very much case-dependent. I see them as likely to be relevant in other postwar contexts, however, as already mentioned, their impact would have to be examined more closely to move beyond the level of assumptions. Conducting the comparative research should not be too complicated, since the design of this study is easily applicable elsewhere.

What do the lines above mean when it comes to broader debates about peacebuilding? They clearly show the limits of the debates. Indeed, if I could make a wish for peacebuilding, I would lobby for broadening of the perspective – both on the academic and practical level. Firstly, by considering new analytical approaches and concepts for the study of postwar interventions. This would bring the hitherto overlooked yet relevant factors in play to the fore and would strengthen the explanatory value of the future analyses. Secondly, it would be useful to broaden the temporal scope and to adopt a long-term perspective of the peacebuilding reforms for the analysis. Thirdly, the analytical lens should stretch beyond institutions and not forget about the ultimate beneficiaries of these reforms – the human beings. Last but not least, as I already suggested earlier in this section, it would be extremely helpful for all parties to open up to the knowledge beyond their own fields: practitioners can learn from the scholars and vice versa, first-track peacebuilders can listen to the middle-range, international staff can learn some lessons from the actors on the ground. Such an exchange would be, in my opinion, beneficial for all.

References

Abasiattai, Monday B. 1988. *African resistance in Liberia: The Vai and the Gola-Bandi.* no. 2 of *Liberia Working Group papers.* Bremen: Liberia Working Group.

Abels, Gabriele, and Maria Behrens. 2014. "Interviewing experts in political science: a reflection on gender and policy effects based on secondary analysis." In *Interviews mit Experten: Eine praxisorientierte Einführung. Qualitative Sozialforschung,* eds. Alexander Bogner, Beate Littig and Wolfgang Menz. Wiesbaden: Springer VS, 138–56.

Abrahamsen, Rita. 2006. *Disciplining democracy: Development discourse and good governance in Africa.* London [u.a.]: Zed Books.

Abramowitz, Sharon A. 2014. *Searching for normal in the wake of the Liberian war.* 1st ed. *Pennsylvania studies in human rights.* Philadelphia: University of Pennsylvania Press.

Adebajo, Adekeye. 2002. *Liberia's civil war: Nigeria, ECOMOG, and regional security in West Africa.* Boulder, Colo.: L. Rienner.

Affa'a-Mindzie, Mireille. 2012. *Preventing Conflicts in Africa: Early Warning and Response.* New York: International Peace Institute. https://www.ipinst.org/wp-content/uploads/publications/ipi_e_pub_preventing_conflicts.pdf (Accessed June 2, 2017).

AFP. 2014. "Corruption continues to linger in Liberian police ranks." *Enca.com,* May 23. http://www.enca.com/corruption-continues-linger-liberian-police-ranks (Accessed June 8, 2017).

Africa Governance Institute. 2014. "AGI Newsletter: How to revitalize the AU Policy on Post-Conflict Reconstruction and Development in Africa?" April. Africa Governance Institute. http://www.iag-agi.org (Accessed June 20, 2015).

African Union. 2006. *Policy on Post-Conflict Reconstruction and Development.*

Akpan, M. B. 1973. "Black Imperialism: Americo-Liberian Rule over the African Peoples of Liberia, 1841-1964." *Canadian Journal of African Studies / Revue Canadienne des Études Africaines* 7 (2): 217.

Allison, Simon. 2012. "Analysis: It's time to reassess Ellen Johnson Sirleaf." *Daily Maverick,* October 10. http://www.dailymaverick.co.za/article/2012-10-10-analysis-its-time-to-reassess-ellen-johnson-sirleaf/#.V-46AvmLS00 (Accessed October 5, 2016).

Alwis, Malathi de, Julie Mertus, and Tazreena Sajjad. 2013. "Women and peace processes." In *Women and wars,* ed. Carol Cohn. Cambridge: Polity, 169–93.

Anastasion, Daniele, and Eric Strauss. 2011. *The Redemption of General Butt Naked.*

Andersen, Morten S. "Governmentalisation of Sovereignty: Ownership and Liberal Governing in Liberia."

Aoláin, Fionnuala N., Dina F. Haynes, and Naomi R. Cahn. 2011. *On the frontlines: Gender, war, and the post-conflict process.* Oxford, New York: Oxford University Press.

Appiayei-Atua, Kwadwo. 2002. *Civil society, human rights and development in Africa: A critical analysis.* https://www.bradford.ac.uk/social-sciences/peace-conflict-and -development/issue-2/CivilSocietyAfrica.pdf (Accessed January 26, 2018).

Aseto, Valerie A. 2013. "Regional Perspectives of Early Warning Systems (EWS): A Case Study of IGAD's Response to Conflicts in the Horn of Africa." Master's Thesis. University of Nairobi.

Austin, Alex, Martina Fischer, and Norbert Ropers, eds. 2004. *Transforming Ethnopolitical Conflict: The Berghof Handbook.* Wiesbaden: VS Verlag für Sozialwissenschaften.

Austin, Alexander. 2004. "Early Warning and The Field: A Cargo Cult Science?" In *Transforming Ethnopolitical Conflict: The Berghof Handbook,* eds. Alex Austin, Martina Fischer and Norbert Ropers. Wiesbaden: VS Verlag für Sozialwissenschaften, 129–50.

Autesserre, Séverine. 2017. *Peaceland: Conflict resolution and the everyday politics of international intervention.* 4th ed.

Baaz, Maria E., and Maria Stern. 2009. "Why Do Soldiers Rape?: Masculinity, Violence, and Sexuality in the Armed Forces in the Congo (DRC)." *International Studies Quarterly* 53 (2): 495–518.

Bach, Daniel, and Mamoudou Gazibo. 2012. *Neopatrimonialism in Africa and beyond.* Vol. 1 of *Routledge studies on African politics and international relations.* New York: Routledge.

Bacon, Laura. 2015. "Liberia's Gender-Sensitive Police Reform: Improving Representation and Responsiveness in a Post-Conflict Setting." *International Peacekeeping* 22 (4): 372–97.

Bahcheli, Tozun. 2004. "Under Turkey's wings: the Turkish Republic of Northern Cyprus, the struggle for international acceptance." In *De facto states: The quest for sovereignty. Politics,* eds. Tozun Bahcheli, Barry Bartmann and Henry F. Srebrnik. London: Routledge, 164–86.

Bahcheli, Tozun, Barry Bartmann, and Henry F. Srebrnik, eds. 2004. *De facto states: The quest for sovereignty. Politics.* London: Routledge.

Bain, William. 2006. "In praise of folly: international administration and the corruption of humanity." *International Affairs* 82 (3): 525–38.

Banister, Elizabeth M. 2016. "Evolving Reflexivity: Negotiating Meaning of Women's Midlife Experience." *Qualitative Inquiry* 5 (1): 3–23.

Barrett, Frank J. 1996. "The Organizational Construction of Hegemonic Masculinity: The Case of the US Navy." *Gender, Work & Organization* 3 (3): 129–42.

Bartelson, Jens. 1995. *A genealogy of sovereignty.* Vol. 39 of *Cambridge studies in international relations.* Cambridge: Cambridge University Press.

Barton, Frederick, and Karin von Hippel. 2008. "Early Warning? A Review of Conflict Prediction Models and Systems." PCR Project Special Briefing. Washington, D.C.: Centre for Strategic and International Studies. https://csis-prod.s3.amazonaws.com/s3fs-public/legacy_files/files/publication/080201_early_warning.pdf (Accessed June 1, 2017).

Basini, Helen S. A. 2013. "Gender Mainstreaming Unraveled: The Case of DDRR in Liberia." *International Interactions* 39 (4): 535–57.

Bastick, Megan, Karin Grimm, and Rahel Kunz. 2007. *Sexual violence in armed conflict: Global overview and implications for the security sector.* Geneva: Geneva Centre for the Democratic Control of Armed Forces.

Baum, Joel A. C., and Frank Dobbin, eds. 2000. *Economics meets sociology in strategic management.* v. 17 of *Advances in strategic management.* Bingley: Emerald Group Publishing Limited.

Bayart, Jean-Francois. 1986. "Civil society in Africa." In *Political domination in Africa: Reflections on the limits of power.* Vol. 50 of *African studies,* ed. Patrick Chabal. Cambridge: Cambridge University Press, 109–25.

Bayart, Jean-François. 2009. *The state in Africa: The politics of the belly* [Translated from French]. 2nd ed. Cambridge, Malden, MA: Polity.

Bayart, Jean-François, Ellis, Stephen. 2000. "Africa in the World: A History of Extraversion." *African Affairs* 99 (395): 217–67.

Beber, Bernd, Michael J. Gilligan, Jenny Guardado, and Sabrina Karim. 2017. "Peacekeeping, Compliance with International Norms, and Transactional Sex in Monrovia, Liberia." *International Organization* 71 (01): 1–30.

Behrends, Andrea, Sung-Joon Park, and Richard Rottenburg, eds. 2014. *Travelling models in African conflict management: Translating technologies of social ordering.* Vol. 13 of *Africa-Europe group for interdisciplinary studies.* Leiden, Boston: Brill.

Bellamy, Alex J. 2004. "The 'next stage' in peace operations theory?" *International Peacekeeping* 11 (1): 17–38.

Bellamy, Alex J., and Paul Williams. 2004. "Introduction: Thinking anew about peace operations." *International Peacekeeping* 11 (1): 1–15.

Belloni, Roberto. 2012. "Hybrid peace governance. Its emergence and significance." *Global Governance* 18 (1): 21–38.

Belur, Jyoti. 2013. "Status, gender and geography: Power negotiations in police research." *Qualitative Research* 14 (2): 184–200.

Berger, Roni. 2014. "Now I see it, now I don't: Researcher's position and reflexivity in qualitative research." *Qualitative Research* 15 (2): 219–34.

Bergsmo, Morten, ed. 2012. *Understanding and proving international sex crimes.* Vol. 12 of *FICHL Publication Series.* Beijing: Torkel Opsahl Acad. EPubl.

Berkeley, Bill. 2001. *The graves are not yet full: Race, tribe and power in the heart of Africa.* New York: Basic Books.

Bernath, Tania. 2015. *Evaluation of the Norwegian Refugee Council's GBV Programme in Liberia 2009-2014.* Norwegian Refugee Council. https://reliefweb.int/sites/reliefweb.int/files/resources/9191044.pdf (Accessed October 24, 2017).

Besada, Hany. 2010. *Crafting an African security architecture: Addressing regional peace and conflict in the 21st century. The international political economy of new regionalisms series.* Farnham, Surrey, England, Burlington, Vt.: Ashgate Pub.

Blattman, Christopher, Alexandra Hartman, and Robert Blair. 2011. *Can we teach peace and conflict resolution?: Results from a randomized evaluation of the Community Empowerment Program (CEP) in Liberia: A program to build peace, human rights, and civic participation.* Yale University, Innovations for Poverty Action. http://www.poverty-action.org/publication/evidence-randomized-evaluations-peacebuilding-liberia-can-we-teach-peace-and-conflict (Accessed August 16, 2017).

Bøås, Morten. 2005. "The liberian civil war: new war/old war?" *Global Society* 19 (1): 73–88.

Bøås, Morten. 2009. "Making Plans for Liberia—a Trusteeship Approach to Good Governance?" *Third World Quarterly* 30 (7): 1329–41.

Bøås, Morten. 2009. ""New" nationalism and autochthony - tales of origin as political cleavage." *Africa Spectrum* 44 (1): 19–38. http://citeseerx.ist.psu.edu/viewdoc/download?doi=10.1.1.467.1611&rep=rep1&type=pdf (Accessed August 12, 2017).

Bøås, Morten. 2015. *The Politics of Conflict Economies: Miners, merchants and warriors in the African borderland. Routledge advances in international relations and global politics.* Hoboken: Taylor and Francis.

Bøås, Morten, and Kevin Dunn. 2013. *Politics of origin in Africa: Autochthony, citizenship and conflict.* London: Zed Books.

Boege, Volker, Anne Brown, Kevin Clements, and Anna Nolan. 2009. "Building Peace and Political Community in Hybrid Political Orders." *International Peacekeeping* 16 (5): 599–615.

Bogner, Alexander, Beate Littig, and Wolfgang Menz, eds. 2014. *Interviews mit Experten: Eine praxisorientierte Einführung. Qualitative Sozialforschung.* Wiesbaden: Springer VS.

Bogner, Alexander, and Wolfgang Menz. 2014. "Der Zugang zu den Experten: die Vorbereitung der Erhebung." In *Interviews mit Experten: Eine praxisorientierte Einführung. Qualitative Sozialforschung*, eds. Alexander Bogner, Beate Littig and Wolfgang Menz. Wiesbaden: Springer VS, 27–47.

Bogner, Alexander, and Wolfgang Menz. 2014. "Wer ist ein Experte? Wissenssoziologische Grundlagen des Expertinneninterviews." In *Interviews mit Experten: Eine praxisorientierte Einführung. Qualitative Sozialforschung*, eds. Alexander Bogner, Beate Littig and Wolfgang Menz. Wiesbaden: Springer VS, 9–15.

Bombande, Emmanuel. 2016. "The role of WANEP in crafting peace and security architecture in West Africa." In *Civil society, peace, and power. Peace and security in the 21st century*, eds. David Cortright, Melanie C. Greenberg and Laurel Stone. Lanham, Boulder, New York, London: Rowman & Littlefield, 119–42.

Booth, David, and Diana R. Cammack. 2013. *Governance for development in Africa: Solving collective action problems.* London, New York: Zed Books.

Box-Steffensmeier, Janet M., ed. 2010. *The Oxford handbook of political methodology.* 1st ed. [4] of *The Oxford handbooks of political science.* Oxford: Oxford University Press.

Brinkerhoff, Derick W., ed. 2007. *Governance in post-conflict societies: Rebuilding fragile states. Contemporary security studies.* London, New York: Routledge.

Brownmiller, Susan. 1975. *Against our will: Men, women and rape.* New York: Fawcett.

Bugingo, Emmanuel. 2002. "Missing the mark? Participation in the PRSP process in Rwanda." Christian Aid. http://reliefweb.int/report/rwanda/missing-mark-par ticipation-prsp-process-rwanda (March 15, 2017).

Burchill, Scott, ed. 2001. *Theories of International Relations.* 3rd ed. Basingstoke: Palgrave Macmillan Ltd.

Butler, Judith. 1990. *Gender trouble: Feminism and the subversion of identity.* 2nd ed. *Routledge classics.* New York, NY: Routledge.

Carvalho, Benjamin de, and Andrea Paras. 2015. "Sovereignty and Solidarity: Moral Obligation, Confessional England, and the Huguenots." *The International History Review* 37 (1): 1–21.

Carvalho, Benjamin de, and Niels N. Schia. 2011. *Local and national ownership in post-conflict Liberia: Foreign and domestic inside out?* Norwegian Institute of International Affairs, Department of Security and Conflict Management. NUPI Working Paper, 787. https://brage.bibsys.no/xmlui/handle/11250/276458 (Accessed January 26, 2018).

Carvalho, Benjamin de, Niels N. Schia, and Xavier Guillaume. 2018. "Everyday sovereignty: International experts, brokers and local ownership in peacebuilding Liberia." *European Journal of International Relations* 67 (4): 135406611875917.

Centre for Civil Society. 2006. *Report on activities July 2005-August 2006.* London School of Economics and Political Science. http://eprints.lse.ac.uk/29398/1/CCS Report05_06.pdf (Accessed January 26, 2018).

Chabal, Patrick, ed. 1986. *Political domination in Africa: Reflections on the limits of power.* Vol. 50 of *African studies.* Cambridge: Cambridge University Press.

Chabal, Patrick. 2009. *Africa: The Politics of Suffering and Smiling (World political theories).* ZED.

Chabal, Patrick, and Jean-Pascal Daloz. 1999. *Africa Works: Disorder as political Instrument / Patrick Chabal; Jean-Pascal Daloz.* 1st ed. *African issues.* London: Villiers Publications.

Chandler, David. 2000. *Bosnia: Faking democracy after Dayton.* 2nd ed. London, Sterling, Va.: Pluto Press.

Chandler, David. 2006. *Empire in denial: The politics of state-building.* London, Ann Arbor, MI: Pluto.

Chang, Ha-Joon. 2002. *Kicking away the ladder: Development strategy in historical perspective.* London: Anthem.

Charbonneau, Bruno, and Geneviève Parent, eds. 2012. *Peacebuilding, memory and reconciliation: Bridging top-down and bottom.* London, New York: Routledge.

Chea-Annan, Melissa. 2014. "National Symbols Review Project Launched." *The Inquirer,* June 10. http://monroviainquirer.com/2014/06/10/national-symbols-rev iew-project-launched (Accessed April 30, 2015).

Chereji, Christian-Radu, and Charles Wratto King. 2013. "West Africa. A comparative study of traditional conflict resolution methods in Liberia and Ghana." *Conflict Studies Quarterly* (5): 3–18.

Chinkin, C. M., and Freya Baetens, eds. 2015. *Sovereignty, statehood and state responsibility: Essays in honour of James Crawford.* Trans. James Crawford. Cambridge: Cambridge University Press.

Chopra, Jarat. 2000. "The UN's kingdom of East Timor." *Survival* 42 (3): 23–40.

Chopra, Jarat. 2002. "Building State Failure in East Timor." *Development and Change* 33 (5): 979–1000.

CIA. 2015. "CIA World Factbook." https://www.cia.gov/library/publications/the-w orld-factbook/geos/li.html (Accessed September 30, 2016).

CIA. 2016. "World Factbook." https://www.cia.gov/library/publications/the-world-f actbook/geos/li.html (Accessed September 30, 2016).

Cilliers, Jakkie. 2005. *Towards a Continental Early Warning System for Africa.* Institute for Security Studies. ISS Paper, 102. https://issafrica.s3.amazonaws.com/site/ uploads/PAPER102.PDF (Accessed June 2, 2017).

Clapham, Christopher. 1978. "Liberia." In *West African states: Failure and promise: a study in comparative politics.* Vol. 23 of *African studies series,* ed. John Dunn. Cambridge, New York: Cambridge University Press, 117–31.

Clements, Kevin, Amelia Hoover Green, and Elisabeth J. Wood. 2013. *Wartime sexual violence: Misconceptions, implications, and ways forward.* Washington DC: United States Institute of Peace. Special Report 323. https://www.usip.org/publi cations/2013/02/wartime-sexual-violence-misconceptions-implications-and-ways -forward (Accessed October 24, 2017).

Cohen, Neal P., Charles Mohan, Kpedee Woiwor, James Whawhen, Sheku Daboh, and David Snelbecker. 2010. *Final Evaluation of USAID GEMAP Activities.* US-AID. http://www.gemap-liberia.org/doc/library/Evaluation%20of%20USAID%2 0Liberia%20GEMAP.pdf (Accessed January 18, 2018).

Cohen, Dara K. 2013. "Explaining Rape during Civil War: Cross-National Evidence (1980–2009)." *American Political Science Review* 107 (03): 461–77.

Cohen, Dara K., and Ragnhild Nordås. 2014. "Sexual violence in armed conflict: Introducing the SVAC Dataset." *Journal of Peace Research* 51 (3): 418–28.

Cohn, Carol, ed. 2013. *Women and wars.* Cambridge: Polity.

Collier, Paul e. a. 2003. *Breaking the Conflict Trap: Civil War and Development Policy.* The World Bank.

Commission on Global Governance. 1995. *Our Global Neighbourhood: The report of the Commission on Global Governance.* Oxford: Oxford University Press.

Corriveau-Bourque, Alexandre. 2010. "Confusions and Palava: The logic of land encroachment in Lofa County, Liberia." Norwegian Refugee Council (November 27, 2013).

Cortright, David, Melanie C. Greenberg, and Laurel Stone, eds. 2016. *Civil society, peace, and power. Peace and security in the 21st century*. Lanham, Boulder, New York, London: Rowman & Littlefield.

Cummings, Kate. 15th 2012. Ushahidi. http://blog.ushahidi.com/index.php/2011/1 2/02/un-and-ushahidi-collaboration-suggests-an-interwoven-future-is-inevitable/ (Accessed May 30, 2012).

Darby, John, and Roger M. Ginty, eds. 2003. *Contemporary Peacemaking: Conflict, Violence and Peace Processes*.

Davidson, W. D., and J. V. Montville. 1981. "Foreign policy according to Freud." *Foreign policy* 45: 145–57.

d'Azevedo, Warren. 1989. "Tribe and chiefdom on the Winward Coast." *Liberian Studies Journal* xiv (2): 90–116.

DCAF. 2011. *Gender and security system reform: Examples from the ground*. Center for security, development and the rule of law. http://www.poa-iss.org/kit/Gender-SS R-E.pdf (Accessed October 24, 2017).

Debiel, Tobias, Thomas Held, and Ulrich Schneckener, eds. 2016. *Peacebuilding in crisis: Rethinking paradigms and practices of transnational cooperation. Routledge global cooperation series*. Abingdon, Oxon, New York, NY: Routledge.

Debiel, Tobias, and Ulf Terlinden. 2005. "Promoting good governance in post-conflict societies." Eschborn. http://inef.uni-due.de/page/documents/GG_PConfl_T D-UT.pdf (Accessed September 20, 2016).

DeLargy, Pamela. 2013. "Sexual violence and women's health in war." In *Women and wars*, ed. Carol Cohn. Cambridge: Polity, 54–79.

Deng, Francis M., Sadikiel Kimaro, Terrence Lyons, Donald Rothchild, and William I. Zartman. 1996. *Sovereignty as responsibility: Conflict management in Africa*. Washington, DC: Brookings Inst.

DeRouen, Karl, JR., and Edward Newman. 2015. "Postscript." In *Gender, peace and security: Implementing UN Security Council Resolution 1325. Routledge Studies in Peace and Conflict Resolution*, eds. Theodora-Ismene Gizelis and Louise Olsson. London, New York, NY: Routledge, 232–44.

Diller, Janelle M. 1997. *Handbook on human rights in situations of conflict*. Minneapolis, MN: Minnesota Advocates for Human Rights.

Dixon, Winnie. 2015. "Land Commission sets up dispute center for Montserrado." *Liberia News Agency*, January 24. http://www.liberianewsagency.org/pagesnews.p hp?nid=3928 (Accessed July 5, 2017).

Dobbins, James, Seth G. Jones, Keith Crane, and Beth C. DeGrasse. 2007. "The Beginner's Guide to Nation-Building." RAND Corporation. http://www.rand.or g/content/dam/rand/pubs/monographs/2007/RAND_MG557.pdf (Accessed May 22, 2015).

Donais, Timothy. 2009. "Empowerment or Imposition?: Dilemmas of Local Ownership in Post-Conflict Peacebuilding Processes." *Peace & Change* 34 (1): 3–26.

Doornbos, M. 2001. "'Good Governance': The Rise and Decline of a Policy Metaphor?" *Journal of Development Studies* 37 (6): 93–108.

Doyle, Michael W., and Nicholas Sambanis. 2006. *Making war and building peace: United Nations peace operations*. Princeton paperbacks. Princeton, N.J.: Princeton University Press.

Driscoll, Ruth, and Alison Evans. 2005. "Second-Generation Poverty Reduction Strategies: New Opportunities and Emerging Issues." *Development Policy Review* 23 (1): 5–25.

Dugan, Maire. 1996. "A nested theory of conflict." *A leadership journal: Women in leadership - Sharing the vision* 1: 9–20. https://www.emu.edu/cjp/resources/free/D ugan_Maire_Nested-Model-Original.pdf (Accessed March 14, 2017).

Dunn, John, ed. 1978. *West African states: Failure and promise: a study in comparative politics*. Vol. 23 of *African studies series*. Cambridge, New York: Cambridge University Press.

Dunne, Timothy, Milja Kurki, and Steve Smith, eds. 2016. *International relations theories: Discipline and diversity*. Oxford: Oxford University Press.

Dzinesa, Gwinyayi A., and Devon Curtis, eds. 2012. *Peacebuilding, power, and politics in Africa. Cambridge Centre of African Studies series*. Athens: Ohio University Press.

Eagleton-Pierce, Matthew. 2011. "Advancing a Reflexive International Relations." *Millennium: Journal of International Studies* 39 (3): 805–23.

Early Warning Early Response (EWER) Working Group. 2013. *Liberia Early-Warning and Response Network (LERN) Trend Analysis Report*. Monrovia, Liberia.

Early Warning Early Response (EWER) Working Group. 2014. *Liberia Early-Warning and Response Network (LERN) Trend Analysis Report*. Monrovia, Liberia.

Eizenstat, Stuart, John E. Porter, and Jeremy Weinstein. 2005. "Rebuilding weak states." *Foreign Affairs* 84 (1): 134–46.

Ellerby, Kara. 2013. "(En)gendered Security?: The Complexities of Women's Inclusion in Peace Processes." *International Interactions* 39 (4): 435–60.

Ellis, Stephen. 2007. *The mask of anarchy: The destruction of Liberia and the religious dimension of an African civil war*. 2nd ed. New York: New York University Press.

Elman, Miriam F. 1997. "Introduction: The need for a qualitative test of the democratic peace theory." In *Paths to peace: Is democracy the answer? CSIA studies in international security*, ed. Miriam F. Elman. Cambridge Mass.: MIT Press, 1–58.

Elman, Miriam F., ed. 1997. *Paths to peace: Is democracy the answer? CSIA studies in international security*. Cambridge Mass.: MIT Press.

Elshtain, Jean B. 1995. *Women and war*. Chicago: Univ. of Chicago Pr.

Englebert, Pierre. 2009. *Africa: Unity, sovereignty, and sorrow*. Boulder: Lynne Rienner.

Enloe, Cynthia. 1983. *Does khaki become you?: The militarisation of women's lives*. London: Pluto Press.

Enloe, Cynthia. 2000. *Maneuvers: The international politics of militarizing women's lives*. Berkeley Calif. u.a.: Univ. of California Press.

Enloe, Cynthia H. 2014. *Bananas, beaches and bases: Making feminist sense of international politics*. Berkeley, Los Angeles, California, London: University of California Press.

Etyang, Oita, Tapera H. Chinemhute, and Taye Abdulkadir. 2016. "Conflict Prognosis: The COMESA Early Warning System in Perspective." *International Journal of Scientific Research and Innovative Technology* 3 (11). http://www.ijsrit.com/uplo aded_all_files/1889653824_h1.pdf (Accessed June 2, 2017).

Etzioni, Amitai. 2007. *Security first: For a muscular, moral foreign policy*. New Haven: Yale University Press.

Executive Mansion. 2014. *President Sirleaf Chairs Special Liberia Development Alliance Steering Committee Meeting*. Monrovia.

Executive Mansion. 2018. *President Weah Signs Local Government, Land Right Acts into Law*. Monrovia.

Falkman, Edwin G. 1972. "Liberia's Struggle with Western Land Tenure." *The Journal of Legal Pluralism and Unofficial Law* 4 (6): 1–33 (Accessed July 1, 2017).

Flaherty, Maureen P., Sean Byrne, Hamdesa Tuso, and Thomas G. Matyók, eds. 2015. *Gender and peacebuilding: All hands required. Peace and conflict studies*. Lanham: Lexington Books.

Foblets, Marie-Claire, ed. 2004. *Healing the wounds: Essays on the reconstruction of societies after war. Oñati international series in law and society*. Oxford: Hart.

Fofana, Umaru. 2014. *Fear, suspicion undermine West Africa's battle against Ebola*.

Ford, Tamasin. 2012. "Liberia land deals with foreign firms 'could sow seeds of conflict'." *The Guardian*, February 29. https://www.theguardian.com/global-de velopment/2012/feb/29/liberia-land-deals-could-seed-conflict (Accessed June 2, 2017).

Foster, David. 2012. Ushahidi. http://blog.ushahidi.com/index.php/2011/12/02/un-a nd-ushahidi-collaboration-suggests-an-interwoven-future-is-inevitable/ (Accessed May 2, 2012).

G7+ Group. *A New Deal for Engagement in Fragile States*. https://www.pbsbdialogue .org/media/filer_public/07/69/07692de0-3557-494e-918e-18df00e9ef73/the_new_ deal.pdf (Accessed December 13, 2016).

Galtung, Johann. 1964. "Editorial." *Journal of Peace Research* 1 (1): 1–4.

Galtung, Johann. 1969. "Violence, Peace and Peace Research." *Journal of Peace Research* 6 (3): 167–91.

Galtung, Johann, ed. 1976. *Peace, War and Defense: Essays in peace research*. Vol. 2. Copenhagen: Christian Ejlers.

Galtung, Johann. 1976. "Three approaches to peace: Peacekeeping, Peacemaking, and Peacebuilding." In *Peace, War and Defense: Essays in peace research*. Vol. 2, ed. Johann Galtung. Copenhagen: Christian Ejlers, 282–304.

Gbowee, Leymah, and Carol Mithers. 2011. *Mighty be our powers: How sisterhood, prayer, and sex changed a nation at war: a memoir*. Sydney, N.S.W.: HarperCollins Publishers.

George, Alexander L., and Andrew Bennett. 2005. *Case studies and theory development in the social sciences*. BCSIA studies in international security. Cambridge Mass. u.a.: MIT Press.

Gerdes, Felix. 2013. *Civil war and state formation: The political economy of war and peace in Liberia*. [v. 9] of *Mikropolitik der Gewalt Micropolitics of violence*. Frankfurt, New York: Campus.

Gerring, John. 2004. "What is a case study and what is it good for?" *American Political Science Review* 98 (2): 341–54.

Gerring, John. 2010. In *The Oxford handbook of political methodology*. 1st ed. [4] of *The Oxford handbooks of political science*, ed. Janet M. Box-Steffensmeier. Oxford: Oxford University Press, 645–84.

Gizelis, Theodora-Ismene, and Louise Olsson, eds. 2015. *Gender, peace and security: Implementing UN Security Council Resolution 1325*. Routledge Studies in Peace and Conflict Resolution. London, New York, NY: Routledge.

Glanville, Luke. 2013. *Sovereignty and the Responsibility to Protect*. University of Chicago Press.

Global Witness. 2012. *Signing their Lives away: Liberia's Private Use Permits and the Destruction of Community-Owned Rainforest*. https://www.globalwitness.org/sites/default/files/library/Signing%20their%20Lives%20away%20-%20Liberian%20Private%20Use%20Permits%20-%204%20Sept%202012%20U_0.pdf (Accessed August 12, 2017).

Global Witness. 2016. *The Deceivers*. https://www.globalwitness.org/thedeceivers/ (Accessed August 16, 2017).

Goldstein, Joshua S. 2006. *War and gender: How gender shapes the war system and Vice Versa*. 2nd ed. Cambridge: Cambridge Univ. Press.

Gomes, Carla, Francisco Leandro, and Dias Mónica, eds. 2013. *Gender violence in armed conflict*. Lisboa: Instituto da Defesa Nacional.

Governance Commission. 2012. *Liberia National Vision 2030.: Summary report*. http://governancecommissionlr.org/pg_img/VISION%202030%20%20%20summary%20for%20the%20conference%20(25%20pgs)%20for%20GC%20%20Website.pdf (Accessed December 13, 2016).

Governance Reform Commission. 2007. *The way forward: land and property rights issues in the republic of Liberia*. Monrovia, Liberia: Governance Reform Commission.

Government of Liberia, Civil Society Organizations. 2016. *GOL-CSOs Partnership Policy*.

Government-UN GBV Joint Program. 2011. *In-depth Study on Reasons for High Incidence of Sexual and Gender Based Violence in Liberia: Recommendations on Prevention and Response*. https://doj19z5hov92o.cloudfront.net/sites/default/files/resource/2012/11/5876-final_high_incidence_of_sgbv_15_may.pdf (Accessed October 27, 2017).

Government-UN GBV Joint Program. 2013. *Exploring GBV Prevention in Liberia*.

Grant, Tom. 2015. "How to recognize a state (and not)." In *Sovereignty, statehood and state responsibility: Essays in honour of James Crawford*, eds. C. M. Chinkin and Freya Baetens. Trans. James Crawford. Cambridge: Cambridge University Press, 192–208.

Green, Maia. 2006. "Representing poverty and attacking representations: Perspectives on poverty from social anthropology." *Journal of Development Studies* 42 (7): 1108–29.

Grindle, Merilee. 2010. *Good governance: The inflation of an idea*. J. F. Kennedy School of Government, Harvard University. Faculty Research Working Papers. https://dash.harvard.edu/handle/1/4448993 (Accessed February 20, 2017).

Grindle, Merilee S. 2004. "Good Enough Governance: Poverty Reduction and Reform in Developing Countries." *Governance* 17 (4): 525–48.

Grindle, Merilee S. 2007. "Good Enough Governance Revisited". *Development Policy Review* 25 (5): 533–74. http://onlinelibrary.wiley.com/doi/10.1111/j.1467-7679.2007.00385.x/pdf (Accessed September 20, 2016).

Gunda Werner Institute. "UN Resolution 1820." Heinrich Böll Stiftung. https://www.gwi-boell.de/en/2010/09/07/un-resolution-1820 (Accessed October 5, 2018).

Handrahan, Lori. 2004. "Conflict, Gender, Ethnicity and Post-Conflict Reconstruction." *Security Dialogue* 35 (4): 429–45.

Hansen, Lene. 2000. "Gender, Nation, Rape: Bosnia and the Construction of Security." *International Feminist Journal of Politics* 3 (1): 55–75.

Hawkins, Robert L. 2010. "Outsider in: Race, Attraction, and Research in New Orleans." *Qualitative Inquiry* 16 (4): 249–61.

Hayden, Robert M. 2000. "Rape and rape avoidance in ethno-nationalist conflicts: Sexual violence in liminalized states." *American Anthropologist* 102 (1): 27–41.

Hearn, Sarah, Alexandra Kubitschek Bujones, and Alischa Kugel. 2014. "The United Nations "Peacebuilding Architecture": Past, Present and Future." New York University Center on International Cooperation. http://cic.nyu.edu/sites/default/files/un_peace_architecture.pdf (Accessed November 27, 2015).

Heathershaw, John. 2009. *Post-conflict Tajikistan: The politics of peacebuilding and the emergence of legitimate order*. Vol. 16 of *Central Asian studies series*. London, New York: Routledge.

Heidenheimer, Arnold J., and Michael Johnston, eds. 2002. *Political corruption: Concepts & contexts*. 3rd ed. New Brunswick, NJ: Transaction Publ.

Herbst, Jeffrey. 2004. "Let them fail: State Failure in Theory and Practice: Implications for Policy." In *When states fail: Causes and consequences*, ed. Robert I. Rotberg. Princeton, N.J.: Princeton University Press, 302–18.

Hesselbein, Gabi. 2008. "Good governance in fragilen Staaten: Konzepte, Fallstricke, Erfahrungen." In *Good governance and developing countries: Interdisciplinary perspectives*. Bd. 21 of *Schriften zur internationalen Entwicklungs- und Umweltforschung*, eds. Kerstin Kötschau and Thilo Marauhn. Frankfurt am Main, New York: Lang, 35–41.

Hewitt de Alcantara, Cynthia. 1998. "Uses and abuses of the concept of governance." *International Social Science Journal* 50 (155): 105–13.

Higate, Paul, and Marsha Henry. 2016. "Engendering (In)security in Peace Support Operations." *Security Dialogue* 35 (4): 481–98.

Holzgrefe, J. L., and Robert O. Keohane, eds. 2003. *Humanitarian Intervention.* Cambridge: Cambridge University Press.

Honwana, Alcinda M. 2007. *Child Soldiers in Africa.* University of Pennsylvania Press, Inc.

Hooghe, Liesbet, and Gary Marks. 2003. "Unraveling the central state, but how?: Types of multi-level governance." *American Political Science Review* 97 (2): 233–43.

Huband, Mark. 1998. *The Liberian Civil War.* London, Portland, Or.: F. Cass.

Hudson, Heidi. 2009. "Peacebuilding Through a Gender Lens and the Challenges of Implementation in Rwanda and Côte d'Ivoire." *Security Studies* 18 (2): 287–318.

Hughes, Caroline, Joakim Öjendal, and Isabell Schierenbeck. 2015. "The struggle versus the song – the local turn in peacebuilding: An introduction." *Third World Quarterly* 36 (5): 817–24.

Hunt, Swanee. 2002. "The critical role of women waging peace." *Columbia Journal of Transnational Law* 41 (3): 557–72.

Hydén, Göran. 1992. "Governance and the Study of Politics." In *Governance and politics in Africa,* eds. Göran Hydén and Michael Bratton. Boulder, Colo.: L. Rienner, 1–26.

Hydén, Göran, and Michael Bratton, eds. 1992. *Governance and politics in Africa.* Boulder, Colo.: L. Rienner.

International Monetary Fund. 2012. *Liberia: Poverty Reduction Strategy Paper - Annual Progress Report.* IMF Country Report No. 12/45. https://www.imf.org/external/pubs/ft/scr/2012/cr1245.pdf (Accessed December 13, 2016).

ISS Africa. 2014. "Spotlight on post-conflict reconstruction and development in Africa." ISS Africa. http://www.issafrica.org/pscreport/addis-insights/spotlight-on-post-conflict-reconstruction-and-development-in-africa (Accessed May 22, 2015).

Isser, Deborah, Stephen Lubkemann, and Saah e. a. N'Tow. 2009. *Looking for justice: Liberian experiences with and perceptions of local justice options.* United States Institute of Peace. Peaceworks, 63. https://www.usip.org/sites/default/files/resources/liberian_justice_pw63.pdf (Accessed August 12, 2017).

Jackson, Robert H., and Carl G. Rosberg. 1982. "Why Africa's Weak States Persist: The Empirical and the Juridical in Statehood." *World Politics* 35 (01): 1–24.

Jahn, Detlef. 2006. *Einführung in die vergleichende Politikwissenschaft.* 1st ed. *Lehrbuch.* Wiesbaden: VS Verl. für Sozialwissenschaften.

Jallow, Baba G., ed. 2014. *Leadership in Postcolonial Africa. Palgrave Studies in African Leadership.* New York: Palgrave Macmillan.

Jenkins, Rob. 2013. *Peacebuilding: From concept to commission. Routledge global institutions series.* New York: Routledge.

Jennings, Kathleen, and Vesna Nikolić-Ristanović. 2009. *UN peace-keeping economies and local sex industries: Connections and implications.* Brighton. MICROCON Research Working Paper, 17.

Jeong, Ho-Won. 2005. *Peacebuilding in postconflict societies: Strategy and process.* Boulder, Colo.: L. Rienner.

Johnson, Thomas T. 2016. "Peacebuilding Office gets new director." *Daily Observer,* May 26. https://www.liberianobserver.com/news/peace-building-office-gets-new -director/ (Accessed January 29, 2018).

Kaba, Ali, and Gaurav Madan. 2014. *Walking with villagers: How Liberia's Land Rights Policy was shaped from the grassroots.* Sustainable Development Institute and Namati. http://pubs.iied.org/pdfs/G03832.pdf (Accessed July 1, 2017).

Kaldor, Mary. 2012. *New and old wars.* 3rd ed. Cambridge [England], Malden, MA: Polity Press.

Karmo, Henry. 2017. "Liberian Senate Amends Rape Law - Makes It Bailable Offense." *Front Page Africa,* October 10. https://www.frontpageafricaonline.com /index.php/news/5675-liberian-senate-amends-rape-law-makes-it-bailable-offense (Accessed October 24, 2017).

Kartas, Moncef. 2007. *Post-conflict peace-building - Is the hegemony of the 'Good Governance' discourse depoliticising the local?* Odense, Denmark: Paper for the Annual Conference of the Nordic International Studies Association. https://pdfs.seman ticscholar.org/64e2/265a39aefae1c32d2b7375bb8d9e248dd2f8.pdf (Accessed February 20, 2017).

Kasfir, Nelson. 1998. "Civil society, the state and democracy in Africa." *Commonwealth & Comparative Politics* 36 (2): 123–49.

Kaufmann, Andrea. 2011. "Mobilizing for improvement. An empirical study of a women's movement in West Point, Liberia." *Stichproben. Wiener Zeitschrift für kritische Afrikastudien* 11 (20): 163–88.

Keohane, Robert O. 2003. "Political authority after intervention: gradations in sovereignty." In *Humanitarian Intervention,* eds. J. L. Holzgrefe and Robert O. Keohane. Cambridge: Cambridge University Press, 275–98.

Kieh, George K. 2008. *The first Liberian civil war: The crises of underdevelopment.* v. 17 of *Society and politics in Africa.* New York: Peter Lang.

Kjellman, Kjell E., and Kristian B. Harpviken. 2010. "Civil society and the state." In *Civil society and peacebuilding: A critical assessment,* ed. Thania Paffenholz. Boulder, Colo.: Rienner, 29–42.

Kötschau, Kerstin, and Thilo Marauhn, eds. 2008. *Good governance and developing countries: Interdisciplinary perspectives.* Bd. 21 of *Schriften zur internationalen Entwicklungs- und Umweltforschung.* Frankfurt am Main, New York: Lang.

Krasner, Stephen D. 2004. "Sharing Sovereignty: New Institutions for Collapsed and Failing States." *International Security* 29 (2): 85–120.

Krause, Jana. 2015. "Revisiting protection from conflict-related sexual violence: Actors, victims and power." In *Gender, peace and security: Implementing UN Security Council Resolution 1325. Routledge Studies in Peace and Conflict Resolution*, eds. Theodora-Ismene Gizelis and Louise Olsson. London, New York, NY: Routledge, 99–115.

Land Commission of Liberia. 2011. *2010 Annual Report*. Monrovia, Liberia.

Land Commission of Liberia. 2012. *2011 Annual Report*. Monrovia, Liberia.

Land Commission of Liberia. 2014. *Annual Report 2014*. Monrovia, Liberia.

Land Commission of Liberia. 2015. *2014 Annual Report*. Monrovia, Liberia.

Landsberg, Chris. 2012. "Peacebuilding as Governance: The Case of the Pan-African Ministers Conference for Public and Civil Service." In *Peacebuilding, power, and politics in Africa. Cambridge Centre of African Studies series*, eds. Gwinyayi A. Dzinesa and Devon Curtis. Athens: Ohio University Press, 121–39.

Last, David. 2000. "Organizing for effective peacebuilding." In *Peacekeeping and Conflict Resolution*, eds. T. Woodhouse and O. Ramsbotham. F. Cass, 80–96.

Layne, Christopher. 1994. "Kant or Cant: The Myth of the Democratic Peace." *International Security* 19 (2): 5.

Lederach, Angela J. 2015. "Mothers at the tree of frustration. Locating healing in Liberia." In *Gender and peacebuilding: All hands required. Peace and conflict studies*, eds. Maureen P. Flaherty, Sean Byrne, Hamdesa Tuso and Thomas G. Matyók. Lanham: Lexington Books, 53–68.

Lederach, John P. 1997. *Building peace: Sustainable reconciliation in divided societies*. Washington, D.C.: United States Institute of Peace Press.

Lederach, John P., ed. 2002. *A handbook of international peacebuilding: Into the eye of the storm*. 1st ed. San Francisco Calif.: Jossey-Bass.

Levitt, Jeremy I. 2005. *The evolution of deadly conflict in Liberia: From 'paternaltarianism' to state collapse*. Zugl.: Cambridge, Univ., Diss., 2001. Durham, NC: Carolina Acad. Press.

Lewin, Kurt. 1952. *Field theory in social science: Selected theoretical papers*. London: Tavistock.

Lewis, David. 2002. "Civil Society in African Contexts: Reflections on the Usefulness of a Concept." *Development and Change* 33 (4): 569–86.

Liberia Comprehensive Peace Agreement: CPA. 18th August 2003.

Liberia. 2005. *An act to establish the Truth and Reconciliation Commission (TRC) of Liberia*.

Liberia Institute of Statistics and Geo-Information Services (LISGIS). 2009. *2008 Population and housing census: Final results*. Monrovia. https://www.lisgis.net/pg_img/NPHC%202008%20Final%20Report.pdf (Accessed November 28, 2018).

Liberia Peacebuilding Programme. Final draft/revised 3rd draft: LPP. 2011.

Liberia's Revised Peacebuilding Priority Plan (September 2013-August 2016): PPP II. 2013.

Liebenow, J. G. 1969. *Liberia: the evolution of privilege. Africa in the modern world*. Ithaca (N.Y.), London: Cornell University Press.

Liebenow, J. G. 1987. *Liberia: The quest for democracy.* Bloomington, Ind.: Indiana University Press.

Liebling Kalifani, Helen, Victoria Mwaka, Ruth Ojiambo-Ochieng, Juliet Were-Oguttu, and Eugene Kinyanda. 2011. "Women War Survivors of the 1989-2003 conflict in Liberia: The impact of sexual and gender-based violence." *Journal of International Women's Studies* 12 (1): 1–21.

Lister, Ruth, and Jo Campling, eds. 1997. *Citizenship: Feminist perspectives.* Washington Square, N.Y: New York Univ. Press.

Livingston, Steven, ed. 2014. *Bits and atoms: Information and communication technology in areas of limited statehood. Oxford studies in digital politics.* Oxford: Oxford Univ. Press.

Mac Ginty, Roger. 2010. "Hybrid peace: The interaction between top-down and bottom-up peace." *Security Dialogue* 41 (4): 391–412.

Mac Ginty, Roger, ed. 2013. *Routledge handbook of peacebuilding. Routledge handbooks.* London: Routledge.

Mac Ginty, Roger, ed. 2015. *Routledge handbook of peacebuilding. Routledge handbooks.* London: Routledge.

Mac Ginty, Roger. 2015. "Where is the local?: Critical localism and peacebuilding." *Third World Quarterly* 36 (5): 840–56.

Mac Ginty, Roger. 2016. "What do we mean when we use the term 'local'? Imagining and framing the local and the international in relation to peace and order." In *Peacebuilding in crisis: Rethinking paradigms and practices of transnational cooperation. Routledge global cooperation series,* eds. Tobias Debiel, Thomas Held and Ulrich Schneckener. Abingdon, Oxon, New York, NY: Routledge.

Maclean, Ruth. 2016. "Liberia must pass land rights bill or risk jeopardising peace, campaigners warn." *The Guardian,* July 14. https://www.theguardian.com/global-development/2016/jul/14/liberia-land-rights-bill-risk-jeopardising-peace-campaigners-warn (Accessed August 14, 2017).

Maina, Grace, and Abu Sherif. 2013. "Enhancing security and justice in Liberia: The regional hub model." *Policy & Practice Brief* (23). http://www.accord.org.za/publication/enhancing-security-and-justice-in-liberia/ (Accessed December 14, 2016).

Malmvig, H. 2006. *State Sovereignty and Intervention: A Discourse Analysis of Interventionary and Non-Interventionary Practices in Kosovo and Algeria.* Taylor & Francis.

Mamdani, Mahmood. 1996. *Citizen and subject: Contemporary Africa and the legacy of late colonialism. Princeton studies in culture/power/history.* Princeton, N.J.: Princeton University Press.

Marks, Gary. 1991. "Structural policy in the European Community." In *Euro-politics: Institutions and policymaking in the new European community,* ed. Alberta M. Sbragia. Washington, D.C.: Brookings Institution, 191–225.

Marks, Z. 2014. "Sexual violence in Sierra Leone's civil war: 'Virgination', rape, and marriage." *African Affairs* 113 (450): 67–87.

Marshall, Monty G. 2008. *Fragility, Instability, and the Failure of States. Assessing Sources of Systemic Risk.* New York: Council on Foreign Relations, Center for Preventive Action.

Marten, Kimberly Z. 2004. *Enforcing the peace: Learning from the imperial past.* New York: Columbia University Press.

Mayntz, Renate, and Fritz W. Scharpf. 1995. *Gesellschaftliche Selbstregelung und politische Steuerung.* Bd. 23 of *Schriften des Max-Planck-Instituts für Gesellschafts- forschung, Köln.* Frankfurt, New York: Campus.

Mbembe, Achille. 2001. *On the Postcolony.* Berkeley: University of California Press.

McCandless, Erin. 2008. *Lessons from Liberia: Integrated approaches to peacebuilding in transitional settings.* ISS Paper, 161. https://issafrica.s3.amazonaws.com/site/upl oads/Paper161.pdf (Accessed March 16, 2017).

McKeown, Mary, Mulbah, Edward. 2007. *Civil Society in Liberia: Towards a strategic framework for support: An overview of civil society in Liberia for Search for Common Ground.* https://www.sfcg.org/wp-content/uploads/2014/08/LBR_EV_Apr07_Ci vil-Society-in-Liberia-Towards-a-Strategic-Framework-for-Support.pdf (Accessed March 28, 2017).

Médard, Jean-François. 2002. "Corruption in the Neo-Patrimonial States of Sub-Sa- haran Africa." In *Political corruption: Concepts & contexts.* 3rd ed., eds. Arnold J. Heidenheimer and Michael Johnston. New Brunswick, NJ: Transaction Publ, 379–402.

Medie, Peace A. 2013. "Fighting gender-based violence: The women's movement and the enforcement of rape law in Liberia." *African Affairs* 112 (448): 377–97.

Mehler, Andreas. 2016. "Adapted instead of Imported: Peacebuilding by power- sharing." In *Peacebuilding in crisis: Rethinking paradigms and practices of transna- tional cooperation. Routledge global cooperation series,* eds. Tobias Debiel, Thomas Held and Ulrich Schneckener. Abingdon, Oxon, New York, NY: Routledge.

Meintjes, Sheila, Anu Pilay, and Meredeth Turshen, eds. 2002. *The aftermath: Wom- en in post-conflict transformation.* 1st ed. London: Zed Books.

Meuser, Michael, and Ulrike Nagel. 2014. "Wissens- und Interviewformen – Vari- anten des Experteninterviews." In *Interviews mit Experten: Eine praxisorientierte Einführung. Qualitative Sozialforschung,* eds. Alexander Bogner, Beate Littig and Wolfgang Menz. Wiesbaden: Springer VS, 17–25.

Ministry of Finance and Development Planning, Republic of Liberia. 2016. *Fact Sheet or Short Citizen's Guide to the Fy2016/17 Draft National Budget.* Ministry of Finance and Development Planning, Republic of Liberia. https://www.mfdp.go v.lr/index.php/the-budget (Accessed October 5, 2016).

Ministry of Finance and Development Planning, Republic of Liberia. 2017. *Budget framework paper FY 2017/18.* Ministry of Finance and Development Planning, Republic of Liberia. https://www.mfdp.gov.lr/index.php/the-budget (Accessed May 20, 2018).

Ministry of Gender and Development. 2009. *The National Gender Policy: NGP.*

Monk, Daniel B., and Jacob Mundy. 2014. *The Post-Conflict Environment.* Ann Arbor, MI: University of Michigan Press.

Moran, Mary H. 2006. *Liberia: The violence of democracy. The ethnography of political violence*. Philadelphia, PA.: Univ. of Pennsylvania Press.

Moser, Caroline, and Fiona Clark, eds. 2001. *Victims, perpetrators or actors?: Gender, armed conflict and political violence*. 1ˢᵗ ed. London u.a.: Zed Books.

Mosse, David, and David Lewis. 2005. *The aid effect: Giving and governing in international development. Anthropology, culture, society*. London, Ann Arbor: Pluto.

Muhire, Blaise. 2017. *Land, power and identity. The politics of scale and violent conflict in Masisi, "DR Congo"*. PhD Dissertation. University of Bayreuth, Bayreuth, Germany. https://epub.uni-bayreuth.de/4373/1/Dissertation%20Blaise%20Muhire_Epub_Uni%20BT.pdf.

Mukendi, Bruno. 2010. *Leadership and change in post-conflict states: A case study of Liberia*. UNDP. Capacity is development. Global Event Working Paper. http://www.undp.org/content/dam/aplaws/publication/en/publications/capacity-development/leadership-and-change-in-post-conflict-states—lessons-from-liberia/Leadership%20and%20change%20in%20post-conflict-Liberia.pdf (Accessed December 15, 2016).

Mulbah, Susanne. 2017. *State-building Interventions in Post-Conflict Liberia: Building a State without Citizens*. 1ˢᵗ ed. *African Governance*. Milton: Taylor and Francis.

Nagelhus Schia, Niels. 2015. *Peacebuilding, Ownership, and Sovereignty from New York to Monrovia: A multi-sited Ethnographic Approach*. Ph. D. Dissertation, University of Oslo. Oslo: Akademika Publishing.

Nathan, Laurie. 2007. "Africa's early warning system: An emperor with no clothes?" *South African Journal of International Affairs* 14 (1): 49–60.

Neubert, Dieter. 1997. *Entwicklungspolitische Hoffnungen und gesellschaftliche Wirklichkeit: Eine vergleichende Länderfallstudie von afrikanischen Nicht-Regierungsorganisationen in Kenia und Ruanda*. Vol. 750 of *Campus Forschung*. Zugl.: Berlin, Freie Univ., Habil.-Schr., 1995. Frankfurt/Main, New York: Campus-Verl.

Neubert, Dieter. 2004. "The role of NGO's in processes of peacekeeping in decentralised conflicts." In *Healing the wounds: Essays on the reconstruction of societies after war. Oñati international series in law and society*, ed. Marie-Claire Foblets. Oxford: Hart, 47–82.

Neubert, Dieter. 2014. *Civil societies in Africa?: Forms of social self-organization between the poles of globalization and local socio-political order*. Bayreuth African Studies Working Papers, 12.

Neumann, Hannah, and Joel G. Winckler. 2013. "When Critique is Framed as Resistance: How the International Intervention in Liberia Fails to Integrate Alternative Concepts and Constructive Criticism." *International Peacekeeping* 20 (5): 618–35.

Newman, Edward. 2009. ""Liberal" peacebuilding debates." In *New perspectives on liberal peacebuilding*, eds. Edward Newman, Roland Paris and Oliver P. Richmond. Tokyo, New York: United Nations University Press, 26–53.

Newman, Edward, Roland Paris, and Oliver P. Richmond. 2009. "Introduction." In *New perspectives on liberal peacebuilding*, eds. Edward Newman, Roland Paris and Oliver P. Richmond. Tokyo, New York: United Nations University Press, 3–25.

Newman, Edward, Roland Paris, and Oliver P. Richmond, eds. 2009. *New perspectives on liberal peacebuilding.* Tokyo, New York: United Nations University Press.

Newman, Edward, and Oliver P. Richmond, eds. 2001. *The United Nations and human security.* Houndmills, Basingstoke, Hampshire, New York: Palgrave.

Noh, Jae-Eun. 2017. "Negotiating positions through reflexivity in international fieldwork." *International Social Work* 19 (33): 002087281772514.

Norton, Gregory. 2011. "Searching for soap trees: Norwegian Refugee Council's land dispute resolution process in Liberia." Norwegian Refugee Council (November 28, 2013).

Nyei, Al-bakri I. 2014. "Constitutional Reform in Postwar Liberia - Key issues and actors." http://www.constitutionnet.org/news/constitutional-reform-postwar-liberia-key-issues-and-actors (Accessed September 30, 2016).

Nyei, Al-bakri I. 2016. "Liberia's constitutional future: Religious and centralized?" http://www.constitutionnet.org/news/liberias-constitutional-future-religious-and-centralized (Accessed September 30, 2016).

Nyei, Al-bakri I. 2018. "George Weah's agenda for constitutional reform in Liberia: The incentives for prioritizing citizenship." http://www.constitutionnet.org/news/george-weahs-agenda-constitutional-reform-liberia-incentives-prioritizing-citizenship (Accessed August 24, 2018).

Nyheim, David. 2009. *Preventing Violence, War and State Collapse: The Future of Conflict Early Warning and Response. Conflict and Fragility.* Paris: OECD Publishing.

Obi, Cyril I. 2009. "Economic Community of West African States on the Ground: Comparing Peacekeeping in Liberia, Sierra Leone, Guinea Bissau, and Côte D'Ivoire." *African Security* 2 (2-3): 119–35.

OECD, Department for International Development, and World Bank. 2006. *Deepening voice and accountability to fight poverty: A dialogue of communication implementers.* Paris: OECD, Department for International Development and World Bank. http://www.oecd.org/dac/37041865.pdf (Accessed December 15, 2016).

Oldenburg, Silke. 2014. "Liebe in Zeiten humanitärer Intervention. Sex, Geschlechterbeziehungen und humanitäre Intervention in Goma, DR Kongo." *Peripherie* 133 (46-70).

O'Reilly, Maria. 2013. "Gender and Peacebuilding." In *Routledge handbook of peacebuilding. Routledge handbooks*, ed. Roger Mac Ginty. London: Routledge, 57–68.

Organisation for Economic Co-operation and Development. 1995. "Participatory Development and Good Governance." Development Co-operation Guidelines Series. Organisation for Economic Co-operation and Development. http://www.oecd.org/dac/accountable-effective-institutions/31857685.pdf (Accessed September 30, 2016).

Paffenholz, Thania, ed. 2010. *Civil society and peacebuilding: A critical assessment.* Boulder, Colo.: Rienner.

Paffenholz, Thania. 2015. "Civil society." In *Routledge handbook of peacebuilding*. *Routledge handbooks*, ed. Roger Mac Ginty. London: Routledge, 347–59.

Pailey, Robtel N. 2014. "Patriarchy, power distance, and female presidency in Liberia." In *Leadership in Postcolonial Africa. Palgrave Studies in African Leadership*, ed. Baba G. Jallow. New York: Palgrave Macmillan, 169–88.

Pailey, Robtel N., and Korto R. Williams. 2017. "Is Liberia's Sirleaf really standing up for women?" *Al-Jazeera*, August 31. http://www.aljazeera.com/indepth/opin ion/2017/08/liberia-sirleaf-standing-women-170827092802275.html (Accessed October 24, 2017).

Pankhurst, Donna, ed. 2008. *Gendered peace: Women's struggles for post-war justice and reconciliation*. Vol. 2 of *Routledge/UNRISD research in gender and development*. New York NY u.a.: Routledge.

Paris, Roland. 2001. "Echoes of the 'Mission Civilisatrice': Peacekeeping in the Post-Cold War Era." In *The United Nations and human security*, eds. Edward Newman and Oliver P. Richmond. London: Palgrave Macmillan.

Paris, Roland. 2004. *At war's end: Building peace after civil conflict*. Cambridge, U.K., New York, NY: Cambridge University Press.

Paris, Roland. 2009. "Does liberal peacebuilding have a future?" In *New perspectives on liberal peacebuilding*, eds. Edward Newman, Roland Paris and Oliver P. Richmond. Tokyo, New York: United Nations University Press, 97–111.

Paris, Roland. 2010. "Saving liberal peacebuilding." *Review of International Studies* 36 (02): 337.

Pateman, Carole. 1988. *The sexual contract*. Stanford Calif.: Stanford Univ. Press.

Paye-Layleh, Jonathan. 2005. "Lebanese demand Liberia poll rights." *BBC News*, July 22. http://news.bbc.co.uk/1/hi/world/africa/4703029.stm (Accessed August 12, 2017).

Peacebuilding Commission - Liberia Configuration. *Report of the Chair's Visit to Liberia 7 - 15 November 2010*. Peacebuilding Commission - Liberia Configuration. http://www.un.org/en/peacebuilding/cscs/lib/pbc_visits/LBR_CSC_Chair's _Mission11_2010_Report.pdf (Accessed December 20, 2016).

Pehe, Jiří. 1997. "Politická kultura v české republice." October 26. http://www.pe he.cz/clanky/1997/politicka-kultura-v-ceske-republice (Accessed September 30, 2016).

Peterson, Jenny H. 2010. "'Rule of Law' initiatives and the liberal peace: the impact of politicised reform in post-conflict states". *Disasters* 34 (s1). http://onlinelibrary .wiley.com/doi/10.1111/j.1467-7717.2009.01097.x/pdf.

Pezalla, Anne E., Jonathan Pettigrew, and Michelle Miller-Day. 2012. "Researching the researcher-as-instrument: An exercise in interviewer self-reflexivity." *Qualitative Research* 12 (2): 165–85.

Phillips, Anne. 1991. *Engendering democracy*. 1st ed. University Park Pa.: Pennsylvania State Univ. Press.

Piattoni, Simona. 2010. *The theory of multi-level governance: Conceptual, empirical, and normative challenges*. Oxford: Oxford University Press.

Pietsch, Silke. 2010. "Women's Participation and Benefit of the Liberian Truth and Reconciliation Commission – Voices from the Field." Masterarbeit. Philipps-Universität Marburg.

Porter, Elisabeth J. 2007. *Peacebuilding: Women in international perspective*. Vol. 60 of *Routledge advances in international relations and global politics*. London, New York: Routledge.

Pouligny, Béatrice. 2016. "Civil Society and Post-Conflict Peacebuilding: Ambiguities of International Programmes Aimed at Building 'New' Societies." *Security Dialogue* 36 (4): 495–510.

Pugh, Michael. 2004. "Peacekeeping and critical theory." *International Peacekeeping* 11 (1): 39–58.

Pugh, Michael. 2009. "Towards life welfare." In *New perspectives on liberal peacebuilding*, eds. Edward Newman, Roland Paris and Oliver P. Richmond. Tokyo, New York: United Nations University Press, 78–96.

Raddatz, Rosalind. 2013. "Tempering great expectations: Peacebuilding and transitional justice in Liberia." In *Transitional justice and peacebuilding on the ground: Victims and ex-combatants. Law, conflict and international relations*, ed. Chandra L. Sriram. Milton Park, Abingdon, Oxon, New York: Routledge, 178–99.

Radelet, Steve. 2007. *Reviving economic growth in Liberia*. Center for Global Development. Working paper, 133. https://www.cgdev.org/files/14912_file_Liberia_G rowth.pdf (Accessed November 9, 2017).

Reeves, Ida. 25th 2018. "Senate Passes Land Rights Act." *The Bush Chicken*, 25th August 2018. http://www.bushchicken.com/senate-passes-land-rights-act/ (Accessed August 29, 2018).

Rehn, Elisabeth, and Ellen J. Sirleaf. 2002. *Women, war, peace: The independent experts' assessment on the impact of armed conflict on women and women's role in peace building*. New York, Great Britain: EDS.

Reilly, Niamh. 2007. "Seeking gender justice in post-conflict transitions: Towards a transformative women's human rights approach." *International Journal of Law in Context* 3 (02): 155-172.

Renard, Robrecht, Molenaers, Nadia. 2003. *Civil society participation in Rwanda's Poverty Reduction Strategy*. Antwerp: Institute of Development Policy and Management. https://www.uantwerpen.be/images/uantwerpen/container2143/files/P ublications/DP/2003/05-renard-molenaers.pdf (Accessed March 15, 2017).

Reno, William. 2004. "Sierra Leone: Warfare in a post-state society." In *State Failure and State Weakness in a Time of Terror*, ed. R. I. Rotberg. Brookings Institution Press, 71–100.

Republic of Liberia. *Liberia National Budget for Fiscal Year 2012-13*. http://www.c abri-sbo.org/en/documents/national-budget-for-fiscal-year-2012-13 (Accessed October 28, 2017).

Republic of Liberia. 1984. *Constitution*.

Republic of Liberia. 2006. *National Gender-based Violence Plan of Action*.

Republic of Liberia. 2007. *Act of the legislature to establish the Governance Commission*.

Republic of Liberia. 2009. *Land Commission Act.*

Republic of Liberia. 2012. *Agenda for Transformation. Steps toward Liberia Rising 2030: AfT.*

Republic of Liberia. 2014. *Land Rights Act.*

Republic of Liberia. 2015. *The Economic Stabilization and Recovery Plan.*

Republic of Liberia. 2016. *Liberia Land Authority Act.*

Richards, Paul. 2005. "To fight or to farm?: Agrarian dimensions of the Mano River conflicts (Liberia and Sierra Leone)." *African Affairs* 104 (417): 571–90 (Accessed August 12, 2017).

Richmond, Oliver P. *Failed statebuilding: Intervention and the dynamics of peace formation.*

Richmond, Oliver P. 2009. "A post-liberal peace: Eirenism and the everyday." *Review of International Studies* 35 (03): 557–80.

Richmond, Oliver P. 2009. "Becoming Liberal, Unbecoming Liberalism: Liberal-Local Hybridity via the Everyday as a Response to the Paradoxes of Liberal Peacebuilding." *Journal of Intervention and Statebuilding* 3 (3): 324–44.

Richmond, Oliver P. 2009. "Beyond liberal peace? Responses to "backsliding"." In *New perspectives on liberal peacebuilding*, eds. Edward Newman, Roland Paris and Oliver P. Richmond. Tokyo, New York: United Nations University Press, 54–77.

Richmond, Oliver P., ed. 2010. *Palgrave advances in peacebuilding: Critical developments and approaches. Palgrave advances.* Basingstoke, Hampshire: Palgrave Macmillan.

Risse, Thomas, ed. 2011. *Governance Without a State: Policies and Politics in Areas of Limited Statehood.* New York: Columbia University Press.

Robinson, William I. 1996. *Promoting polyarchy: Globalization, US intervention, and hegemony.* Vol. 48 of *Cambridge studies in international relations.* Cambridge [England], New York: Cambridge University Press.

Rogers, Mark M. 2011. *Ears to the Ground: Anticipating Violence in an Environment of Risk and Uncertainty.* Humanity United.

Röhner, Nora. 2012. "UN peacebuilding - light footprint or friendly takeover?". Freie Universität Berlin and Freie Universität Berlin, Germany.

Ronen, Yaël. 2015. "Recognition of the State of Palestine." In *Sovereignty, statehood and state responsibility: Essays in honour of James Crawford*, eds. C. M. Chinkin and Freya Baetens. Trans. James Crawford. Cambridge: Cambridge University Press, 229–47.

Rosen, David M. 2005. *Armies of the young: Child soldiers in war and terrorism. The Rutgers series in childhood studies.* New Brunswick, N.J: Rutgers University Press.

Rosenau, James N., and Ernst O. Czempiel. 1992. *Governance without government: Order and change in world politics.* Vol. 20 of *Cambridge studies in international relations.* Cambridge [England], New York: Cambridge University Press.

Rotberg, R. I., ed. 2004. *State Failure and State Weakness in a Time of Terror.* Brookings Institution Press.

Rotberg, Robert I., ed. 2004. *When states fail: Causes and consequences*. Princeton, N.J.: Princeton University Press.

Rupesinghe, Kumar. 2009. "FCE Citizen-based Early Warning and Early Response System: A New Tool for Civil Society to Prevent Violent Conflict." Foundation for Co-existence. https://earlywarning.files.wordpress.com/2009/03/fce-citizen-ba sed-early-warning-and-early-response-system.pdf (Accessed June 1, 2017).

Sabaratnam, Meera. 2017. *Decolonising intervention: International statebuilding in Mozambique. Kilombo international relations and colonial questions*. London, New York: Rowman & Littlefield International.

Saunders, Harold. 2000. "Interactive Conflict Resolution: A View for Policy Makers on Making and Building Peace." In *International conflict resolution after the Cold War*, eds. Paul C. Stern and Daniel Druckman. Washington, D.C: National Academy Press, 251–93.

Sawyer, Amos. 1987. *Effective immediately, dictatorship in Liberia, 1980-1986: A personal perspective*. no. 5 of *Liberia Working Group papers*. Bremen: Liberia Working Group.

Sawyer, Amos. 2005. *Beyond plunder: Toward democratic governance in Liberia*. Boulder: L. Rienner Publishers.

Sawyer, Amos. 2009. *Land Governance Challenges: The case of Liberia*. World Bank. http://siteresources.worldbank.org/INTARD/Resources/sawyer.pdf (Accessed August 12, 2017).

Sawyer, Amos. Interview with Graeme Blair, 16 July 2009.

Sbragia, Alberta M., ed. 1991. *Euro-politics: Institutions and policymaking in the new European community*. Washington, D.C.: Brookings Institution.

Schäfer, Rita. 2008. *Frauen und Kriege in Afrika: Ein Beitrag zur Gender-Forschung*. 1st ed. v.145 of *Wissen & Praxis*. Frankfurt am Main: Brandes Apsel Verlag.

Scharpf, Fritz W. 1997. *Games real actors play: Actor-centered institutionalism in policy research. Theoretical lenses on public policy*. Boulder, Colo.: Westview Press.

Schneckener, Ulrich. 2011. "State-building or new modes of governance?" In *Governance Without a State: Policies and Politics in Areas of Limited Statehood*, ed. Thomas Risse. New York: Columbia University Press, 232–61.

Schneckener, Ulrich. 2016. "Peacebuilding in crisis? Debating peacebuilding paradigms and practices." In *Peacebuilding in crisis: Rethinking paradigms and practices of transnational cooperation. Routledge global cooperation series*, eds. Tobias Debiel, Thomas Held and Ulrich Schneckener. Abingdon, Oxon, New York, NY: Routledge, 1–20.

Scott, Joan W. 1996. *Only paradoxes to offer: French feminists and the rights of man*. Cambridge, Mass: Harvard University Press.

Seawright, Jason, and John Gerring. 2008. "Case selection techniques in case study research: A menu of qualitative and quantitative options." *Political Research Quarterly* 61 (2): 294–308.

Senah, Gbatemah. 26th 2017. "Senate Fails to Agree with House of Representatives on Passage of Land Rights Act." *The Bush Chicken,* 26th August 2017. http://ww w.bushchicken.com/senate-fails-to-agree-with-house-of-representatives-on-passag e-of-land-rights-act/ (Accessed August 29, 2018).

Shepherd, Laura J. 2011. "Sex, security and superhero(in)es: From 1325 to 1820 and beyond." *International Feminist Journal of Politics* 13 (4): 504–21.

Skelcher, Chris. 2005. "Jurisdictional Integrity, Polycentrism, and the Design of Democratic Governance." *Governance: An International Journal of Policy, Adminis-tration, and Institutions* 18 (1): 89–110.

Skjelsbaek, Inger. 2013. *Preventing perpetrators: How to go from protection to preven-tion of sexual violence in war?* Oslo: Peace Research Institute. Policy Brief, 03. http://file.prio.no/publication_files/prio/Skjelsbaek-Preventing-Perpetrators-PRI O-Policy-Brief-03-2013.pdf (Accessed October 24, 2017).

Specht, Irma. 2013. "Gender, disarmament, demobilization and reintegration and violent masculinities." In *Gender violence in armed conflict,* eds. Carla Gomes, Francisco Leandro and Dias Mónica. Lisboa: Instituto da Defesa Nacional, 61–90.

Spurk, Christoph. 2010. "Understanding civil society." In *Civil society and peace-building: A critical assessment,* ed. Thania Paffenholz. Boulder, Colo.: Rienner, 3–28.

Sriram, Chandra L., ed. 2013. *Transitional justice and peacebuilding on the ground: Victims and ex-combatants. Law, conflict and international relations.* Milton Park, Abingdon, Oxon, New York: Routledge.

Srivastava, Prachi, and Nick Hopwood. 2009. "A Practical Iterative Framework for Qualitative Data Analysis." *International Journal of Qualitative Methods* 8 (1): 76–84.

Stanley, Christine A., and Patrick Slattery. 2016. "Who Reveals what to whom?: Critical Reflections on Conducting Qualitative Inquiry as an Interdisciplinary, Biracial, Male/Female Research Team." *Qualitative Inquiry* 9 (5): 705–28.

Steady, Filomina C. 2006. *Women and collective action in Africa: Development, democ-ratization, and empowerment, with special focus on Sierra Leone.* 1st ed. New York: Palgrave Macmillan.

Stern, Paul C., and Daniel Druckman, eds. 2000. *International conflict resolution after the Cold War.* Washington, D.C: National Academy Press.

Stewart, Frances. 2000. "Crisis Prevention: Tackling Horizontal Inequalities." QEH Working Paper Series, 33. Oxford Department of International Development. http://www3.qeh.ox.ac.uk/pdf/qehwp/qehwps33.pdf (Accessed May 22, 2015).

Stiglmayer, Alexandra, and Marion Faber, eds. 1994. *Mass rape: The war against women in Bosnia-Herzegovina.* Lincoln: Univ. of Nebraska Press.

Stinchcombe, Arthur L. 2000. "Social structure and organizations." In *Economics meets sociology in strategic management.* v. 17 of *Advances in strategic management,* eds. Joel A. C. Baum and Frank Dobbin. Bingley: Emerald Group Publishing Limited, 229–59.

Talmon, J. L. 1985. *The origins of totalitarian democracy.* Boulder: Westview Press.

Tarr, Byron. 2007. "The Evolution of Deadly Conflict in Liberia: From 'paternaltar-ianism' to state collapse, by Jeremy I. Levitt." *African Affairs* 106 (423): 337–38. https://academic.oup.com/afraf/article-pdf/106/423/337/108002/adm008.pdf (Accessed August 12, 2017).

The New Republic Liberia. 2018. *"Local Government Act Receives Another Setback."* June 7, 2018. http://newrepublicliberia.com/local-government-act-receives-anoth er-setback/ (Accessed December 21, 2018).

The Nordic Africa Institute. 2014. *Distrust lingers in wake of Ebola.*

The Republic of Liberia. *Poverty reduction strategy.* The Republic of Liberia. www.lif tliberia.gov.lr (Accessed November 28, 2013).

Tokpa, Katharina H., Andrea Kaufmann, and Franzisca Zanker. 2015. "The Ebola Outbreak in Comparison: Liberia and Côte d'Ivoire." *GIGA Focus International Edition English* (03). https://www.giga-hamburg.de/en/system/files/publications/g f_international_1503.pdf (Accessed September 15, 2017).

Tokpah, Willie N. 2016. "Liberia Civil Society Demands Changes in Land Authori-ty Act." *Front Page Africa,* June 29. http://www.frontpageafricaonline.com/ind ex.php/news/1221-liberia-civil-society-demands-changes-in-land-authority-act (Accessed July 4, 2017).

Tompkins, Tamara. 1995. "Prosecuting Rape as a War Crime: Speaking the Un-speakable." *Notre Dame Law Review* 70 (4): 845–90. http://scholarship.law.nd.ed u/ndlr/vol70/iss4/3 (Accessed November 11, 2017).

Towards a reconciled, peaceful and prosperous Liberia: A strategic roadmap for national healing, peacebuilding, and Reconciliation. Ministry of Internal Affairs, Ministry of Planning and Economic Affairs, Governance Commission, Independent Nation-al Commission for Human Rights, Liberia Reconciliation Initiative, Representa-tives of Civil Society Organizations, United Nations in Liberia. 2012. http://lern. ushahidi.com/media/uploads/page/3/Reconciliation%20Roadmap%20Draft%20 3-W.pdf (Accessed May 20, 2014).

Tracy, Sarah J. 2013. *Qualitative research methods: Collecting evidence, crafting analy-sis, communicating impact.* 1st ed. Chichester: Wiley-Blackwell.

Tran, Mark. 2012. "Liberia's Johnson Sirleaf defiant over nepotism and corruption claims." *The Guardian,* November 1. https://www.theguardian.com/global-dev elopment/2012/nov/01/liberia-johnson-sirleaf-nepotism-corruption (Accessed October 5, 2016).

True, Jacqui. 2001. "Feminism." In *Theories of International Relations.* 3rd ed., ed. Scott Burchill. Basingstoke: Palgrave Macmillan Ltd, 231–76.

UN. 1992. *Agenda for Peace.*

UN. 2000. *Brahimi Report.*

UN. 2005. *In larger freedom.*

UN. 2008. *United Nations Development Assistance Framework Liberia 2008-2012. Consolidating Peace and National Recovery for Sustainable Development: UNDAF.* Monrovia.

UN. 2017. *Sustaining peace and securing development. Liberia Peacebuilding Plan: PPP.*

UN General Assembly. 2003. *Report of the Advisory Committee on Administrative and Budgetary Questions*. http://www.un.org/ga/search/view_doc.asp?symbol=A/58/59 1), (Accessed January 26, 2018).

UN Office of the High Commissioner for Human Rights, and UNMIL. 2016. *Addressing Impunity for Rape in Liberia: 2016 SGBV Report*. https://unmil.unmissi ons.org/sites/default/files/impunity_report_-_binding.pdf (Accessed October 25, 2017).

UN Office of the Special Representative of the Secretary General for Sexual Violence in Conflict. 2015. *Liberia*. UN. http://www.un.org/sexualviolenceinconflict /countries/liberia/ (Accessed October 25, 2017).

UN Peacebuilding Support Office. 2010. "UN Peacebuilding: An Orientation." UN Peacebuilding Support Office. http://www.un.org/en/peacebuilding/pbso/pdf/pe acebuilding_orientation.pdf (Accessed May 22, 2015).

Underwood, Mair, Leonn D. Satterthwait, and Helen P. Bartlett. 2010. "Reflexivity and minimization of the impact of age-cohort differences between researcher and research participants". *Qualitative health research* 20 (11): 1585–95.

UNDP. 2013. *Proposal for Security Hubs*. https://info.undp.org/docs/pdc/Documents /LBR/Proposal for Hubs 2 3 (Pt 3).pdf (Accessed November 11, 2017).

United Nations. 2003. *Special Humanitarian Coordinator for Liberia calls for immediate end to use of child soldiers, key element for long-term peace*. Monrovia.

United Nations Department of Social and Economic Affairs, United Nations Development Programme. 2007. "The challenges of restoring governance in crisis and post-conflict countries." New York: United Nations. https://publicadministr ation.un.org/publications/content/PDFs/E-Library%20Archives/2007%20The%2 0Challenges%20of%20Restoring%20Governance%20in%20Crisis%20and%20Po st-Conflict%20Countries.pdf (Accessed September 12, 2017).

United Nations Development Programme. 1997. *Governance for sustainable human development: A UNDP policy document*. New York: United Nations Development Programme.

United Nations Economic and Social Commission for Asia and the Pacific. n.d. "What is Good Governance?" http://www.unescap.org/sites/default/files/good-go vernance.pdf (Accessed September 30, 2016).

United Nations in Liberia. 2013. *United Nations Development Assistance Framework 2013-2017*. Monrovia. https://www.unicef.org/liberia/UNDAF_2013-2017.pdf (Accessed December 13, 2016).

United Nations Office for Disaster Risk Reduction. 2009. "Terminology: Early Warning." https://www.unisdr.org/we/inform/terminology (Accessed June 1, 2017).

United Nations Peacebuilding Commission. 2015. *Summary of the visit of H. E. Olof Skoog, Chair of the Peacebuilding Commission Liberia Configuration, to Liberia from 4 to 7 April 2015*. United Nations Peacebuilding Commission. http://www.un.or g/en/peacebuilding/pdf/PBC%20Chair%20trip%20report%20Liberia%20April% 202015.pdf (Accessed December 14, 2016).

United Nations Peacebuilding Support Office/Peacebuilding Fund. 2011. *Peacebuilding Priority Plan (2011-2013): PPP.*

Unruh, J., and R. Williams, eds. 2013. *Land and Post-Conflict Peacebuilding.* Taylor & Francis.

Unruh, Jon D. 2008. "Catalyzing the Socio-Legal Space for Armed Conflict: Land and Legal Pluralism in Pre-War Liberia." *The Journal of Legal Pluralism and Unofficial Law* 40 (58): 1–31.

Utas, Mats. 2008. *Liberia beyond the blueprints:.* http://nai.diva-portal.org/smash/get/ diva2:293641/FULLTEXT01.pdf (Accessed April 10, 2017).

Utas, Mats. 2003. *Sweet battlefields: Youth and the liberian civil war.* Uppsala: DiCA.

Vabah Kazaku Gayflor. Interview with iKNOWpolitics, 16 September 2008.

van der Windt, Peter. 2014. "From Crowdsourcing to Crowdseeding: The Cutting Edge of Empowerment?" In *Bits and atoms: Information and communication technology in areas of limited statehood. Oxford studies in digital politics,* ed. Steven Livingston. Oxford: Oxford Univ. Press, 144–55.

van Tongeren, Paul, ed. 2005. *People building peace II: Successful stories of civil society. A project of the European Centre for Conflict Prevention.* Boulder, Colo: Lynne Rienner.

Verkoren, Willemijn, and Mathijs van Leeuwen. 2013. "Civil Society in Peacebuilding: Global Discourse, Local Reality." *International Peacekeeping* 20 (2): 159–72.

Villellas Arino, María. 2010. *The participation of women in peace processes: The other tables.* 05/2010 of *ICIP Working Papers.* Barcelona: Institut Catala Internacional per la Pau.

Waugh, Colin M. 2011. *Charles Taylor and Liberia: Ambition and atrocity in Africa's Lone Star State.* London, England, New York, NY: Zed Books.

Weinstein, Jeremy. 2005. "Autonomous recovery and international intervention in comparative perspective." CGD Working Papers, 57. Center for Global Development. http://www.cgdev.org/publication/autonomous-recovery-and-internation al-intervention-comparative-perspective-working-paper (Accessed November 21, 2015).

Wessells, Michael G. 2009. *Child soldiers: From violence to protection.* Cambridge, Mass. [u.a.]: Harvard University Press.

Whitworth, Sandra. 2004. *Men, militarism, and UN peacekeeping: A gendered analysis. Critical security studies.* Boulder Colo. u.a.: Lynne Rienner.

Williams, Andrew J. 2010. "Reconstruction: The missing historical link." In *Palgrave advances in peacebuilding: Critical developments and approaches. Palgrave advances,* ed. Oliver P. Richmond. Basingstoke, Hampshire: Palgrave Macmillan, 58–73.

Williams, Gabriel I. H. 2002. *Liberia: The heart of darkness: accounts of Liberia's civil war and its destabilizing effects in West Africa.* Victoria, B.C.: Trafford Publishing.

Wit, Paul de. 2012. *Land Rights, Private Use Permits, and Forest Communities.* Land Commission of Liberia. http://eeas.europa.eu/archives/delegations/liberia/docu ments/press_corner/20130916_01.pdf (Accessed July 1, 2017).

Wood, Elisabeth J. 2009. "Armed Groups and Sexual Violence: When Is Wartime Rape Rare?" *Politics & Society* 37 (1): 131–61.

Wood, Elisabeth J. 2012. "Rape is not inevitable during war: Variation in wartime sexual violence." In *Understanding and proving international sex crimes*. Vol. 12 of *FICHL Publication Series*, ed. Morten Bergsmo. Beijing: Torkel Opsahl Acad. EPubl, 389–420.

Woodhouse, T., and O. Ramsbotham, eds. 2000. *Peacekeeping and Conflict Resolution*. London: Routledge.

World Bank. 1992. *Governance and Development*. Washington, DC.

World Bank. 2008. *Insecurity of Land Tenure, Land Law and Land Registration in Liberia*. World Bank. http://documents.worldbank.org/curated/en/15849146805 0694915/pdf/461340ESW0P10310Box334099B01PUBLIC1.pdf (Accessed August 12, 2017).

World Bank. 2017. *Liberia Land Administration Project*. World Bank. http://docume nts.worldbank.org/curated/en/950201498786361109/pdf/ITM00194-P162893-06 -29-2017-1498786357083.pdf (Accessed July 1, 2017).

Worzi, Alwin. 2017. "FGM excluded from Domestic Violence Act." *Daily Observer*, August 15. https://www.liberianobserver.com/news/fgm-excluded-from-domesti c-violence-act/ (Accessed October 28, 2017).

Wulf, Herbert, and Tobias Debiel. 2009. *Conflict early warning and response mechanisms: Tools for enhancing the effectiveness of regional organizations?: A comparative study of the AU, ECOWAS, IGAD, ASEAN/ARF, and PIF*. Crisis State Research Centre. Regional and Gloal Axes of Conflict, 49. https://assets.publishing.service .gov.uk/media/57a08b8b40f0b64974000bfc/WP49.2.pdf (Accessed June 1, 2017).

Yarsiah, James M. 2016. "Liberia's Land Authority Act: Deadlock ends with unanimous suppoort from Senate." http://www.osiwa.org/liberias-land-authority-act-d eadlock-ends-unanimous-support-senate/ (Accessed August 14, 2017).

Yin, Robert K. 2014. *Case study research: Design and methods*. Los Angeles: Sage.

Yoder, John C. 2003. *Popular political culture, civil society, and state crisis in Liberia*. v. 72 of *African studies*. Lewiston, N.Y.: E. Mellen Press.

Zanker, Franzisca. 2011. "Liberia: Gescheiterte Verfassungsänderung – erfolgreiche Wahlen?" *GIGA Focus Afrika* (05). https://www.giga-hamburg.de/en/system/files/ publications/gf_afrika_1105.pdf (Accessed October 5, 2016).

Zanker, Franzisca. 2017. *Legitimacy in Peacebuilding: Rethinking Civil Society Involvement in Peace Negotiations*. 1ˢᵗ ed. *Routledge Studies in Peace and Conflict Resolution*. Milton: Taylor and Francis.

Zaum, Dominik. 2007. *The sovereignty paradox: The norms and politics of international statebuilding*. Oxford: Oxford University Press.

Zürcher, Christoph. 2006. "Is more better? Evaluating external-led state building after 1989." CDDRL Working Papers, 54. Freeman Spongli Institute for International Studies, Center on Democracy, Development, and the Rule of Law, Stanford University. https://cddrl.fsi.stanford.edu/sites/default/files/Zuercher_N o_54.pdf (Accessed November 21, 2015).

Websites:

American Bar Association https://www.americanbar.org/ (Accessed April 30, 2018).

Early Warning Early Response Group Liberia http://www.ewerliberia.net/ (Accessed June 14, 2017).

eNews Channel Africa http://www.enca.com/ (Accessed October 6, 2018).

G7+ http://www.g7plus.org/ (Accessed December 20, 2016).

GEMAP http://www.gemap-liberia.org/ (Accessed August 20, 2016)

Governance Commission http://governancecommissionlr.org (Accessed December 13, 2016).

Humanity United https://humanityunited.org/ (Accessed June 14, 2017).

Institute for Multi-Track Diplomacy http://imtd.org/ (Accessed November 27, 2018).

International Monetary Fund http://www.imf.org/ (Accessed December 13, 2016).

Internet Live Stats http://www.internetlivestats.com/ (Accessed June 14, 2017).

Internet World Stats http://www.internetworldstats.com/ (Accessed June 14, 2017).

Liberia Institute of Statistics and Geo-Information Services http://www.lisgis.net/ (Accessed December 20, 2016).

Peacebuilding Data http://www.peacebuildingdata.org/ (Accessed December 5, 2018).

UN Peacebuilding Fund http://www.unpbf.org/ (Accessed May 22, 2015).

United Nations. Website. http://www.un.org/ (Accessed December 20, 2016).

UNMIL https://unmil.unmissions.org/ (Accessed September 14, 2017).

World Bank. http://www.worldbank.org/ (Accessed December 20, 2016).

World Health Organization. http://www.who.int/ (Accessed December 20, 2016).

Annex

Annex 1

Interview guiding questions

Introductory statement:

In my study I am looking at the process of post-conflict reconstruction in Liberia, more specifically at the three groups of actors involved in the process: the government of Liberia, international actors, and Liberian civil society. I would like to learn about their interactions, their roles within the reconstruction process, and on places where they meet. I would appreciate the chance to get some insights and opinions from you about these topics, as you are, from your position of …. (affiliation), well-informed.

If you agree, I would like to record our conversation. The information will be treated in a confidential manner and used in line with good scientific practice. The record will be transcribed and in the final study, the data will be presented anonymously.

Questions related to personal background and trajectory of the respondent:

Would you tell me more about your current position and how you got to this field?

Questions related to the research topic:

Could you tell me about your institution, about its creation, tasks, and current structure? What are the projects your institution is working on? Are there any challenges your institution faces?

Is there a platform where you meet other actors involved in post-conflict reconstruction? Would you tell me more about it?

What is the interaction between the government, civil society, and international actors like there? How does it work? What is your overall impression?

What are the strong sides of the cooperation? Are there any challenges?

What is the role of your institution in the reconstruction process?

What is your relation to other actors in the reconstruction process?

What is, in your opinion, the role of the government/civil society/international actors in peacebuilding in Liberia?

Complementary questions:

If a decision has to be made, how does it work?

Is there anything else that comes to your mind as relevant with regard to the issues we have talked about?

Do you have anyone else in mind, to whom I could talk about these issues? Are there any other relevant institutions at which I should not forget to take a closer look?

Questions for respondents without institutional affiliation:

What is your overall impression of the peacebuilding process?

What are the strong sides of the reconstruction process? What are the challenges?

List of interviews

Governmental actors					
# Interview	Name/ Initials (sex)	Category	Institution (if applicable)	Date	Note
21	CD (F)	desk officer GBV Unit	MoGD	1. 5. 2012	Liberian
22	WJ (M), NW (M)	PBO employees	PBO	1. 5. 2012	Liberian
39	EK (F)	Commissioner	Land Commission	8. 6. 2012	Liberian
45	NW (M)	international consultant	PBO	14. 6. 2012	Liberian
46	AD (F)	desk officer	MoGD	6. 11. 2012	Liberian
47	HA (M)	police officer	LNP	6. 11. 2012	Liberian
48	EK (F)	LC employee	Land Commission	9. 11. 2012	Liberian
49	RC (F)	GC employee	Governance Commission	12. 11. 2012	Liberian
50	SJ (M)	desk officer	MPEA	16. 11. 2012	Liberian
52	HB (M), VJ (M)	traditional leader, local government employee	National Traditional Council of Liberia	20. 11. 2012	Liberian
57	EM (F)	GC Commissioner	Governance Commission	28. 11. 2012	Liberian
59	NW (M)	EWWG Chairman/PBO staff	EWWG	28. 11. 2012	Liberian
62	RD (F)	GC employee	Governance Commission	30. 11. 2012	Liberian
63	ED (F), WJ (F)	LC employees	Land Commission	30. 11. 2012	Liberian
64	AJ (M)	desk officer	Ministry of Lands, Mines, and Energy	30. 11. 2012	Liberian

| 65 | DC (M) | MIA employee | Ministry of Internal Affairs | 30. 11. 2012 | Liberian |

International Actors

# Inter-view	Name/ Initials (sex)	Category	Institution (if applicable)	Date	Note
1	TG (F)	INGO	Innovation for Poverty Action (IPAL)	10. 6. 2011	Expatriate (US)
18	SS (M)	INGO	Justice and Peace Commission	22. 6. 2011	Expatriate (DE)
23	CS (M)	international consultant	Land Commission	3. 5. 2012	Expatriate (US)
24	SP (F)	international expert	University of Liberia/AGEH/ KAICT	7. 5. 2012	Expatriate (DE)
25	EW (F)	EWWG member	Justice and Peace Commission	16. 5. 2012	Expatriate (UK)
26	BS (M)	diplomat	Foreign Embassy	16. 5. 2012	Expatriate
29	RR (M)	UN official	Office of the Resident Coordinator	25. 5. 2012	Expatriate
31	AP (F), CM (F)	INGO employees	international human rights NGO	28. 5. 2012	Expatriate
32	AL (M)	INGO employee	American Bar Association	29. 5. 2012	Expatriate (US)
34	SR (M)	development agency officer	GIZ	1. 6. 2012	Expatriate (DE)
35	SR (M)	development agency officer	GIZ	4. 6. 2012	Expatriate (DE)
37	FB (M)	IGO employee	FAO	6. 6. 2012	Expatriate (A)
38	WM (M)	diplomat	Foreign Embassy	7. 6. 2012	Expatriate
40	JW (F)	development agency officer	GIZ	8. 6. 2012	Expatriate (DE)
41	GN (M)	international NGO employee	Norwegian Refugee Council	11. 6. 2012	Expatriate

42		international consultant	Land Commission	13. 6. 2012	Expatriate (US)
51	ML (F)	UN officer	UNDP	18. 11. 2012	Expatriate
53	NK (F)	EU employee	EU delegation in Liberia	20. 11. 2012	Expatriate (A)
55	AG (F)	ECOWAS official	ECOWAS Office in Liberia	26. 11. 2012	Expatriate
58	ML (F)	UN officer	UNDP	28. 11. 2012	Expatriate
60	JW (F)	development agency officer	GIZ	29. 11. 2012	Expatriate (DE)
61	DT (M)	development agency officer	USAID	30. 11. 2012	Expatriate (US)
Civil Society					
# Interview	Name/ Initials (sex)	Category	Institution (if applicable)	Date	Note
3	WA (M)	informal leader		10. 6. 2011	former armed actor, Liberian
6	YP (F)	NGO employee	IPAL	13. 6. 2011	Liberian
8	DS (M)	university lecturer	University of Liberia/KAICT	14. 6. 2011	Liberian
9	WA (M)	informal leader		15. 6. 2011	former armed actor, Liberian
10	WA (M)	informal leader		16. 6. 2011	former armed actor, Liberian
11	CP (F)	NGO employee	freelance	16. 6. 2011	Liberian
19	CR (M)	NGO employee	freelance	23. 6. 2011	Liberian
20	OB (M)	NGO employee	Search for Common Ground	27. 6. 2011	Liberian

27	RC (M)	NGO employee	WANEP	18. 5. 2012	Liberian
28	MF (F)	NGO employee	Foundation for Peace and Development	24. 5. 2012	Liberian
30	VK (F)	NGO employee	Inter-Religious Council of Liberia	28. 5. 2012	Liberian
33	VK (M), JW (M)	NGO employees	Liberia Democracy Watch	30. 5. 2012	Liberian
43	VK (M)	NGO employee	Liberia Democracy Watch	13. 6. 2012	Liberian
44	JT (M)	NGO employee	Slum Dwellers Association	13. 6. 2012	Liberian
56	DS (M)	university lecturer	University of Liberia	27. 11. 2012	Liberian
Others					
# Interview	Name/ Initials (sex)	Category	Institution (if applicable)	Date	Note
2	PJ (M)	unemployed		10. 6. 2011	Liberian
4	GS (M)	unemployed		12. 6. 2011	Liberian
5	RT (M)	unemployed		12. 6 2011	Liberian
7	PL (M)	student		14. 6. 2011	Liberian
12	JJ (M)	unemployed		19. 6. 2011	Liberian
13	AS (M)	unemployed		19. 6. 2011	Liberian
14	GM (F)	market woman		20. 6. 2011	Liberian
15	PJ (M)	unemployed		20. 6. 2011	Liberian
16	SD (F)	market woman		20. 6. 2011	Liberian
17	MR (M)	businessman		22.6. 2011	Liberian

| 36 | SA (F) | researcher | US academic | 5. 6. 2012 | Expatriate (US) |
| 54 | ST (M) | director | LEITI | 22. 11.201 2 | Liberian (diaspora) |

Meetings attended (observation)

Institution	Date	Location
Early Warning Working Group	10. 5. 2012	Ushahidi Building, Sinkor, Monrovia
	24. 5. 2012	Landmine Action, Mamba Point, Monrovia
	30. 5. 2012	Justice and Peace Commission, Sinkor, Monrovia
GBV Taksforce	31. 5. 2012	MoGD, Mamba Point, Monrovia
	5. 6. 2012	MoGD, Mamba Point, Monrovia
	28. 11. 2012	MoGD, Mamba Point, Monrovia
LC Policy Taskforce	29. 5. 2012	Land Commission, Sinkor, Monrovia
	19. 6. 2012	Land Commission, Sinkor, Monrovia
	6. 11. 2012	Land Commission, Sinkor, Monrovia
Land Dispute Resolution Taskforce	12. 6. 2012	Land Commission, Sinkor, Monrovia
	26. 6. 2012	Land Commission, Sinkor, Monrovia
	13. 11. 2012	Land Commission, Sinkor, Monrovia

Annex 3

National budget of Liberia (in mil USD)

Fiscal year	2012/13	2015/16	2016/17	2017/18 (pro-jected)
Total domestic revenues	497,3	416,3	525,0	576,7
Grants	45,1	53,7	30,2	17,9
On-budget grants	N/A	34,8	44,22	12,94
Off-budget grants	515	304,7	245,91	N/A
Grants and loans total (on- and off-budget)	N/A	394,2	343,83	12,94

Source: retrieved from the Budgetary framework paper for 2017/18, and Liberia Citizen's guide to national budget 2012/13.

Annex 4

Map of Monrovia

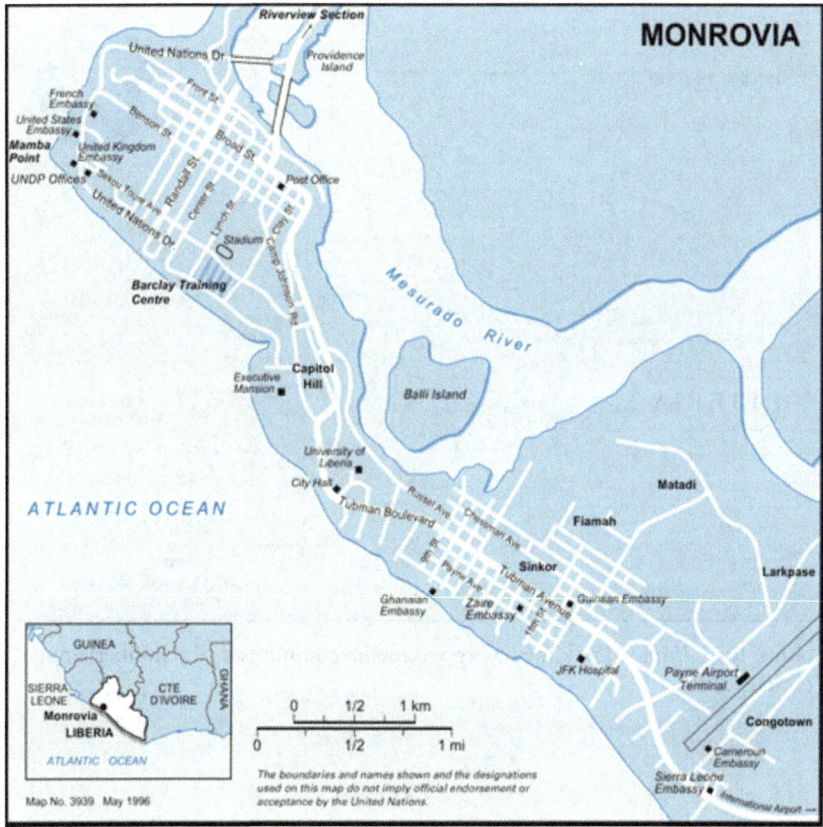

Source: https://de.m.wikipedia.org/wiki/Datei:Map_of_Monrovia.png (7 February 2019).

Annex 5

Map of Liberia

Source: https://upload.wikimedia.org/wikipedia/commons/d/db/Un-liberia.png (7 February 2019).

Bereits erschienen in der Reihe „Bayreuther Studien zu Politik und Gesellschaft in Afrika"

Already published in the series "Bayreuth Studies in African Politics and Societies"

The Peacebuilding Process in Postwar Liberia
A Tortuous Way Forward
by Alžběta Šváblová,
2021, Volume 12

The Rise and Fall of Kenyan Entrepreneurs
Social Mobility in Kisumu
by Maike Voigt,
2021, Volume 11

North to South Migration
Portuguese Labour Migration to Angola
by Asaf Augusto,
2021, Volume 10

Religion und Entwicklungszusammenarbeit
Positionen aus Politik, Praxis und Afrikaforschung
herausgegeben von Sebastian Müller, Eva Spies, Heike Wagner,
2021, Band 9

Hexerei in Nigeria zwischen Christentum, Islam und traditionellen Praktiken
Globale Verflechtungen und lokale Positionierungen bei den Yoruba
von Judith Bachmann,
2021, Band 8

The Making of a Petro-State
Governmentality and Development Practice in Uganda's Albertine Graben
hy Paddy Kinyera,
2020, Volume 7

Diversity Gains
Stepping Stones and Pitfalls
edited by Sarah Böllinger, Carsten Mildner, Ulf Vierke,
2020, Volume 6

Die Welt aus der Perspektive der Entwicklungssoziologie
Festschrift für Dieter Neubert
herausgegeben von Artur Bogner, Reinhart Kößler, Rüdiger Korff, Henning Melber,
2020, Band 5

Medialisierungen Afrikas
herausgegeben von Valerie Hänsch, Johanna Rieß, Ivo Ritzer, Heike Wagner,
2018, Band 4